Alliance Politics, Kosovo, and NATO's War

Alliance Politics, Kosovo, and NATO's War: Allied Force or Forced Allies?

Edited by

Pierre Martin and Mark R. Brawley

palgrave

Alliance Politics, Kosovo, and NATO's War: Allied Force or Forced Allies?
© Pierre Martin and Mark R. Brawley, 2000

All rights reserved. No part of this book may be used or reproduced in any manner whatsoever without written permission except in the case of brief quotations embodied in critical articles or reviews.

First published 2000 by
PALGRAVE
175 Fifth Avenue, New York, N.Y. 10010 and
Houndmills, Basingstoke, Hampshire RG21 6XS.
Companies and representatives throughout the world

PALGRAVE is the new global publishing imprint of
St. Martin's Press LLC
Scholarly and Reference Division and Palgrave Publishers Ltd
(formerly Macmillan Press Ltd).

ISBN 0-312-23817-7 hardback

Library of Congress Cataloging-in-Publication Data

Alliance politics, Kosovo, and NATO's war : allied force or forced allies? / edited by Pierre Martin and Mark R. Brawley.
    p. cm.
   Papers from a conference held at Harvard University Sept. 30–Oct. 1, 1999, titled "Allied Force or Forced Allies—Alliance Politics in Canada and Europe from the End of the Cold War to Kosovo."
   Includes bibliographical references and index.
   ISBN 0-312-23817-7 (cloth)
   1. Kosovo (Serbia)—History—Civil War, 1998—Congresses.
2. North Atlantic Treaty Organization—Congresses. 3. World politics—1989—Congresses. I. Martin, Pierre. II. Brawley, Mark R. (Mark Randal), 1960–
DR2087 .A45 2001   00-068200
949.7103—dc21

A catalogue record for this book is available
from the British Library.

Design by Newgen Imaging Systems (P) Ltd, Chennai, India.

First edition: July 2001
10 9 8 7 6 5 4 3 2 1

Printed in the United States of America.

Contents

Acknowledgments	vii
Foreword, *Stanley Hoffmann*	ix
List of Acronyms and Abbreviations	xiii

Introduction

Kosovo, Alliance Politics, and the Future of NATO   1
    Mark R. Brawley and Pierre Martin

Part I: The Alliance, Security Institutions, and the Nature of New Threats

1. NATO's Future (In Theory)   11
    Stephen M. Walt

2. Challenges to Euro-Atlantic Security   27
    S. Neil MacFarlane

3. The Constraint of Legitimacy: The Legal and Institutional Framework of Euro-Atlantic Security   41
    Alan K. Henrikson

4. The European Union and NATO's War over Kosovo: Toward the Glass Ceiling?   57
    Anne Deighton

Part II: National Perspectives on Operation Allied Force

5. Kosovo and the Future of U.S. Engagement in Europe: Continued Hegemony or Impending Retrenchment?   75
    Charles A. Kupchan

6. Allied Force or Forced Allies? The Allies' Perspective 91
   David G. Haglund

7. France: Kosovo and the Emergence of a
   New European Security 113
   Alex Macleod

8. Germany and the Kosovo Conflict 131
   Peter Rudolf

9. A Force for Good in the World? Britain's Role
   in the Kosovo Crisis 145
   Louise Richardson

10. Italy and the Management of International Crises 165
    Maurizio Cremasco

11. Canada and the Kosovo War: The Happy Follower 181
    Kim Richard Nossal and Stéphane Roussel

12. The Atlantic Alliance and the Kosovo Crisis: The Impact
    of Expansion and the Behavior of New Allies 201
    Milada Anna Vachudová

Conclusion

Balancing Acts: NATO's Unity and the Lessons to Learn 221
Mark R. Brawley and Pierre Martin

Notes on Contributors 235

Index 241

Acknowledgments

The chapters in this book represent the culmination of two sets of presentations. Initially, the contributors met at a conference held at Harvard University on September 30 and October 1, 1999, titled "Allied Force or Forced Allies: Alliance Politics in Canada and Europe from the End of the Cold War to Kosovo." We therefore wish to thank the main sponsor of that conference, the Weatherhead Center for International Affairs. We are both fortunate to have been associated with the Weatherhead Center during the preparation of this volume. In 1999–2000, Pierre Martin was the William Lyon Mackenzie King Visiting Associate Professor of Canadian Studies at Harvard, and Mark Brawley was a visiting professor in Harvard's Department of Government in 2000-2001. The Weatherhead Center—particularly its director, Jorge Domínguez, and executive director, James Cooney—gave us unfailing support from the project's inception. We are also grateful to the project's two cosponsors, Harvard's European Union Center and the Université de Montréal/McGill University Research Group in International Security. We specifically wish to thank Beth Hastie, assistant to the Mackenzie King Chair and conference coordinator, for her work in making the conference a success.

We were honored to have Canada's defense minister, Art Eggleton, deliver the opening address for this conference. Special thanks go to Stanley Hoffmann, who commented on Minister Eggleton's address and also agreed to write a brief foreword to this volume. Other participants in the conference we would like to thank are Daniel Bon, Lawrence Broz, Marc Busch, James Cooney, Jonathan Day, Jorge Domínguez, George Ross, and Daniel Turp. Several contributors gathered again at the March 2000 meeting of the International Studies Association in Los Angeles. We were able to refine certain sections in this later gathering and we are grateful to the audience for valuable insights.

As members of the Université de Montréal/McGill University Research Group in International Security, we would also like to thank Canada's Department of National Defence for its support over the years. Through the Security and Defence Forum, the DND has supported our group and other centers throughout Canada, while entrusting them with all the autonomy that is vital for independent scholarly pursuits.

We would like to thank the contributors for cooperating so fully. We should also thank Karen Wolny and Gabriella Pearce at Palgrave, as well as Palgrave editors and production staff. A product such as this one truly is a team effort. In the end, however, all errors remain our responsibility.

Pierre Martin and Mark R. Brawley
Montréal and Cambridge

Foreword

Stanley Hoffmann

The war in Kosovo has raised a very large number of issues, many of which are addressed in this book. Most of its chapters deal with one of the major problems for students of international relations: the connection between domestic factors and foreign policy—in this case, the divisions within public opinion in certain countries; the contrast between a hostile or skeptical public and a government that cooperated with its NATO allies (as in the case of Italy or Greece); or the effects on the public of apparently unsuccessful or inadequate ways of waging the war.

Here, I shall concentrate on two other sets of issues. The first one concerns military interventions for humanitarian purposes. One specific question is that of the proper authority for launching such enterprises. There is no doubt that in the current architecture of world governance, it is the Security Council that is the legitimate authority and that regional bodies can act only with the Security Council's consent. However, here as in many other respects the architecture is flawed. There are five powers with a right of veto in the Security Council, and the legality of humanitarian interventions is a major bone of contention among them—two, Russia and China, are fierce defenders of state sovereignty in theory, and in practice oppose interventions to support oppressed minorities or peoples claiming a right to self-determination, because these two powers have far too many potential rattlers of chains on their own territories. Thus, often if not always, respect for the supremacy of the Security Council would make humanitarian interventions impossible or submit them to crippling limitations. This explains why Washington and London have favored "coalitions of the willing"—either as the effective secular arm of the Security Council, as in the case of Iraq's aggression against Kuwait, or instead of a Security Council that was likely to be paralyzed, as in Kosovo.

Were the allies right to act without resorting to a Council vote first? Was it better, in other words, to ignore the Council than to ignore one or two vetoes? Was polite avoidance better than an outright challenge to a demonstrably paralyzed Council? On these questions, observers, commentators, and public officials will continue to differ. More important, however, is the need, in cases of egregious violations of human rights, not to be deterred from timely action by the incapacity of the Security Council to resort to Chapter VII of the Charter—and the fact that a collective intervention in such cases remains preferable to a unilateral one, although one can conceive of a tragedy of such proportions that a quick unilateral intervention would still be better than none at all or than a collective one that would come together too late (Rwanda would have been such a case, had any state able to intervene been willing to do so).

Another question relates to two other requirements of the traditional "just war" theory: a reasonable chance of success and the proportionality of means to ends. The war in Kosovo showed how difficult it is to meet these imperatives in humanitarian interventions. If the operation begins when genocide or ethnic cleansing or political massacres are already going on, war risks adding victims—either among the civilians whom one wants to help or among civilians in the country whose government is the villain, something that can be justified only if the effect is to put a rapid end to the atrocities committed by it. For a while, it looked as if the air war in Kosovo could neither succeed nor meet the proportionality standard. If, as many students of intervention have suggested, preventive action is preferable to action after the disaster has begun, NATO's intervention in Kosovo, which began after some killings had occurred but was aimed at deterring the Serbs from massive ethnic cleansing, could be rated a failure, insofar as the bombing led to the wholesale expulsion of the Albanian population of Kosovo. We may know someday whether or not NATO merely accelerated something Milosevic had planned to do anyhow, as there are good reasons to suspect. What allows one to judge that, on balance, the intervention was a success is the fact that the Albanians were able to return and to obtain a statute (still undefined) of autonomy. NATO reversed the two decisive Serbian actions against them: the revocation of autonomy in 1989 and the ethnic cleansing of 1999.

The second set of issues I would like to raise concerns NATO. The essays in this volume prove decisively that it did act as a "coalition of the willing," as what Karl Deutsch called a security community and not simply as the defensive alliance against the very specific Soviet threat it had been between 1950 and 1991. Nevertheless, two questions must be asked about NATO's future. The first one, discussed at length in chapters 1 and 2, is that of the agenda of threats NATO may have to face—and to which it would owe its persistence. It is difficult to imagine an instance of interstate aggression that would shock NATO into action. Russia is not a likely threat for many years (and is busy reducing its military power). A Turkish-Greek conflict would be an intra-NATO affair. A new aggression by, say, Iraq or Iran would require a new "coalition of the willing" that would, in all likelihood, involve non-NATO members and probably not all of NATO's. Another Arab-Israeli war might require observers or peacekeepers from outside the area after the hostilities, but NATO is not the most likely candidate for the task. As for more interventions in domestic crises, à la Kosovo, the reader will find in this volume compelling reasons to believe that after Bosnia and Kosovo the return of the Balkans to the dark ages of ethnic horrors may fortunately have come to an end, and that an enlarged European Union will serve as a pacifier.

This means, in effect, that the main role of NATO would be to serve as an insurance policy for the Europeans and the Canadians—a guarantee of American support should some unexpected threat that exceeds their capacities somehow and somewhere appear—and as an instrument of U.S. foreign policy, triply useful to Washington: as a means of control over allies that might otherwise be tempted either to revive old hostilities or to emancipate themselves from the *gouvernante américaine,* as a deterrent of attempts by Europeans to "balance" the American "hyperpower," and as an essential component of America's hegemony in world affairs.

The problem lies in the imbalance between the two roles. The more nebulous the need for the insurance policy becomes, the less compelling the argument for continuing European submissiveness. Indeed, the kinds of threats Europeans often have nightmares about—flows of refugees from the East and the South, turmoil and terrorism created by Islamic fundamentalism around the Mediterranean are either not the kinds of threats that the United States would consider dangerous for itself or are more likely to be addressed on a basis other than NATO. Even the improbable revival of ethnic tragedies in eastern Europe is more likely to implicate the EU than the United States, where battle fatigue against interventions and the willingness to dump these issues on the Europeans are on the rise. This is precisely one of the reasons why the EU is now trying to put in place a security system of its own. There are, indeed, two reasons for this new determination under French and British leadership; they are apparently contradictory but point in the same direction. The one reason, just mentioned, is America's withdrawal symptoms. The other is increasing European reluctance to bear the burden of American hegemony, which, as this book documents, dictated the course of the war in Kosovo in ways many European governments disliked. Both reasons are leading Europeans to prefer the cost of building up their forces to that of letting the gap between America's technological and military capacity and Europe's remain as huge as it has been since 1945.

It is very hard to kill an international organization. They would rather fade away than die. Nobody has any reason to kill NATO: the Europeans can use an insurance policy, the United States a handle on Europe, and Canada a vast alliance that can act as a moderating force on Washington. But how often will NATO be a manifest actor in international and internal crises? Above all, will the imbalance between the country that has been the sole leader since 1950 and its allies persist, and if it does not, what will that leader's reaction be: reassertion (i.e., voice) or exit? This is what is at stake after Kosovo.

List of Acronyms and Abbreviations

BSEC	Black Sea Economic Cooperation Pact
CEI	Central European Initiative
CFSP	Common Foreign and Security Policy (European Union)
CIS	Commonwealth of Independent States
CoE	Council of Europe
EAPC	Euro-Atlantic Partnership Council
EDC	European Defense Community
EMU	Economic and Monetary Union
EP	European Parliament
ESDI	European Security and Defense Identity
EU	European Union
G7/G8	Group of seven leading industrial nations, or eight including Russia
FRY	Federal Republic of Yugoslavia
FYROM	Former Yugoslav Republic of Macedonia
HCNM	High Commissioner for National Minorities
IFOR	Intervention Force (Bosnia)
IOM	International Organization for Migration
KFOR	Kosovo Force
KLA	Kosovo Liberation Army
NACC	North Atlantic Cooperation Council
NATO	North Atlantic Treaty Organization
NBC	Nuclear, Biological, and Chemical (weapons)
NORAD	North American Aerospace Defense Command
OPEC	Organization of Petroleum Exporting Countries
OSCE	Organization for Security and Co-operation in Europe
PfP	Partnership for Peace
PGM	Precision-Guided Missile
SEECI	South-East European Co-operation Initiative
SEECP	South Eastern Europe Co-operation Process
SFOR	Stability Force (Bosnia)

SHAPE	Supreme Headquarters Allied Powers Europe
SPD	Social Democratic Party (Germany)
UNHCR	United Nations High Commissioner for Refugees
UNMIK	United Nations Interim Mission in Kosovo
UNPROFOR	United Nations Protection Force (in the former Yugoslavia)
UNSC	United Nations Security Council
USAF	United States Air Force
WEU	Western European Union
WMD	Weapons of Mass Destruction

INTRODUCTION

Kosovo, Alliance Politics, and the Future of NATO

Mark R. Brawley and Pierre Martin

The Kosovo crisis underscored important issues for the foreign policies of NATO allies, and raised questions with serious theoretical and policy implications. What range of autonomy does U.S. leadership in—or, as some prefer to call it, hegemony over—Euro-Atlantic security institutions leave for other NATO members? Is American unilateralism in security matters as pervasive as some would lead us to believe, or can other Western democracies maintain some degree of autonomy vis-à-vis the United States, even in the context of severe crises?[1] What are the lessons of the crisis from the point of view of America and its NATO allies? Beyond the Alliance itself, what are the lessons to be drawn from the crisis about the articulation of the various components of the so-called architecture of European security? The following chapters explore these questions from the often neglected perspective of Alliance followers. The findings offer some insights into broader theoretical issues regarding Alliance politics in the post–Cold War period, but they will also highlight important factors for policymakers to consider before undertaking another multilateral military intervention under the NATO umbrella.[2]

Part I: The Alliance, Security Institutions, and the Nature of New Threats

The first set of articles establish the theoretical issues that have caused academics to remain focused on NATO even after the demise of its ideological enemy, the Soviet Union. These begin with an assessment of the expectations regarding NATO's future that have been generated by prominent theories of international relations. But the authors also consider the role of likely threats NATO will confront in the foreseeable future, and the legal/institutional environment that drove many—but not all—Alliance members to select NATO as the instrument for action in this crisis. Each contribution provides us with a particular aspect of the difficulties confronting NATO as both it and its institutional and international milieus have changed in recent years.

Stephen Walt provides the assessment of the various theoretical points of view on NATO's continued survival into the 1990s and evolution as an alliance. Walt notes that while realists would expect NATO to disintegrate after the threat posed by the Soviet Union disappeared, there is no specific time frame regarding this outcome; it is therefore hard to say whether NATO's survival is an anomaly for the realists—at least up to this point. In fact, NATO's attempt to locate new responsibilities, and the deep concerns expressed that NATO had to fulfill its new responsibilities in the Balkans successfully lest it be delegitimated and abandoned as a result, can best be understood via the realists' thinking. Institutionalism provides insights into the reason members would value an already established military alliance. Constructivism draws attention to the shared identities (and therefore shared interests) that tie NATO members together.[3] Thus Walt concludes that different paradigms contribute to our understanding of the Alliance's persistence and evolution.

Providing some details to these discussions, Neil MacFarlane begins his contribution by noting that NATO's success in deterring a Soviet attack—indeed, success in turning back the Soviet ideological challenge—undercut the organization's primary purpose. Why does western Europe need this alliance, when the potential military threats to western Europe appear to be so few and far between? It is no surprise then that NATO would accept different responsibilities outside those of its original jurisdiction. Yet even in looking beyond the geographic periphery of NATO's members, Kosovo may well be the last of a series of incidents associated with the breakup of Yugoslavia, rather than the first of a wave of opportunities for NATO to exercise its military prowess. We are left with a paradox: NATO's strength and cohesion has lessened the threats its members face, but in the face of declining threats, will NATO maintain that strength and cohesion?

The third chapter in Part I discusses the legal friction between NATO and the United Nations generated by Operation Allied Force. Alan Henrikson notes the conflicting norms and principles at work in international law in this case. The case for intervention was based on certain aspects of international law, but ultimately NATO argued that it was acting in the common interest when it undertook military action. Yet, who should determine the common interest of the international community if not the

United Nations? Since approval for action from either the Russians or the Chinese was unlikely to be forthcoming in the Security Council, and even an endorsement within the General Assembly was considered problematic, NATO acted without the sanction of the United Nations. Not only did this raise questions about the legitimacy of Operation Allied Force, it set a dangerous precedent by claiming that there were legitimate grounds for offensive military action without United Nations authorization. Henrikson offers potential avenues for overcoming these frictions and thereby resolving some of these legal issues before the need for future interventions arise.

Finally in Part I, Anne Deighton discusses some of the disagreements about, and frustrations with, the EU in the Kosovo crisis. Some NATO members argued that the EU was the correct body to undertake action in the Balkans, yet the EU had already lost its claim to primacy to other international organizations before Operation Allied Force began. The conflict has reignited or reenergized several disputes about the EU and its role in European defense. The need for a European Security and Defense Identity (ESDI) may be more widely felt than before—but this does not make achievement of such a common identity any easier. As Deighton notes, on this and other issues that were under discussion during the Cold War, NATO was the "glass ceiling" through which European collective defense efforts were not to go—but the situation may now have changed.

Part II: National Perspectives on Operation Allied Force

Whereas Part I set the scene, the contributions in Part II develop perspectives on Operation Allied Force as seen by various member states. These pieces illustrate variation from one ally to the next in terms of domestic support for the war, the depth of desire for action on Kosovo, and the need for NATO to succeed. The contributions in Part I necessarily tend to stress systemic factors and international causes or consequences; those in Part II naturally place greater emphasis on domestic factors, though they mostly draw our attention to the challenges that decision-makers faced in balancing foreign policy aims with domestic concerns. It was this matching of domestic concerns and attitudes in the crisis, plus the mix of systemic incentives and constraints (especially but certainly not only those posed by the United States), that allows us to answer questions regarding the relative autonomy of the NATO members. Rather than finding evidence of "forced allies," we would argue that the other members of NATO fall into several quite different categories. There were "the front-runners" out ahead of the United States on many issues, "the faithful" who stuck by American policy decisions, "the followers" who reluctantly mimicked American leadership in the Alliance, and "the frustrated" who followed U.S. leadership but were unhappy with particular aspects of the conduct of the conflict.

The first national perspective we assess is the American. When we consider the questions central to the analysis here, we must remember that many cut two ways. The perspective outside the United States may be that the latter plays too prominent a role in making decisions, while within the United States, concerns remain that it carries a disproportionate share of the burdens. Recent analyses suggest that the rising cost of weaponry, the increased research and development necessary, and the changing focus of NATO's mission toward the projection of force will all lead to a greater exploitation of the larger members by the smaller. Exploitation is expected to increase as NATO expands, since the newer members will be unlikely to contribute forces toward operations, and new expenditures will be necessary simply to modernize their forces.[4] Moreover, the need for America to guarantee members' immediate security now varies considerably, as does acceptance of American "strategic priorities."[5] These tensions can be observed in the actions of some NATO allies, but also in the Americans' perspective on the Alliance as well.

Charles Kupchan argues that the United States led its allies in Operation Allied Force for both humanitarian and strategic interests. Events in Kosovo did threaten to spill over into other regional conflicts, so the United States acted to prevent the spread of such conflicts. Once willing to lead the Alliance into conflict, the United States provided the bulk of the military forces and ensured that military victory was attained. NATO works well when its strongest member is willing to lead, but how much longer will this be the case? Kupchan rightly asks whether the United States will be willing to maintain or even increase its share of the burden of defending Europe now that the Cold War is over; it surely cannot be safe to assume that the United States will do so indefinitely. Even if one judges NATO's performance as an alliance to have been superb, it may be time to discuss new security arrangements.

In looking to the various allies and their interactions with the United States, some were clearly out ahead on a variety of issues. Britain, for instance, was much more keenly interested in expressing the threat of using troops on the ground than was the United States. As Louise Richardson points out, Britain described its own policy as being "a force for good in the world"—a phrase also used by the Blair team to describe American foreign policy. The two countries largely shared interests and aims in this endeavor. Much the same could be said of Canada. As Stéphane Roussel and Kim Nossal argue in their description of Canada's participation in Operation Allied Force, the principles motivating NATO's action were those that Canada has long been promoting. Indeed, one of the persons most closely associated with the "human security agenda" internationally has been Lloyd Axworthy, Canada's foreign minister during the Kosovo conflict. Thus it should be no surprise that Canada would be right alongside Britain and the United States in declaring the need to intervene in this case.

David Haglund examines Canada as well as Spain in a comparison of two of NATO's smaller members. He finds little evidence of either having been under external pressure to participate in NATO's first offensive military action. Public opinion in Canada supported the government's position, but the Spanish public was much more divided. Yet the Spanish government also contributed military forces in the end. If the Spanish government felt compelled to participate, it was more an "internal compellence"—a desire to carry their share in the joint effort, or to prove their reliability to other allies.

This same sort of desire appears to have driven Germany's decisions, according to Peter Rudolf's description. He notes, however, that the German government desired that the Alliance handle its relations with Serbia and Russia in a different manner than actually occurred under U.S. leadership. Therefore Germany's SPD-led government approved participation in the air campaign of Operation Allied Force to prove it was a reliable ally, but it simultaneously pursued diplomatic overtures to find other solutions to the crisis, as well as to bring Russia back into the diplomatic discussions.

The country most unhappy with the way things were handled was undoubtedly France. As Alexander Macleod sets the scene, the French government's thinking on security issues has been unsettled in the post–Cold War era. Its basic premises have been removed, and it has yet to find new moorings. One consistency has been the French interest in ensuring that France is considered an international power of the first rank. This may lead to a ready bristling whenever American leadership is exercised, as in the case of Operation Allied Force. Yet this is not quite the same as saying that the French disputed the aims of its other Alliance partners; what was more galling, perhaps, was the inability of the French government to provide a coherent and feasible alternative to the policies coming from Washington.

On the surface, some of the rhetoric coming from the Italian government sounded similar to the words emanating from Paris. Yet these statements were soon followed by others with a different point of view. Maurizio Cremasco helps make sense of the apparent swings in Italian positions on Operation Allied Force by unraveling the mix of domestic concerns confronting the top political decision-makers there. As leaders of a coalition government that included parties from the left (who traditionally pushed to distance Italian from American foreign policy), the top policymakers in the Italian government used their public statements to maneuver both their internal allies and their external allies. They sought, with some success, to reconcile their internal and external needs.

Among NATO's newest members, some of the same balancing of internal and external pressures can be observed. Still, as Milada Vachudová argues, the need to remain in NATO for reasons driven by international insecurity took precedence over any internal divisions. In the Czech Republic, the public and many prominent politicians expressed strong disapproval of the air strikes; nevertheless, the government satisfied all of its formal commitments to the Alliance. In Poland, by contrast, the public and the political class were staunchly in favor of the air strikes and of an active role in the prosecution of the distant war. More striking, however, was the strong political consensus in Hungary that allowed it to meet NATO's higher expectations—despite the higher risks arising from its geographic proximity to the conflict. For NATO's new members, and even more so for its aspiring members, the international environment drove governments to do what was necessary to preserve NATO's favor.

Conclusion: Understanding NATO's Strength and Cohesion

One challenge for further research will be to come to a better understanding of why each country fell into one particular category rather than another, so as to gain a better sense of how NATO's members might behave in a future non–Article 5 operation. In the concluding chapter we seek to integrate the findings from the systemic and domestic levels into a single framework. This framework will provide a simple way to compare and contrast the differences observed in the NATO members' relations with the United States. By showing how one could understand the subtle variances in the actions of NATO's members, it will also provide a point of contrast to those who argue that a shared security and defense identity drove the Alliance members to act together in this instance.

Of course, we will also try to draw out one or two key lessons concerning the politics of NATO's first experience in conducting offensive operations. Should we expect NATO to handle future non–Article 5 operations with ease? Should we expect the Alliance to hold together well into the future? By bringing together the domestic and international factors drawn from the cases analyzed in the individual chapters, we hope to develop convincing answers to these questions.

Notes

1. This is not simply conjecture. As Robert Cottrell argued about Operation Allied Force, "Once begun, this became an American war run from the White House

and the Pentagon over which the Europeans had little political influence." See "A Work in Progress: A Survey of Europe," *Economist,* October 23, 1999, p. 9.
2. We hope to shed light on theoretical issues as well as inform debates on specific policies, thereby avoiding Robert Rothstein's old assessment of the literature in this area. In Rothstein's words: "... alliances seem fated to remain the subject either of generalizations which are too ambiguous to enlighten the analyst or of empirical studies which are too narrow to provide theoretical guidance." See *Alliances and Small Powers* (New York: Columbia University Press, 1968), p. 57.
3. One perspective not given much attention here, however, is that of bureaucratic politics. As Edward Luttwak observed in an article for the *Los Angeles Times* ("A Not So Splendid War," March 25, 2000), "NATO is not just an alliance, it is an organization" offering paths for career advancement and often higher pay for military and diplomatic personnel. In Luttwak's view, these factors shaped decision-making as much as, if not more than, strategic considerations.
4. See Todd Sandler and Keith Hartley, *The Political Economy of NATO* (New York: Cambridge University Press, 1999), especially pp. 48 and 117.
5. This is the assessment provided by *The Strategic Survey 1998/1999,* produced by IISS, edited by Sidney Bearman (New York: Oxford University Press, 1999). See "NATO Celebrates Its Fiftieth Year," pp. 31–39. As argued in this piece's concluding sentence, "a healthy transatlantic alliance requires an alliance of equals: this is the principal challenge for NATO as it enters middle age."

PART ONE

The Alliance, Security Institutions, and the Nature of New Threats

CHAPTER ONE

NATO's Future (In Theory)

Stephen M. Walt

During the Cold War, theorists of international relations paid surprisingly little attention to NATO. Although the Alliance did inspire seminal work on pluralistic security communities in the 1950s and helped advance the theory of collective goods in the 1960s and 1970s, these works were never part of the central theoretical debates in the field.[1] This lack of attention is not hard to explain: NATO's basic structure and its rationale remained largely unchanged from the early 1950s until the 1990s, so there were few theoretical issues that seemed to be worth studying. We all knew that NATO had been formed to keep Russia out of Europe (and the United States in), and that was that. Although the fine details of NATO's military strategy provided ample material for a generation of deterrence theorists and defense analysts, the political issues of NATO's origins, evolution, and future lay dormant so long as the overall structure of world politics remained static.

Since the end of the Cold War, however, the future of NATO, the likely effects of its changing character, and the broader lessons to be drawn from its history have reemerged as central topics for international relations theorists. As one might expect, representatives of different theoretical traditions have been quick to view events since 1991 as confirming their own positions. Critics of realism have been especially eager to interpret NATO's persistence as a decisive refutation of balance-of-power theory and a convincing demonstration that alternative theoretical approaches are superior.

This paper does not attempt to adjudicate this irresolvable interparadigmatic debate. Rather, it pursues the more modest objective of identifying what several important theories of alliances tell us about NATO's likely evolution in the near-to-medium term. This course makes sense because the various competing theories are not mutually exclusive, and because each is likely to provide different but complementary insights into the forces that will shape transatlantic security relations over the next several decades.

The remainder of the paper is organized as follows. I begin by considering the broad family of realist theories, focusing in particular on some recent work that is especially relevant to NATO's future course. I then consider the role of institutionalist theory, which several scholars have recently invoked to explain NATO's capacity to adapt to the post–Cold War environment. Subsequent sections examine the potential contributions of collective-goods theory and several types of liberal and cultural theory. I conclude by suggesting what these theories predict for NATO's future and highlight some of their practical implications. In particular, I suggest that NATO's future will be determined primarily by domestic developments in the United States and Europe, and by the potentially increasing costs that the commitment should entail over time.

Realist Approaches

Balance of Power/Balance of Threat Theory

According to realist theory, alliances commonly form in response to external threats. Such threats, in turn, are a function of relative power, geographic proximity, specific offensive capabilities, and perceived intentions. The logic is straightforward: because there is no central authority to protect states from each other, each is forced to fend for itself. When strong states arise, others will band together to prevent the most powerful from dominating. This tendency will increase if a powerful state is nearby, if it possesses capabilities that facilitate conquest (such as large, mobile military forces), and if it appears to have especially dangerous intentions (such as enduring territorial ambitions or an expansionist ideology).[2]

From this perspective, shifts in the level of threat will alter the nature of existing alliances significantly. If a strong state becomes weaker or is defeated in war, alliances formed to check its ambitions will be less necessary and more likely to dissolve. If a strong state abandons its revisionist ambitions (due to a regime change or some other internal shift), its neighbors will fear it less and be less inclined to ally against it. A defensive alliance may also collapse if its members begin to question each other's credibility, although this tendency has probably been exaggerated in the past.[3]

Contrary to what several critics have suggested, however, balance-of-threat theory does not predict that an existing alliance will immediately dissolve once the threat it was formed to counter disappears. Rather, the theory predicts that such alliances will become more fragile and less coherent and will devote less effort and attention to matters of mutual defense. Over time, such an alliance is more likely to dissolve, or at least to lapse into irrelevance. But realist theory does not specify how fast and how far the adjustment process will proceed; it predicts only the general direction the adjustment will take. The smaller the threat, the less cohesive and strong the alliance will be, unless forces lying outside the theory (see below) intervene to counter these tendencies. Although balance-of-threat theory cannot explain the persistence of an alliance whose original defensive purpose is gone, persistence by itself does not invalidate the theory.

This perspective reveals several important things about NATO's evolution over the past decade and its likely course in the years to come. First, NATO's decision to adopt a new set of missions in the 1990s reflected the widespread consensus that the collapse of the Soviet Union had eliminated NATO's original rationale. And though one could justify the Alliance as a hedge against Russia's future resurgence, that danger looked less and less compelling with the passage of time. Elites on both sides of the Atlantic were increasingly aware of NATO's fragility, and the fear that NATO might well collapse played an important role in the eventual decisions to intervene in Bosnia and Kosovo. Second, as realism predicts, NATO's various members are devoting less and less effort to common defense. The U.S. presence in Europe has declined steadily since 1990 (despite its grudging involvement in the Balkans), and European defense spending continues to fall. Third, the recent war in Kosovo has underscored Europe's continued dependence upon U.S. military power. When coupled with Europe's growing recognition that Uncle Sam might not be around forever, this realization has sparked a new effort to create a stronger European defense capability and a more unified European foreign policy. European leaders claim that these efforts will not undermine NATO, but a stronger and more unified Europe would have less need for U.S. backing and be much less willing to defer to U.S. "leadership." Under these circumstances, further erosion of transatlantic solidarity would be hard to forestall. Although officials and publics on both sides of the Atlantic remain committed to the idea of a transatlantic partnership, the cracks in the edifice are increasingly apparent.[4]

Alternative Realist Predictions

Realism is a broad theoretical tradition rather than a single specific theory, and different scholars working within this tradition reach somewhat different conclusions regarding NATO's future. For realists such as Kenneth Waltz, John Mearsheimer, and Christopher Layne, the end of the Cold War marks the dawn of a new multipolar era. Although the United States is the sole remaining superpower, these writers argue that America's "unipolar moment" will be short-lived and that the familiar dynamics of great-power rivalry will soon reemerge. The United States and Europe will drift apart, and security competition will return to Europe as soon as the "American pacifier" is withdrawn.[5]

William Wohlforth, who presents a very different perspective while remaining within the broad realist tradition, recently challenged this view. First, Wohlforth argues that the present unipolar structure is likely to last a long time.[6] Defining "unipolarity" as a condition in which "one state's capabilities are too great to be counterbalanced," he argues that the United States now enjoys a preponderance of power that is historically unprecedented. It has the world's largest and most productive economy, it spends more on defense than the next five powers combined, and it possesses a clear lead in the advanced technologies on which power is likely to rest in the future.

Unlike those realists who believe that other powers will soon rise or combine to check U.S. preponderance, Wohlforth believes that the present structure is likely to endure for at least several decades. Furthermore, geography helps reinforce America's existing advantages by discouraging other states from challenging the United States directly or from combining against it. Medium powers may grumble about U.S. dominance and offer symbolic resistance on occasion, but none of them is going to invite the focused enmity of the United States by organizing a countervailing coalition or engaging in significant territorial expansion.

The good news, according to Wohlforth, is that unipolarity is likely to be tranquil. The bloodiest world conflicts have arisen when two or more great powers were struggling for dominance, but that danger is eliminated now that one state is so obviously number one. U.S. power can also have a dampening effect on many regional rivalries. Thus, the present unipolar structure is likely to be more peaceful than the bipolar or multipolar orders that preceded it and is likely to last a long time.

Wohlforth's analysis carries several obvious implications for NATO. First, it helps us understand why NATO's European members complain about U.S. dominance but are unwilling to challenge it. Not only would Europe have to achieve unprecedented levels of political cohesion to truly balance the United States, but NATO's European members would also have to make major economic sacrifices in order to match U.S. military power. And because the United States is still committed to NATO but does not threaten to physically dominate Eurasia, its allies are still content to let Uncle Sam do the heavy lifting.

This argument also implies that NATO's fate will be determined largely by the evolution of U.S. domestic politics. In a sense, the entire notion of a "transatlantic community" has rested on the willingness of the United States to commit its power and prestige to the defense of territory on the other side of the ocean. "Atlanticism" has always been a one-way street: the United States deployed its power to protect its European allies but neither needed nor expected the Europeans to help it out in its own backyard. Thus, NATO's persistence depends largely on whether the United States will remain willing to pay the price of alliance leadership, and in particular, to risk blood and treasure to defend a set of wealthy and stable countries who no longer face a significant external threat.

The difference between these alternative realist perspectives is both striking and informative. For Wohlforth, the key to NATO's persistence is the willingness of the United States to remain actively involved, even though its vital interests are no longer at stake. For realists such as Waltz, Mearsheimer, and Layne, this is a vain hope. The central issue that divides them is the question of whether the American people will continue to support the Alliance if this commitment requires real sacrifices in blood or treasure. Wohlforth believes the costs will be low and the domestic will can be found; the other theorists are more skeptical.

Institutionalist Theory

A second theoretical perspective on alliances is derived from theories of international institutions. In the dominant "neoliberal" version of this approach, formal and informal institutions encourage cooperation by reducing transaction costs and facilitating compliance with existing agreements.[7] Institutions also create formal bureaucracies with a vested interest in keeping themselves in business, and provide decision-making procedures that can make it easier for the alliance members to adapt to new conditions. A highly institutionalized alliance may also create capacities that are worth keeping even after their original rationale is gone, especially when it costs less to maintain them than it did to create them in the first place. In other words, institutions are "sticky"; once established, they tend to endure even if the conditions that led to their creation are no longer present. From the perspective of institutionalist theory, in short, the more highly institutionalized the alliance, the more likely it is to endure even in the face of a significant shift in the array of external threats.

As a number of writers have recently emphasized, NATO is by far the most heavily institutionalized alliance in history. Not surprisingly, they also see this as a central source of its durability.[8] NATO is supported not only by the common interests of its members but by an elaborate transatlantic network of former NATO officials, defense intellectuals, military officers, journalists, and policy wonks whose professional lives have been devoted to the security issues of the Atlantic community. This elite community is unlikely to advocate dissolving NATO, and has labored hard to keep it alive. Moreover, as we saw in the Gulf War and in the Balkans, the capabilities and assets that NATO created in order to deal with the Soviet threat are still useful in the post–Cold War world. It would surely cost more to create these capacities from scratch than to keep them intact today, which makes preserving NATO both a prudent hedge and the path of least resistance. Finally, NATO has had 40 years to learn how to make decisions in peacetime, including decisions on how to adapt to new conditions. Although the lethargic response to events in the Balkans reminds us that NATO's elaborate decision-making apparatus can be a barrier to timely action, the existence of well-established rules and procedures made it easier to achieve and sustain a consensus within the Alliance on many issues.

In sum, NATO's highly institutionalized character facilitated its ability to adapt and endure following the disappearance of the Soviet Union. Here again, the more interesting question is whether the adjustments that have been made will be sufficient to keep the partnership intact well into the twenty-first century. On this score, perhaps the most worrisome development is the additional burdens created by the new Strategic Concept adopted in 1991 (and expanded further in 1999). For most of its history, NATO was a purely defensive alliance whose primary aim was to deter a Soviet attack on Western Europe. Its members were obliged to take action only if a foreign power attacked one of them directly, which meant that the Alliance in fact did not have to do much except prepare for a conflict that (fortunately) never occurred. Problems arising beyond NATO territory were not its responsibility, which meant that the Alliance could safely ignore peripheral conflicts without casting doubt on its credibility.

By contrast, NATO's new Strategic Concept has shifted its primary mission from deterrence or defense against direct external attack and toward the more expansive goal of combating potential sources of instability (e.g., terrorism, ethnic conflict, etc.), even if they lie outside NATO's formal boundaries. This decision in effect transformed NATO from a coherent and credible defense pact to a vaguer and more loosely defined regional militia. Unfortunately, the new strategic concept makes it impossible for NATO to ignore events in neighboring areas—such as the former Yugoslavia—without casting doubt on its claim to be the main guarantor of regional stability. Thus, NATO was forced to intervene in Bosnia and Kosovo in part because failing to act would have exposed its growing irrelevance. In a sense, NATO's stated purpose now rests on a perverse circular logic. We are told that NATO is needed in order to handle low-level security problems such as Bosnia or Kosovo, but we are also told that intervention in these regions is necessary in order to demonstrate that NATO is still needed.

Finally, institutionalist theory is most applicable when states already have strong common interests. It implies that institutions can overcome various impediments to cooperation and thus help states reach higher levels of welfare. But as several prominent institutionalists have acknowledged, they cannot prevent tensions from degenerating once sharp conflicts of interest arise. Although Europe and the United States are fortunate that neither threatens the other's vital interests, the number of shared interests is declining and the number of potential points of conflict is probably growing.[9] For the past ten years, NATO was a valuable institution in part because the future security environment looked ambiguous and because NATO membership eliminated another obvious form of uncertainty. To note but one example, NATO was a valuable hedge against the possibility of a resurgent Russia, which made keeping the Alliance intact especially appealing. With the passage of time, however, many of these ambiguities may be resolved (i.e., Russia looks less and less like a future threat). And as it becomes clear that Europe no longer needs U.S. protection, centrifugal tendencies are bound to increase. Although the presence of a large set of overlapping institutions is likely to slow a tendency for Europe and America to drift apart, nothing in neoliberal institutionalism suggests that these formal arrangements can prevent it from occurring.

Ideological and Cultural Solidarity

A third family of theories explains alliance formation and alliance cohesion by focusing on the shared domestic characteristics of the member states. Other things being equal, states usually prefer to ally with governments whose ambitions are compatible with their own. This sort of ideological or cultural solidarity can also reduce intra-alliance conflicts and help sustain an alliance even when its original rationale is gone.

Democratic Peace Theory

An obvious example of this sort of explanation derives from the well-known literature on the "democratic peace." In addition to arguing that democracies rarely (if ever) fight each other, democratic peace theorists also suggest that democracies tend to form especially stable alliances and are uniquely able to resolve conflicts within them.[10] Democratic states are also said to be able to make more credible commitments to one another, based on the claim that domestic audiences will punish leaders who fail to live up both to their own commitments and to those made by previous governments.[11] From this perspective, NATO's longevity and its capacity to adapt to new conditions is not merely a function of U.S. leadership or NATO's highly institutionalized character; it is also due to the fact that NATO is an alliance of states with stable and well-ordered democratic governments.[12]

Culture and Common Identities

In theory, an alliance could persist because its members come to see themselves as integral parts of a larger political community. Here the member states no longer regard themselves as wholly separable units, and thus find it difficult to imagine dissolving the partnership. According to this perspective, alliances are strengthened whenever members share similar political perspectives.[13]

An alliance sustained by a powerful sense of shared identity stands in sharp contrast to the traditional conception of an alliance as a purely instrumental compact between sovereign states. When independent states form an alliance to advance separate national interests, a significant change in the balance of threats should lead each state to reconsider its commitment(s). But when an alliance either reflects or creates a common identity, then the entire notion of an individual "national interest" becomes less appropriate. If key officials or mass publics begin to view their own societies as inextricable parts of a larger political community, then the members will tend to define their interests as identical even if the external environment changes dramatically. As a result, this sort of alliance—if that is even the correct term—is likely to be extremely robust.

This possibility resembles Karl Deutsch's notion of a "pluralistic security community," defined as a group of formally sovereign states enjoying a "sense of community" sufficient to "assure, for a long time, [...] the resolution of social problems without recourse to force."[14] Deutsch's work focuses primarily on social processes that could eliminate the possibility of violent conflict among the member states, but the same logic can also apply to alliances formed primarily to oppose others. If a group of formally sovereign states develop a powerful sense of shared identity, then a threat facing one of them by definition becomes a problem facing them all, and a mutual commitment is likely to be sustained even when there is no immediate challenge to be faced.

Deutsch argues that the formation of a security community rests on compatible values, expectations of economic gain, a wide range of mutual transactions (trade, communications flows, etc.), broad elite networks, and high levels of social communication. Drawing upon this logic, a number of scholars have recently suggested that the Atlantic Alliance is becoming a security community in the Deutschian sense. If so, then NATO (or something very much like it) is likely to endure even in the absence of a major external threat, simply because the member states no longer draw a firm distinction between their own interests and those of their alliance partners.[15]

This vision of transatlantic partnership is undeniably appealing, for it suggests that past patterns of competition will not recur and implies that Europe and America will continue to work together for ends that are widely shared. Not surprisingly, therefore, a number of prominent authors have recently invoked this sort of argument to underscore the importance of keeping NATO together. In *The Clash of Civilizations and the Remaking of World Order,* for example, Samuel Huntington calls for the "liberal" West (plus Japan) to preserve its unity against a growing threat from the Islamic world and from China. Although Huntington's prescription relies in part on the logic of the balance of power, the criteria used to identify friends or foes are explicitly cultural. The West should hang together because it shares certain liberal political and social values, values that place it at odds with the Islamic and Sinic "civilizations" in particular.[16]

Thus, theories that emphasize domestic characteristics—and especially the unifying force of shared democratic traditions—imply that NATO's future is bright despite the collapse of its principal adversary. Elite opinion and mass opinion continue to support the Alliance, there are a wealth of commercial interests binding Europe and America together, and the liberal traditions that have taken root on both sides of the Atlantic may make for more credible commitments and facilitate conflict resolution within the Alliance itself. At the very least, these common characteristics should slow the process of devolution.

Unfortunately, there are good reasons to question whether this vision is an accurate account of the past or a useful guide to the future. To begin with, even if there is a growing sense of community among particular states, such bonds are far weaker than the ties of nationalism *within* most modern states. Even in Europe itself, where the process of integration is most advanced, there is little evidence that loyalty to some larger political community has superseded the idea of a "national interest."[17] Politicians still owe their careers to how well they satisfy their own electorates, not to how well they advance the larger interests of the EU or the Atlantic community. These two goals do not necessarily conflict, of course, and may even reinforce each other on occasion. When they do conflict, however, most leaders will give greater priority to national preferences than to foreign ones. And as Robert Art has shown, European elites do not regard the possibility of "renationalization" as far-fetched, which suggests that identities have not merged enough to guarantee maintenance of the Alliance.[18] Indeed, German chancellor Gerhard Schroeder has recently called for Germany to take up its rightful role as a "great power in Europe," based on the pursuit of Germany's individual self-interest.[19]

Second, we are likely to exaggerate the importance of common ideologies and shared identities if we take the rhetoric of national leaders and foreign policy elites too seriously. Statesmen are prone to describe their allies in overly flattering terms, and to overstate the level of compatibility and identification between them, both to convince adversaries that the alliance is firm and to sustain domestic support for potentially costly commitments. During World War II, for example, the requirements of alliance solidarity led U.S. leaders to transform Joseph Stalin from a bloodthirsty tyrant into the benevolent "Uncle Joe." Similarly, Soviet and East European elites repeatedly emphasized the bonds of "socialist fraternity" that allegedly bound the Warsaw Pact together, and politicians on both sides of the Atlantic habitually invoke the rhetoric of community to describe U.S.-European relations. But it is difficult to know if such sentiments are robust enough to sustain the Alliance in the absence of other motivations. The litmus test comes not at summit meetings—which are designed for the ritual incantation of unifying rhetoric—but when the member states are actually called upon to do something for each other. And as NATO's erratic responses to the Bosnian and Kosovo crises suggest, unity can no longer be taken for granted.[20]

Third, and following from the second point, we should not assume that attitudes and identities formed in one context will continue to thrive once the circumstances in which they emerged are altered. A long-lived alliance may foster a sense of community among its members, and this sense of community is likely to delay its dissolution, but a dramatic change in the external environment will eventually strain the sense of community and shared identity as well. New political structures create new possibilities, new possibilities provoke new debates, and these debates frequently lead to different appraisals of where one's interest lies. There is no guarantee that today's allies will continue to feel a powerful sense of identity with their current partners now that the material conditions that brought them together have radically changed. To repeat: a sense of common identity may slow the process of dissolution, but the present level of mutual identification will not prevent the member states from pursuing an independent course should tangible conflicts of interest intrude.

Moreover, to the extent that new transnational identities are emerging, it does not bode well for NATO. The most important and dynamic example of this phenomenon is clearly the European Union, but its long-term effects on transatlantic solidarity are likely to be negative. If the EU continues to expand and deepen, it will make Europe a more powerful rival in economic matters and facilitate efforts to give Europe a common foreign and defense policy. The more unified Europe becomes, the less it will need U.S. protection, the less it will listen to Washington's guidance, and the less willing Americans will be to expend blood and treasure on Europe's behalf.

Conclusion

Several conclusions may be drawn from this brief summary of alternative theoretical perspectives. First, most realist theories explain why NATO's members have been and remain worried about NATO's long-term survival, and help us understand why the Alliance decided to take on a set of new missions in the aftermath of the Soviet collapse. Barring some unforeseen deterioration in the security environment in Europe, most realist theories also imply that NATO will continue to grow more fragile over time. Because realism sees alliances as primarily a response to external threats, the absence of a major threat will inevitably weaken the glue binding the member states together, and will allow previously suppressed conflicts of interest to reemerge. In Kenneth Waltz's memorable phrase, "NATO's days may not be numbered, but its years are."[21]

Although it also falls within the realist tradition, Wohlforth's analysis of unipolarity offers a more optimistic scenario. So long as the unipolar power (the United States) continues to exercise hegemonic leadership and remains committed to Europe's defense even though its own vital interests are less than fully engaged, there is no reason why the Alliance cannot continue for several more decades. From this perspective, NATO has ceased to be an instrument for collective defense and has become a tool of "great power management."[22] NATO has always been an instrument of U.S. influence, of course, but this vision implies that that role has now become paramount. And the critical question is whether U.S. leaders can sustain popular support for such a policy, particularly if America's European allies are increasingly resentful and if economic or political differences between Europe and America become more salient.

Second, institutionalist theories help explain why NATO has been able to redefine itself successfully, and why the collapse of the U.S.S.R. did not lead to NATO's immediate dissolution. Formal organizations rarely go out of business voluntarily, and NATO was no exception to this rule. If NATO had not existed in 1991, the United States and Europe would not have created it. But given that most of the costs were already sunk, keeping it going has seemed like the least risky option ever since.

Taken together, realist and institutionalist theories suggest a paradoxical conclusion. Because everyone recognizes that NATO is increasingly fragile, and because NATO's leaders remain fearful of allowing it to go out of business "on their watch," its members are increasingly reluctant to do anything that might weaken it further. As a result, they are willing to do things they might otherwise avoid merely to keep the Alliance from unraveling further. The United States tried to stay out of both Bosnia and Kosovo, for example, but eventually agreed to intervene because it was convinced that NATO might be finished if nothing was done. A leader such as Charles de Gaulle could take NATO for granted and act unilaterally, but today's leaders run the risk of destroying the Alliance if they indulge themselves as de Gaulle did. So long as the costs of maintaining the status quo remain small, therefore, we should expect NATO to continue. Thus, the key issue that divides NATO optimists from NATO pessimists is each group's estimate of how much keeping the Alliance together is likely to cost.

Third, and following from the second point, the "paradox of fragility" is likely to be exacerbated by the new "Strategic Concept" adopted in 1999. The new Strategic Concept commits NATO to a much more active role in shaping the global security environment.[23] Having formally taken on this ill-defined mission, however, NATO cannot ignore events like Bosnia or Kosovo without casting doubt on its continued relevance. Similarly, the new Strategic Concept creates the expectation of mutual support for a host of potential out-of-area missions, thereby sowing the seeds of future disagreement and resentment. By forcing NATO to act even when the vital interests of its members are not at stake, such a policy could easily generate a powerful backlash should any of these activities go awry.

Fourth, theories that emphasize the importance of shared political or ideological traditions help explain why the ideal of Western unity retains its hold on Western elites and publics alike. There is something to the idea of a common Western culture (even if it was no barrier to conflict in the past), and this factor probably retarded the centrifugal tendencies emphasized by realist approaches. The question is how durable and powerful such perceptions will be, particularly in the absence of more tangible motives for cooperation.

Ironically, each of the theories discussed here suggests that the key to NATO's future lies in the domestic politics of its largest member. If Americans continue to support a substantial international role, and if U.S. leaders can reverse the unilateralist trend that increasingly dominates U.S. foreign policy, then NATO's current features are likely to endure.

But we can hardly assume that these prerequisites will be met. Although NATO's leaders have responded energetically and for the most part skillfully to the new circumstances facing the Alliance, NATO has also been extremely lucky. The U.S. economy has performed exceptionally well over the past decade, which muted concerns about burden sharing and reinforced American perceptions that it is somehow destined to lead. NATO has also been lucky that its military activities in Bosnia, Kosovo, and the Persian Gulf have cost very few U.S. lives. But everyone's luck runs out sooner or later, and the real question is whether the United States will be willing to bear the burdens of leadership once its economy slows or its commitments entail tangible human costs.

Notes

1. See Karl W. Deutsch et al., *Political Community in the North Atlantic Area: International Organization in Light of Historical Experience* (Princeton: Princeton University Press, 1957); Mancur Olson and Richard Zeckhauser, "An Economic Theory of Alliances," *Review of Economics and Statistics* 48 (August 1966): pp. 266–79.
2. See Stephen M. Walt, *The Origins of Alliances* (Ithaca: Cornell University Press, 1987).
3. See Stephen M. Walt, "Why Alliances Endure or Collapse," *Survival* 39 (spring 1997): pp. 156–79.
4. See Stephen M. Walt, "The Ties That Fray: Why Europe and America Are Approaching a Parting of the Ways," *The National Interest* 54 (winter 1998): pp. 3–11.
5. See Kenneth N. Waltz, "The Emerging Structure of International Politics," *International Security* 18 (fall 1993): pp. 44–79; John J. Mearsheimer, "Back to the Future: Instability in Europe after the Cold War," *International Security* 15 (summer 1990): pp. 5–56; and Christopher Layne, "The Unipolar Illusion: Why New Great Powers Will Rise," *International Security* 17 (spring 1993): pp. 5–51.
6. See William C. Wohlforth, "The Stability of a Unipolar World," *International Security* 24 (summer 1999): pp. 5–41. For similar views, see Michael Mastanduno, "Preserving the Unipolar Moment: Realist Theories and U.S. Grand Strategy after the Cold War," and Ethan B. Kapstein, "Does Unipolarity Have a Future?" in *Unipolar Politics: Realism and State Strategies after the Cold War,* eds. Ethan B. Kapstein and Michael Mastanduno (New York: Columbia University Press, 1999).
7. The canonical text of neoliberal institutionalism is Robert O. Keohane, *After Hegemony: Cooperation and Discord in the World Political Economy* (Princeton: Princeton University Press, 1984). Applications to security affairs include John S. Duffield, *Power Rules: Explaining NATO's Conventional Force Posture* (Stanford: Stanford University Press, 1995); and Celeste A. Wallander, *Mortal Friends, Best Enemies: German–Soviet Cooperation after the Cold War* (Ithaca: Cornell University Press, 1999).
8. See especially Robert McCalla, "NATO's Persistence after the Cold War," *International Organization* 50 (summer 1996): pp. 445–75; John Duffield, "NATO's Functions after the Cold War," *Political Science Quarterly* 109 (winter 1994): pp. 763–88; and Celeste A. Wallander, "Institutional Assets and Adaptability: NATO After the Cold War," *International Organization* 54 (autumn 2000): pp. 705–35.
9. For example, if China does emerge as a rival great power in the next century, the United States will probably take steps to contain its influence. It is not clear whether NATO's European members would have much interest in doing so, however, and they have few assets to contribute. One can even imagine the United States moving closer to Russia to balance China, while China responds by courting Europe.

10. A useful survey of democratic peace findings is Steve Chan, "In Search of Democratic Peace: Problems and Promise," *Mershon International Studies Review* 41, supplement 1 (May 1997): pp. 59–91.
11. See, for example, Kenneth A. Schultz, "Do Democratic Institutions Constrain or Inform?" *International Organization* 53 (spring 1999): pp. 233–66.
12. See Thomas S. Risse-Kappen, *Cooperation Among Democracies: The European Influence on U.S. Foreign Policy* (Princeton: Princeton University Press, 1995).
13. Important exceptions are alliances in which a shared ideology prescribes that the members form a centralized, hierarchical movement. As the history of international communism and the pan-Arab movement suggest, centralized ideological movements tend to provoke leadership struggles within the movement and are therefore prone to bitter and protracted schisms. See Walt, *Origins of Alliances,* pp. 35–36, 206–12.
14. See Deutsch et al., *Political Community in the North Atlantic Area,* p. 5 and passim.
15. See Emanuel Adler and Michael Barnett, eds., *Security Communities* (Cambridge: Cambridge University Press, 1998); G. John Ikenberry and Daniel Deudney, "The Logic of the West," *World Policy Journal* 10 (winter 1993): pp. 17–26; and Ole Waever, "Integration as Security: Constructing a Europe at Peace," in *Atlantic Security: Contending Visions,* ed. Charles A. Kupchan (Washington, D.C.: Council on Foreign Relations/Brookings Press, 1998).
16. See Samuel P. Huntington, *The Clash of Civilizations and the Remaking of World Order* (New York: The Free Press, 1997). For a critique of Huntington's arguments, see my "Building Up New Bogeymen," *Foreign Policy* 106 (spring 1997): pp. 177–89.
17. See Anthony Smith, "National Identity and the Idea of European Unity," *International Affairs* 68, no. 1 (1992): pp. 55–76. If anything, "national loyalties" are devolving into more particularistic or ethnic identities, rather than expanding into some sort of all-encompassing "Western" or "Atlantic" identity.
18. Indeed, European elites wanted to preserve the U.S. presence in Europe primarily to prevent a return to interstate competition. See Robert J. Art, "Why Western Europe Needs the United States and NATO," *Political Science Quarterly* 111 (spring 1996): pp. 1–40.
19. See "A New German Assertiveness on Its Foreign Policy Stance," *New York Times,* September 12, 1999, p. A8.
20. It is interesting to speculate on what might have happened had the Kosovo crisis not erupted on the eve of NATO's fiftieth anniversary. Had the crisis occurred at a less embarrassing moment, a forceful allied response would have been less likely.
21. See Waltz, "The Emerging Structure of International Politics," p. 76.
22. See Paul Schroeder, "Alliances, 1815–1945: Weapons of Power or Tools of Management?" in *Historical Dimensions of National Security Problems,* ed. Klaus Knorr (Lawrence: University Press of Kansas, 1976).

23. The Strategic Concept adopted at NATO's fiftieth anniversary summit explicitly calls for the Alliance to prepare for crisis response operations outside the territory of the Alliance, because "instabilities on NATO's periphery could lead to crises or conflicts requiring an Alliance military response." See "The Alliance's Strategic Concept," press release NAC–S(99)65, April 23–24, 1999, available from the NATO webpage (http://www.nato.int/docu/pr/1999/p99-065e.htm).

CHAPTER TWO

Challenges to Euro-Atlantic Security

S. Neil MacFarlane

This volume is, in a general sense, about the structure of Euro-Atlantic security relations, and in particular about how the distribution of power in the North Atlantic Treaty Organization (NATO) affects Alliance decisions regarding the use of force. This presumes a shared perspective on threats and challenges to security, since alliances are generally conceived to be cooperative responses to a shared perception of threat.[1]

The structure of Euro-Atlantic security cooperation was constructed around the perceived threat of Soviet expansionism. This required West German recovery in order that that country's latent power could be deployed as part of an effort to deter the Union of Soviet Socialist Republics (U.S.S.R.) and its unwilling allies. Both the essential Soviet threat and the derivative necessity of German recovery implied a further requirement—that the United States be tightly associated with Western European security.

At the end of the 1980s, the noted Soviet Americanist, Georgii Arbatov, declared to the West: "We are going to do you a great disservice. We are going to deprive you of an enemy." And that they did, though not quite in the way that Academician Arbatov had in mind. The root purpose of the Alliance has disappeared. As a meeting of NATO put it in Rome in 1991:

> All the countries that were formerly adversaries of NATO have dismantled the Warsaw Pact and rejected ideological hostility to the West. They have, in varying degrees, embraced and begun to implement policies aimed at achieving pluralistic democracy, the rule of law, respect for human rights and a market economy. The political division of Europe that was the source of the military confrontation of the Cold War period has thus been overcome […]. The monolithic, massive and potentially immediate threat that was the principal concern of the Alliance in its first forty years has disappeared.[2]

What was true in 1991 is even more true today after a decade of Russian economic and military deterioration. The wars in Chechnya in 1994–96 and 1999–2000 suggest that the Russian military has great difficulty in handling operations against a guerrilla force of some 10,000 men in an area smaller than the state of Massachusetts. There is no theater military threat from Russia. It will probably be decades before Russia can recover to the point that it could mount such a threat once again.

Moreover, the evolution of relations between former adversaries inside western Europe—and in particular the multiplication of multilateral and transnational linkages amongst them—renders the notion of NATO as a necessary form of containment of Germany somewhat quaint. With these factors in mind, this chapter addresses three questions:

1. How does the Alliance perceive its security environment?
2. What are the challenges to regional security in Europe to which Euro-Atlantic structures of military-political cooperation are to respond?
3. Is NATO an appropriate forum in which to address these challenges?

As a preliminary step, however, it is useful to agree on some definitions. In considering challenges to European security, the first question one must address is what Europe we are talking about. In this chapter, the identity on which I focus is the Euro-Atlantic security community institutionalized in NATO—the developed and prosperous democracies of North America and western Europe and their new partners in central Europe.

A second conceptual question is what we mean by security. The meaning of security has been a subject of intense debate for at least two decades.[3] However, despite the contested nature of the concept in modern international relations, a survey of documents from NATO (1991 and 1999), the European Union (1999), the Western European Union (1992 and 1995), and the Organization for Security and Cooperation in Europe (1990) suggests that, whatever its merits, the European community has come to accept a rather broad and multidimensional conception of security, going well beyond traditional preoccupations with defense and focusing on conflict prevention, crisis management, peacekeeping, peacemaking, and humanitarian roles.[4]

Two questions need to be answered here. The first is "whose security?" In this chapter, I am talking primarily about the security of NATO member *states*, particularly those in Europe. This seems appropriate in a volume dealing with the nature of an alliance amongst states. The second is "what is being secured?" My focus in this context is on the core values of these states and their citizens, which I consider to be: defense of sovereignty (both internal—supremacy over all other authorities within a state's territory—and external—independence of outside authorities),[5] personal freedom and democratic representative institutions, economic welfare, social stability, and environmental quality.

Some elaboration might be useful here, first and foremost with regard to the relationship between the security of the state and that of the individual, and also with regard to sovereignty. Although in many instances it is problematic to conflate the security of the state with the security of individuals and groups within it, in the Euro-Atlantic context such an equation is at least plausible given the representative quality of the political institutions of the NATO member states (with the qualified exception of Turkey). Second, it may seem odd to count sovereignty as an essential core value when the western European states are integrated to the extent that conventional understandings of sovereignty can be applied only with difficulty and when the EU members of this community for many years now have arguably been ceding elements of their sovereignty upward to community institutions. However, this process of transfer is itself the product of sovereign state decision. It may culminate in a more or less sovereign regional entity. It is also possible for members to pull back. There is little doubt that European states continue to value sovereignty.

Finally, "challenges" are not synonymous with "threats." In this chapter, I spend considerable time on evolving threats to European security. But I shall also include a discussion of major institutional challenges. How "Europe" deals with these institutional questions is likely to have an important impact on the landscape of threats to European security and on the evolution of Euro-Atlantic cooperation in the field of security.

NATO Strategic Concepts, 1991 and 1999

In beginning a discussion of challenges to European security, it is useful to compare the 1991 and 1999 NATO Strategic Concepts. The 1991 Strategic Concept focused on threats emanating from "instabilities that may arise from the serious economic, social and political difficulties, including ethnic rivalries and territorial disputes, which are faced by many countries in central and eastern Europe." While not constituting in any sense a direct military threat to the Alliance, they could lead to instability in Europe, including armed conflict. This in turn could involve outside powers and spill over into NATO countries. The document also pointed to the potential problems associated with substantial remaining Soviet military capability. As it noted: "Even in a non-adversarial and cooperative relationship, Soviet military capability and build-up potential, including its nuclear dimension, still constitute the most significant factor of which the Alliance has to take account in maintaining the strategic balance in Europe."[6]

It then looked farther afield, noting the importance of stability and the consequences of instability in the Middle East and Mediterranean for NATO, citing in this context the military buildup and proliferation of weapons technologies including weapons of mass destruction (WMD) and ballistic missile capabilities. Finally, it noted the significance for the Alliance of global risks (proliferation, disruption of the flow of vital resources, and terrorism).[7] In view of this rather multifaceted threat assessment, it is striking that the emphasis of the Rome document rested strongly—and in rather conventional terms—on the function of collective defense. A second notable element—given the focus on out-of-area threats—was the absence of serious discussion of out-of-area operations.

The 1999 Strategic Concept provides an interesting contrast. In the first place, and for obvious reasons, the language concerning the need to deter remaining conventional military threats has disappeared. So, too, has that on the fundamental purpose of maintaining the balance in Europe. The function of collective defense is correspondingly played down (shifting from part 2—"Alliance Objectives and Security Functions"—to part 4—"Guidelines for Alliance Forces"), while the emphasis on partnership has grown. This reflects factors to which I shall return below. The emphasis on conflict prevention and crisis management is also far more prominent, as too is that on the need for cooperation with other multilateral structures (the EU, the OSCE, and the United Nations).

Turning to the identification of risks, the focus is on the emergence of "uncertainty and instability in and around the Euro-Atlantic area and the possibility of regional crises at the periphery of the Alliance, which could evolve rapidly." The document goes on to mention political, social, and economic difficulties, ethnic and religious rivalries, territorial disputes, inadequate or failed efforts at reform, the abuse of human rights, and the dissolution of states, all of which could "lead to local and even regional instability." This in turn could produce "crises affecting Euro-Atlantic stability, human suffering, and armed conflicts." Again, the document stresses the problem of spillover.

In this context, it is interesting, but not surprising, that no explicit mention is made of the possibility that the policies and actions of specific European states may constitute a threat to the Alliance. Russia, for example, is rather blithely characterized as a partner with a unique role to play. This contrasts rather starkly with the mention of the substantial military capability of the U.S.S.R.—which was potentially threatening despite the entente between East and West—in the 1991 Strategic Concept.

Turning to global concerns, the risk assessment then goes on to emphasize the existence of nuclear forces outside the Alliance area and the proliferation of weapons of mass destruction and the means for their delivery, mentioning the difficulty of controlling these processes and the possible spread of these capabilities to nonstate actors. This is part of a more general problem—the spread of technology that could be used in the production of weapons and the risks associated with information warfare. Strong emphasis is placed on the global challenges facing the Alliance (terrorism, international crime, and the possibility of disruption in flows of natural resources).[8]

The next section comments on the principal challenges highlighted by NATO in its Strategic Concepts. It assesses how serious these are and what role NATO (as opposed to other actors) might play in them.

Ethnic Conflict and Civil War

It would appear that the emphasis on this problem—present in the 1991 Strategic Concept—has grown over time. It strongly informs the focus on conflict prevention and crisis management in the purposes and tasks section of the 1999 Strategic Concept, as well as the commentary on the maintenance of military capability and missions there. One key policy issue within the Alliance at the moment is the development of the capacity of the European (and Canadian) allies to participate effectively in such operations alongside U.S. forces.[9] This is not surprising, since the two largest operations ever undertaken by NATO "out-of-area" (IFOR in Bosnia and KFOR in the Kosovo region of the Federal Republic of Yugoslavia) were responses to wars with ethnic dimensions.

In evaluating this emphasis, the key question is whether similar challenges are likely to emerge in the future. There is some prospect that a similar sequence of events could emerge in Montenegro if that jurisdiction chooses to exercise its option to exit the FRY. Should it choose to do so in the face of resistance from Belgrade, there is some prospect that NATO might find itself engaged in a third former Yugoslav theater. The likelihood of such an outcome appears to have diminished as a result of the overthrow of Slobodan Milosevic in October 2000. Beyond this, the question worth asking is: Where next? This is a difficult question to answer.

The logical venues are those in which territorially compact minority populations may challenge the territorial integrity of central European states. The most "promising" cases in this regard are those affecting Hungarian diaspora populations in southern Slovakia and Transylvanian Romania, and various (Serb, Albanian) minorities in Macedonia. With regard to the first two, it is striking how much progress has been made (by minority populations, majority-dominated central governments, and "kin-country" governments) to defuse these potential security challenges. This reflects in part the success of conditionalities employed by European institutions (the EU, NATO, and the CoE), and the mediating efforts of the OSCE (and particularly the High Commissioner on National Minorities) in the realm of conflict prevention.

As for Macedonia, this is more problematic. Kosovo may become independent, despite the democratic changes in Serbia. It may then seek unification with Albania. This raises serious problems for Macedonia, which possesses a rather compactly settled Albanian minority that constitutes approximately 23 percent of the population. The ethnic balance in the country is unstable, given that the natural growth rate of the Albanian minority is higher than that for other ethnic groups in the country. The sensitivity of the ethnic balance in Macedonia was evident during the Kosovo crisis of 1999. The massive influx of Kosovar Albanians led to mass demonstrations in Skopje and to the sudden expulsion of several tens of thousands of refugees to Albania in the early stages of the crisis.

There is some prospect that in the event that Kosovo joined Albania, the Albanian minority in Macedonia might also seek entry into a greater Albania. On the other hand, it is likely that substantial NATO forces will be in place in immediate proximity to Macedonia for the foreseeable future. So the means to respond will exist in the vicinity of the problem, should the problem occur.

Beyond these cases, there is no substantial prospect of ethnic-civil conflict in central Europe. Indeed, to judge from the recent record of France (Corsica), the United Kingdom (Northern Ireland), and Spain (the continuing activities of the ETA in pursuit of Basque independence), the issue is of greater significance in western Europe than it is in Europe's center.

Territorial Challenges

Another issue raised in the 1991 and 1999 Strategic Concepts was that of territorial conflict amongst the states recently freed from Soviet domination. The number of potential *irredenta* was impressive in 1991 and included potential disputes between Latvia and Russia, Estonia and Russia, Poland and Lithuania, Germany and Poland, Poland and the then Czechoslovakia, Slovakia and Hungary (over rights in the Danube watercourse), Hungary and Romania, Bulgaria and Macedonia, Bulgaria and Romania, Ukraine and Slovakia, Ukraine and Poland, Ukraine and Hungary, and Ukraine and Romania, not to mention the numerous territorial issues enlivening relations among the CIS members.

Again, it is striking after ten years of post–Cold War reality how little actual conflict has emerged out of the rather messy post–World War II (and post-Soviet collapse) territorial dispensations. Most of the outstanding territorial issues mentioned above have been resolved by treaty or by unilateral renunciation, even in instances when the claim was quite sound (as, for example, with Estonian claims on Russia). The key here has been the desire of these states to enter European institutions, notably NATO and the EU. In order to make a credible case for doing so, they have had to get their house in order. Both institutions have made it reasonably clear that they would not seriously consider a membership application by a state with unresolved territorial claims. In the case of the split in Czechoslovakia, the external incentives for conducting this process in a voluntary and orderly fashion were likewise clear.[10] A further, though probably less important, factor has been the OSCE norm concerning territorial integrity and the inviolability of internationally recognized frontiers.

Spillover, Migration, and Terror

A third area of concern mentioned in both the 1991 and 1999 Strategic Concepts and in much associated literature is the issue of spillover from conflict or state collapse in central and eastern Europe. The principal form that spillover has taken over the past decade is forced migration (for example, the massive flow of former Yugoslav citizens to Germany in 1991–93 or the flood of Albanians to Italy in 1997). As has been evident in the link between migration and the growth of the extreme right in Germany, Austria, and Switzerland, such flows can have deeply disturbing effects on recipient states. The reactions of the EU to the 1999–2000 arrival in government of Austria's Freedom Party amply illustrate the sensitivity of this issue in European capitals.

Several qualifications are important here, however. First, the dangers of spillover are related to the incidence of conflict. To the extent that conflict is less likely in the future in central Europe, then so too is spillover from it. Second, the experience of Germany in radically curtailing the flow of asylum seekers in 1993–94 suggests that states have effective means of managing this problem unilaterally. The evolution of the Schengen regime indicates further that western European states are developing multilateral mechanisms to address the migration issue more effectively.

More generally, the "international community" is, willy-nilly and right or wrong, revising the international refugee regime in order to prevent people from fleeing conflict, notably through increased efforts to deal with migrant populations inside their own countries or in contiguous states.[11] Finally, the effects of specific episodes of mass migration are often concentrated in single states rather than constituting a regional problem, as was more or less evident in the case of Albanians crossing the Adriatic. Not surprisingly, this asymmetry of interest complicates multilateral response. This explains the lack of a NATO response to the Albanian crisis and the decision of the Italians to lead a "coalition of the willing" instead.[12]

The problem of refugees from conflict is only one aspect of the issue of migration. The second is economic migration. Here, it is noteworthy that the dimensions of the problem of south-north and east-west economic migration have turned out to be smaller than most anticipated in the early years of the decade, while state and regional capacities (e.g., Schengen) have turned out to be more robust than initially anticipated in dealing with this problem.

The second major aspect of spillover is the spread of violence to the Euro-Atlantic community. This may involve disputes between immigrant communities (such as those between Kurds and Turks in Germany and between Greeks and Macedonians in Canada), or efforts to influence host government policy on the conflict in question, either through protest (Kurds in Germany) or through terror (for example, the bombings in France attributed to Algerian Islamic militants or, for that matter, the bombing of New York's World Trade Center). The effects of such activities—so far—are not so much direct and material as psychological. There is little indication that terror and wider conflict spillovers constitute fundamental threats to the sociopolitical fabric of the Euro-Atlantic community.

With regard to responses to terrorism, so far as one can tell, national rather than multilateral means predominate. U.S. actions against Osama bin Laden suggest, moreover, that military force is a rather blunt, ineffectual, and controversial instrument. Intelligence and police agencies play a more important role than does the military. In the multilateral realm, cooperation amongst such agencies has played and is likely to play a more substantial role than cooperation in the Alliance context in addressing this type of threat. All of this leaves one with the question of just what the role of the Alliance is or should be with regard to terrorism.

Similar doubts could be raised regarding the relevance of the Alliance to migration as a security issue. The preferred means of managing it have been through U.N. agencies (e.g., the United Nations High Commissioner for Refugees and the International Organization for Migration), the Schengen apparatus, and national policies. Where NATO has played an effective role is in the stabilization of crises producing migrants, thereby stemming the flow and permitting return.

In short, the challenges to specifically European security that the two concepts focus upon are underwhelming. The regional security context of Europe, although hardly problem-free, is more threat-free than it has been at any time in its history. This itself is a problem to which I shall return later.

Global Threats

Before discussing institutional challenges, some comment may be useful on the "global" dimensions of Europe's threat environment mentioned in the

Strategic Concepts. I have already touched briefly on terrorism. Two other factors are particularly important. The first is the proliferation of weapons of mass destruction. The second is threats to resource flows. The proliferation of weapons of mass destruction and the means for their delivery, particularly toward the Middle East, is a matter of deep and persistent concern to security planners on both sides of the Atlantic. It is linked to terrorism, given the increasing access that nonstate actors appear to be gaining to these capabilities. It is difficult, however, to base alliance cohesion on threats linked to WMD proliferation, as these threats are by nature diffuse, sporadic, limited, and they vary widely in their probable effects on NATO partners. Moreover, it is not entirely clear what value added the Alliance would bring in this area to the already substantial state-based involvement (e.g., U.S. sanctions on "rogue" states and efforts to move toward deployment of limited ballistic missile defense) and multilateral involvement (e.g., the Missile Technology Control Regime and the chemical and biological weapons conventions, as well as the nuclear nonproliferation regime).

Concerning threats to flows of essential resources, it is hard to view these as compelling. No one is in a position to contest U.S. dominance of sea lines of communication. As to constriction at source, it is hard to see the development of market power on the part of any particular producer or group of producers sufficient to constrain the supply of natural resources sufficiently to cause significant dislocation. It would be difficult for producers to sustain such constraint, since they have as much need of the revenues from their sale as consumers have for the resources themselves.

The one potential exception is hydrocarbon energy, given the concentration of reserves in the Persian Gulf. Indeed, OPEC enjoyed considerable success in pushing oil prices upward through reduction in production and export in 1999 and 2000. However, if history is any indication, the capacity of the OPEC members to sustain this success is likely to be limited, not least because the rise in prices will accelerate the development of alternative energy provinces (e.g., the Caspian Basin and offshore West African deposits).

It is worth noting that NATO has demonstrated its utility in responding to threats to energy security. The Gulf War of 1990–91 was in part about sustaining secure access to hydrocarbon reserves in the Persian Gulf and preventing Iraq from establishing an unacceptable degree of control over the region's resources. NATO staff and infrastructure played a very important part in planning and implementing the coalition response to the invasion of Kuwait, and forces otherwise committed to NATO roles were central to the successful operation. Prior training in joint operations no doubt enhanced the effectiveness of cooperation amongst NATO allies in the field. Yet a repeat of this scenario seems unlikely. Iraq will not be in a position to mount a conventional challenge to the status quo in the Gulf for some time to come, if ever. There are no obvious alternative challengers to the balance in the Gulf region.

It is also noteworthy that the possibility of a role for NATO in ensuring the security of energy infrastructure in and from the Caspian Basin has been raised frequently both by policymakers in the southern Caucasus and by Western analysts. In 1999, for example, Vafa Gulu-zade (Azerbaijani president Aliev's then principal foreign policy adviser) raised the possibility of a NATO base on Azerbaijan's territory, one purpose of which would be the protection of pipelines from the Caspian Sea to Georgia. The eventual membership in NATO of at least Azerbaijan and Georgia has been mooted as a way to protect what some U.S. policymakers have come to identify as a vital interest in the free flow of hydrocarbons from the Caspian. Georgian policymakers, including the president, have deployed the energy argument as a justification for NATO to repeat its Kosovo operation in the region to restore the territorial integrity of Georgia.[13]

On the other hand, the level of reserves in the region is too low to justify this kind of engagement. The extension of membership to the Caucasus, or the permanent deployment of NATO forces there would have a profoundly negative impact on the Alliance's relationship with Russia. It would risk involving the Alliance in local conflicts that have proven to be very intractable and have little to do with Alliance interests. Not surprisingly, in Brussels there is no obvious interest in or enthusiasm about the accession of these newly independent states and no evidence of the development of contingency plans for deployment in the region. NATO activities in the southern former U.S.S.R. are limited to PfP and are likely to continue to be so limited for the foreseeable future.[14]

The Russian Problem

Turning from threats that NATO does talk about to those that it avoids in official documentation, the most obvious problem is Russia. The NATO-Russia Founding Act notwithstanding, the Euro-Atlantic security community has not managed to discover a way to manage the Russian problem effectively. Despite the effort to paper over the impact of NATO enlargement, the Russian foreign policy and defense elites continue to display considerable consensus that this process is at odds with Russia's national interest. Opinion in Russia seems to range from the visceral hostility to NATO characteristic of the nationalist/communist right to the more nuanced criticisms of liberals. The latter argue that for NATO to play a positive role in European security, it needs to transform itself from an essentially collective defense organization to a cooperative security mode as part of an authoritative pan-European structure.

Further enlargement, particularly if it embraces former Soviet republics (e.g., Lithuania, Latvia, Estonia), will reinforce this alienating effect. Russian concerns over NATO have been deepened by the Alliance's actions in Kosovo and by the clear effort on the part of NATO to circumvent the U.N. Charter's provisions concerning the use of force by regional associations (Chapter VIII), particularly when such use is directed at internal issues facing member states (Article 2, paragraph 7).

One might argue that this does not really matter—that, when push comes to shove, Russia has to play ball, and if it doesn't, so what? From a narrow and short-term security perspective, such a position is appropriate. However, it discounts the future heavily. Russia will probably recover. When it does so, it would be preferable for it to do so within a framework of European security whose legitimacy it accepts. It would not be an exaggeration to argue that the principal security challenge facing the Euro-Atlantic community in the longer term is what to do with Russia, and the associated issue of how to deal with the security problems of the non-Russian newly independent states. Here we run into a Catch-22. To the extent that NATO attempts to address these issues through reaching out to the former Soviet republics, it enhances Russian perceptions of insecurity and victimization further. To the extent that NATO does not respond to the security needs of these republics, they remain dependent and vulnerable.

Institutional and Identity Challenges

This is closely related to a further point. If one looks at Europe as a whole, it is striking how institutionally dense the West is and how institutionally deficient the East is. This is being addressed to some extent in central Europe through processes of enlargement. But it is improbable that this process will proceed substantially into the former Soviet Union. The institutional deficit is both a product and a producer of instability. This instability in turn may engender many of the more immediate challenges discussed above. The deficit will grow increasingly serious as Russia begins to recover in economic and security terms. The problem here, I suspect, is the lack of a widely accepted vision of institutional architecture, and the partly consequent problem of institutional rivalry. The result is an incrementalism that contributes to the alienation of Russia while doing little to address the security problems of the other former Soviet states.

A second significant institutional challenge concerns identities within the Alliance, and notably the emergence and institutionalization of a European identity in security within the context of the Euro-Atlantic connection.[15] It is hard to see how the first institutional challenge can be properly addressed without resolving this central question. Here too, however, there is a problem. The development of a shared European perspective on security might conduce to a weakening of the transatlantic link, since such a perspective might well not correspond to American conceptions of the purposes of the Alliance. Such tensions are already obvious with regard to potential global roles of NATO structures, in the relationship of NATO to the United Nations, and in the defense industrial relationship between Europe and the United States. On the other hand, the absence of an ESDI is an impediment to the development of regional capabilities for action in instances in which the United States prefers not to take a leading role. The failure of the European allies to coordinate their national defense and procurement policies merely widens the gap between U.S. and European capabilities, creating significant interoperability problems and diminishing the value of the Alliance to the United States.

Third, and finally, NATO and the Euro-Atlantic security identity may in part be the victims of their own success. The Alliance's cohesion over the long term played a significant role in the disappearance of the major threats in response to which it had coalesced. The reputation of NATO in turn has been of considerable utility in tamping down anticipated post–Cold War threats. Aspirant members of European structures strive to resolve their interstate disputes and internal problems so that they can join. However, although the staying power of these cooperative structures in the absence of the forces that caused them to appear is impressive, realists have a point in asking just how long these structures can endure in the absence of compelling threats. The strains are evident in the long delays in response to the Bosnia and Kosovo crises, in the ruminations of leading presidential candidates that the time has come for America to focus in a more disciplined way on matters of direct interest to the United States, and in European concerns that NATO may become an instrument of an American global agenda that European powers do not necessarily share.

Conclusion

The comparatively "threat-free" security environment in western and central Europe is in part a product of the accumulated reputation of NATO as an effective producer of security for member states. In this respect, perhaps the key role of the Alliance in western and central Europe is the symbolic one of reassurance. The Alliance's reputation depends in turn on the cohesion of members and their willingness to invest in Alliance structures.

On the other hand, the weakness of imminent "threats" may weaken the cohesion and diminish members' investment in Alliance structures. This will in turn draw into question its reputation and its associated dampening effect on potential and incipient processes of conflict on the margins. In this respect, one of the more compelling challenges to European security may be the absence of compelling challenges to European security. The weakening of the Alliance, in turn, may produce the threats that the Alliance could be useful in addressing.

Notes

1. See Stephen M. Walt, *The Origins of Alliances* (Ithaca: Cornell University Press, 1987).
2. NATO, "Strategic Concept" (November 7–8, 1991). Text available at: http://www.nato.int/docu/comm/49–95/c911107.a.htm.
3. Useful contributions to this debate include notably: Jessica Tuchman Mathews, "Redefining Security," *Foreign Affairs* 68 (spring 1989): pp. 162–77; Barry Buzan, *People, States and Fear: An Agenda for International Security Studies in the Post–Cold War Era* (London: Harvester Wheatsheaf, 1991); Richard Ullman, "Redefining Security," *International Security* 8 (summer 1983): pp. 129–53; Peter J. Katzenstein, *The Culture of National Security: Norms and Identity in World Politics* (New York: Columbia University Press, 1996); Keith Krause and Michael Williams, "Broadening the Agenda of Security Studies: Politics and Methods," *Mershon International Studies Review* 40 (October 1996): pp. 229–54; Muthiah Alagappa, *Asian Security Practice: Material and Ideational Influences* (Stanford, CA: Stanford University Press, 1999).
4. NATO, "Strategic Concept," November 7–8, 1991; NATO, "The Alliance's Strategic Concept," April 23–24, 1999 (http://www.nato.int/docu/pr/1999/p99-065e.htm); European Union, "European Council Declaration on Strengthening the Common European Policy on Security and Defense," (Cologne: European Council, June 1999); Western European Union, "Western European Union Council of Ministers Petersberg Declaration" (Bonn: WEU, June 1992); ibid., "European Security: A Common Concept of the 27 WEU Countries" (Madrid: WEU, November 1995); and Organization for Security and Co-operation in Europe (OSCE), "Charter of Paris for a New Europe" (Paris: OSCE, 1990).
5. Hedley Bull, *The Anarchical Society* (New York: Columbia University Press, 1977), pp. 8–9.
6. NATO, "Strategic Concept," November 7–8, 1991, p. 4.
7. Ibid.
8. NATO, "The Alliance's Strategic Concept," April 23–24, 1999, pp. 4–7.
9. Elizabeth Becker, "Deep Disparity in NATO: U.S. Allies Accept Need to Improve Capability," *International Herald Tribune,* September 23, 1999, pp. 1, 7.
10. For a brief, but useful, discussion of the role of the European Community in the management of the process of dissolution in Czechoslovakia, see Robert A. Young, *The Breakup of Czechoslovakia* (Kingston, Ont.: Queen's University Institute of Intergovernmental Relations, 1994), pp. 51–52.

11. Adam Roberts, "More Refugees, Less Asylum: A Regime in Transformation," *Journal of Refugee Studies* 11 (December 1998): pp. 375–95.
12. Ettore Greco, *Delegating Peace Operations: Improvisation and Innovation in Georgia and Albania* (New York: United Nations Association of the United States, 1998), pp. 19–21.
13. For a broader discussion of American policy in the Caspian area, see S. Neil MacFarlane, "Amerikanische Politik in Zentralasien und im Transkaukasus," *Aus Politik und Zeitgeschichte* B43-44/98 (October 1998): pp. 3–12.
14. I discuss these activities in more detail in S. Neil MacFarlane, "New Military Missions for NATO: Peacekeeping Partnership in the CIS," in *Quatrièmes conférences stratégiques annuelles de Paris: L'avenir de l'OTAN* (Paris: Institut de recherches internationales et stratégiques, 1999), pp. 53–62.
15. For a very useful account of the origins and significance of this process, see Peter Van Ham, "Europe's Common Defense Policy: Implications for the Trans-Atlantic Relationship," *Security Dialogue* 31 (June 2000): pp. 215–28.

CHAPTER THREE

The Constraint of Legitimacy: The Legal and Institutional Framework of Euro-Atlantic Security

Alan K. Henrikson

The United Nations Charter, in its preamble, states that "armed force shall not be used, save in the common interest."[1] According to this constraint, nations cannot employ force unless they do so in a way that reflects, and is widely seen to reflect, the needs, wishes, and values of the international community—if not the entirety of it, then at least the main part of it. In the absence of a world government capable of making globally binding decisions, only one organ is empowered to authorize the use of military force at the international level, and that is the U.N. Security Council.[2] Nations are generally skeptical, even hostile, toward subjecting themselves to someone else's decision. But the Security Council, as in the cases of the Korean War and the Gulf conflict, "has taken decisions in the name of, and binding upon, the entire international community."[3]

The 1998–99 crisis over Kosovo was also a crisis of international legitimacy.[4] The question was the authorization of the use of force with regard to an internal situation, inside the Federal Republic of Yugoslavia.[5] The focus of attention, initially, was the U.N. Security Council. It soon became evident, however, that Russia and China would veto the military action needed to stop the violence being carried out against the Kosovar Albanians. The Security Council thus could not authorize action. Nor, in the end, could it prevent NATO from acting, with Operation Allied Force.

To some critics of Operation Allied Force, the United States and its allies were a new "Holy Alliance," and their intervention in the internal affairs of

Yugoslavia was reminiscent of the "Brezhnev Doctrine." Far from having received a legitimizing mandate from the United Nations, they had taken responsibility for action upon themselves. "It's not good for NATO to arrogate to itself what sounds like a unilateral right—if only because it might give similar ideas to the Russians or the Chinese about invading some small neighbor of theirs," a British official recognized.[6] Arguably, the NATO allies had fragmented the structure of international authority. They had threatened the world order with "moral relativism."[7]

"Unless the Security Council is restored to its preeminent position as the sole source of legitimacy on the use of force," U.N. Secretary-General Kofi Annan stated in May 1999 as NATO was in its second month of bombing, "we are on a dangerous path to anarchy." Unless the Council's members "can unite around the aim of confronting massive human rights violations and crimes against humanity on the scale of Kosovo, then we will betray the very ideals that inspired the founding of the United Nations." Annan rejected having to choose between "unity and inaction in the face of genocide"—as in the case of Rwanda—and "division and regional action"—as in the case of Kosovo. The Security Council should be able to "find common ground in upholding the principles of the Charter, and find unity in defense of our common humanity." He cited "the preference for so-called coalitions of the willing" as having contributed to the increasing resort to unauthorized force.[8]

Annan's frank raising of the issue of authorization arguably compounded the very problem of the illegitimacy of the use of force that he lamented. He thus exposed the gap between the agreed-upon structures and processes for approving military action such as that against Yugoslavia and what actually had been done. In theory, a Security Council resolution still was needed. In practice, the legitimizing of international force by the Security Council was not a strict necessity, as the constraint of international legitimization as defined in the U.N. Charter had not held back NATO.

In September 1999, with the crisis over, Secretary-General Annan further inquired whether it was "legitimate for a regional organization to use force without a U.N. mandate." In his judgment, this is what occurred when NATO waged its war against Yugoslavia: "In Kosovo a group of countries intervened without seeking authority from the United Nations Security Council." To those who saw in the Kosovo action the sign of a new trend in international law enforcement, he asked: "Is there not a danger of such interventions undermining the imperfect, yet resilient, security system created after the second world war, and of setting dangerous precedents for future interventions without a clear criterion to decide who might invoke these precedents and in what circumstances?"

It is important to note that Annan did not challenge the idea of "humanitarian intervention" as such. "Nothing in the U.N. charter precludes a recognition that there are rights beyond borders," he stated. "What the charter does say is that 'armed force shall not be used save in the common interest.'" He then posed a series of questions, to him obviously still open ones, in the context of examining the legal and institutional frameworks for forcible action: "But what is that common interest? Who shall define it? Under whose authority? And with what means of intervention?"[9]

NATO as an "Alternative" to the United Nations

Can it ever be truly legitimate, one must ask, for the North Atlantic Treaty Organization or any other nonuniversal group of states to employ military force outside their own jurisdictions and inside the territory of another country? The main question is one not so much of the substantive reason or legal-moral justification for allied intervention as it is of the *source* and the *scope* of the authority claimed for such action. Alliances, almost by definition, represent something *less than* "the common interest" that Secretary-General Annan, on the basis of the U.N. Charter, says must be served if the use of armed force is to be legitimated.

Alliances are arrangements made in relation to a balance of power. They remain *mere* alliances, no matter how apparently inclusive, nonthreatening, or beneficial their formation and their maintenance may be. The efforts that occasionally have been made by the North Atlantic Treaty Organization to present itself as an instrument of a wider international general will, whether that of the Cold War "West" or of the post–Cold War "international community," probably never can be entirely convincing. "Collective self-defense," the inherent right of which is acknowledged in Article 51 of the U.N. Charter and is cited in Article 5 of the North Atlantic Treaty, is conceptually different from "collective security," U.N.-style.

Some commentators, making a very sharp conceptual distinction between "collective defense" and "collective security," have contended that they are logically inconsistent and actively compete with each other. Most famously, in "Collective Defense versus Collective Security," Arnold Wolfers observes that they "clash," as they did when the United States was obliged by its subscription to the principles of the United Nations at the time of the 1956 Suez crisis to oppose the aggression carried out against Egypt by two of its closest NATO allies, Great Britain and France.[10] Similarly, though from a realistic pro-U.N. rather than a realistic pro-NATO perspective, Inis Claude writes that NATO "can do only what an alliance can do." It "cannot do what collective security theoretically could do if collective security were a feasible achievement."[11]

As one who has attempted to make the case for the compatibility of NATO with the U.N. Charter and the United Nations Organization, I am well aware of the difficulty in legal and political theory, as well as in historiographical analysis, of demonstrating their consistency.[12] It is hard to deny that during the decades of the Cold War there was no cooperation between them.[13] My own argument for the compatibility of NATO and the United Nations—more particularly, of the potential congruence of the former's power and the latter's authority—is a long-term, historically oriented one. It emphasizes the factor of political strategizing, in which legal and institutional considerations, being relatively static, are secondary. The role of politics, of sheer political opportunism and sometimes necessity, is a more dynamic phenomenon, and is primary. NATO and the United Nations simply *have* to work together. The legal and institutional structures of the United Nations in particular, however, frame, and thereby constrain, any discussion of what they can do together in confronting situations such as that concerning Kosovo.

The United Nations' "Collective Legitimization" Function

"Collective legitimatization," as Inis Claude has pointed out, has emerged to become one of the major political functions of the United Nations.[14] So successful has the United Nations become at this novel activity that it became recognized, even during the Cold War years, as "the custodian of the seals of international approval and disapproval." Today, however, this sole custodial possessor of the seals of international legitimacy is being challenged, in fact if not in intent, by NATO.

It should be emphasized that the collective legitimization function acquired by the United Nations is not mainly a matter of legality or of judicial proceeding, although international law is hardly irrelevant to the process. The key elements of it, as Claude points out, are its *collective* and its *political* aspects. Although states can justify their actions on their own, he claims, they need the approval of as many other states as possible in order to gain what he calls collective legitimacy. Moreover, adds Claude, "it is a political judgment by their fellow practitioners of international politics that they primarily seek, not a legal judgment rendered by an international judicial organ."[15] Legal rulings in support of internationally held political positions can, of course, buttress a political case. Lawfulness enhances rightfulness.[16]

In the euphoria over the end of the Cold War and the appearance of East-West comity and even cooperation at the center of the United Nations, which the Security Council effectively is, the role of that U.N. organ in particular as the collective legitimizer of international enforcement arguably has become accepted as part of the "new world order."[17] The Security Council's portentous authorization on November 29, 1990, of "all necessary means" usable by member states to reverse the Iraqi invasion of Kuwait was historic. And indeed, never again, it was widely assumed, would significant military action be taken without Security Council authorization. This implied that the veto power possessed by the five permanent members of the Security Council might well never again be exercised, at least on a matter of major international importance, such as the Kosovo issue became.

The Veto Question

The very existence of the Security Council veto system, the way it "privileges a group of five states," is bound to be contentious. As Adam Roberts rightly has pointed out, the system does have merits. Without the veto, the United Nations might not have been born at all. Its existence may have defused many potential conflicts among the United Nation's major members and saved the organization from impossible missions. Finally, and more positively, Roberts notes, "it may have contributed to a sense of responsibility and a habit of careful consultation among the permanent five." Although the permanent members' veto is widely perceived as having long prevented the United Nations from fulfilling its functions, it has contributed to making "UN decision-making procedures superior to those of its predecessor, the League of Nations, and of many regional organizations."[18] A historical and comparative perspective is necessary.

Nonetheless Roberts shares a widespread view that the Security Council cannot retain its legitimacy or, by extension, its legitimization function without adapting. Given the considerable institutional and procedural obstacles involved in modifying the Security Council, only minor changes in it might be possible, however. Reforming the Security Council through revision of the Charter would be difficult. Easier to achieve would be strengthening of the Council through non-permanent-membership election, by vote of the General Assembly, less according to "equitable geographical distribution" and more in accordance with the "contribution" that prospective members could make to the maintenance of international peace and security, as well as other purposes of the organization (Article 23, paragraph 1). Changes in the procedures of the Security Council could help, the most important being "more regular Security Council consultations" with major states not on the Council, and with the parties that are interested in particular issues.[19]

Bringing the General Assembly more directly into deliberations regarding the maintenance of international peace and security also would be desirable. In extreme cases, the General Assembly is even empowered to take over from the Security Council, should the latter become deadlocked. During the Korean War, the U.S.-sponsored "Uniting for Peace" plan gave the General Assembly the authority to recommend, though not order, collective measures to be taken. If Article 24 of the Charter conferred upon the Security Council "primary responsibility" for maintaining international peace and security, that did not prevent the General Assembly from exercising a kind of reserve power.[20]

Although widely considered to be a departure from what the drafters of the Charter had in mind in 1945, the Uniting for Peace plan was passed. It was judged valid by the International Court of Justice. And it remains on the books. It was an expedient, but it has been a useful expedient. And it could, conceivably, be used again, as the Canadian and some other governments briefly contemplated doing during the Kosovo crisis. Apart from bypassing the obstruction of the Security Council veto, use by member states of the Uniting for Peace procedure in the General Assembly could enable the United Nations to *continue* to exercise its collective legitimization function, though in a way that could and probably would be institutionally divisive.

The "Legitimacy" Debate over Kosovo

During the Kosovo crisis, NATO forces took forcible action against Yugoslavia without any endorsement by the Security Council, because Russia had stated that it would veto such action and because China was plainly opposed as well. The Security Council could not act. This has put the Council's "primary responsibility" for maintaining international peace and security in doubt. In theory, it held to that position; in practice, it was at risk of losing it.

This issue of trying to get Security Council approval posed a terrible dilemma for the Western powers. On one horn of the dilemma, the United States and its NATO allies could seek a Security Council mandate, fail to get it, and thus expose a political division at the heart of the United Nations. This might not heal over. The allies might thereby ruin an institution on which they ostensibly relied for legitimacy they obviously still needed. On the other horn of the dilemma, the United States, Britain, and France could refrain from all further discussion of using military force in the Security Council. They would thereby preserve a superficial comity with the Russians and Chinese and others who might be opposed to NATO action, but they would in so doing marginalize the United Nation's central organ for the management of international conflict. In short, they could debilitate the organization by trying but failing to use it. Or they could discredit the organization by effectively ignoring it.

In these circumstances, it was natural to ask, and many did: What, really, *is* "legitimacy"? What does it *do*? Does authorization *have* to come only from the United Nations? Could not a mandate be achieved in some *other* way? Could not even a decision by the NATO Council, as a kind of surrogate for the U.N. Security Council, be fairly presented as the will of "the international community," providing a moral-political warrant of sorts? Would an institutional endorsement truly be needed at all if the cause were manifestly just and recognized the world over as being so? Could not an extra-institutional action, if situationally necessary and justified by reference to international norms, be made acceptable to others? Conceivably, a group of leading states, if not the six-nation Contact Group (which includes Russia), then perhaps the Group of Seven (or Eight, if Russia should decide to go along), might assert themselves, either directly or through the various organizations to which they belonged. Even a single leader—the "sole surviving superpower," the United States—might command a general following, if it acted altruistically and assumed an international mantle.

All these speculations regarding imaginable alternatives to obtaining a resolution of the U.N. Security Council indicate that legitimacy does indeed operate as a *constraint*. Legitimacy belongs to a system, mechanical as well as ideological. Certain channels have to be passed through in order to create legitimacy. Certain principles have to be invoked and certain premises have to be established for the reasoning, as well as the organizational, process that is international legitimization to be considered perfected.

When the long-simmering crisis over Kosovo grew violent early in 1998, the immediate recourse of the Western powers had to be to the Security Council. The result was Resolution 1160 of March 31. This placed an arms embargo on the Federal Republic of Yugoslavia that would remain in effect until the FRY and the Kosovar Albanians began a substantive political dialogue, the Serbs removed their forces from Kosovo, and international organizations were allowed entry into the province. Despite Resolution 1160, the situation worsened. On September 23, by a vote of 14 to 0 (China abstaining), Resolution 1199 was passed, when Russia finally accepted a resolution under Chapter VII (Action with Respect to Threats to the Peace, Breaches of the Peace, and Acts of Aggression) that did not, however, actually provide for the use of force if Belgrade failed to comply. The Security Council's demands included: cessation of action by the Yugoslav security forces against the civilian population in Kosovo; unimpeded access and freedom of movement there for EU monitors and diplomatic missions; facilitation of the safe return of refugees and displaced persons and of entry of humanitarian organizations and supplies; and rapid progress in a dialogue between the FRY and the Kosovar Albanian leadership, without preconditions and with international involvement, aimed at finding a political solution. If concrete measures were not taken to meet these demands, the Council would "consider further action and additional measures to maintain or restore peace and stability in the region."[21]

NATO followed the Security Council's step with suggestions of military force that neither Russia nor China would allow the Council to authorize. On September 24, the very day after passage of Resolution 1199, the NATO Council issued an activation warning (ACTWARN) for limited air strikes and a phased air campaign. "It is not a decision to use force," stated a senior Pentagon official, "but it is a sign of the recognition by the Alliance and all of its members of the increasing urgency and seriousness of the situation."[22] Beyond this indication of readiness, some allies simply were not willing to go without an explicit Security Council authorization. In early October, moreover, Russia's foreign minister Igor Ivanov declared that his country would "definitely" use its veto to block any U.N.-sanctioned strike against Yugoslavia. President Boris Yeltsin himself made phone calls to Western leaders and U.N. Secretary-General Kofi Annan urging diplomacy over force.[23] That China would use its veto also was quite certain.

In these circumstances, how could "further action and additional measures"—that is, the actual launching of the planned NATO air assault against Yugoslavia—be justified? As countries dedicated to democracy and the rule of law, the NATO allies found it difficult, intellectually and politically, to resort to force without any international legal basis. Thus, in the absence of an explicit U.N. Security Council resolution, they considered a number of other ways to legitimize their action. These were as follows.

One idea was to cite the 1948 U.N. Declaration of Human Rights and the 1949 Geneva Conventions regarding warfare, and to assert an *erga omnes* obligation (to be respected by all states in all circumstances without exception) to provide assistance that the Kosovar Albanians, as victims of human rights offenses, could claim as a right. These documents, unfortunately, are "silent on preventive measures," which the allied military intervention in Kosovo, even if not aimed against the territorial integrity or political independence of Yugoslavia (protected by the U.N. Charter's Article 2, paragraph 4), clearly would be.[24]

A second idea was to argue that while Resolutions 1160 (the arms embargo) and 1199 (the call for an end to violence) did not authorize force, the threat of military enforcement was contained in, as German foreign minister Klaus Kinkel said, the "sense and logic" of those resolutions. Similarly, Germany's new chancellor, Gerhard Schroeder, contended that NATO, in referring to UNSC Resolution 1199, was not giving itself a mandate but was "acting within the reference framework of the United Nations."[25] A weakness of this argument is that proposals for using force or even sanctions were not being introduced at the time those resolutions were passed, and the reference to "additional measures" in them was generally understood to mean, on the basis of the language used, that the Security Council would have to authorize any further action.[26]

A third way of justifying outside intervention in Kosovo was through reference to the principles and norms that had progressively been adopted by the Organization for Security and Co-operation in Europe (OSCE), particularly those related to minority rights. Though not universal in scope, these texts covered the European continent, Russia, the United States, and Canada. Moreover, the documents are relatively "advanced" in their substance, suggesting that states in the OSCE area might allow a greater degree of mutual interference in each other's internal affairs than might countries in other regions of the world, "well beyond what general international law permits."[27] Yet the 1975 Helsinki Final Act and subsequent texts that constitute the OSCE body of doctrine do not provide for enforcement. Moreover, the OSCE (unlike NATO) is a self-declared "regional arrangement" in the sense of Chapter VIII of the U.N. Charter, and under the terms of Article 53, paragraph 1, therein, enforcement action requires Security Council authorization.

A fourth way of justification, more political and moral than legal, was the stark proposition that the urgency of the humanitarian situation in Kosovo warranted an "exception" being made to the requirement of a Security Council resolution authorizing the use of force. President Jacques Chirac of France, for one, advanced this argument. Although he expressly recognized the constraint of Resolution 1199, he insisted that "the humanitarian situation constitutes a ground that can justify an exception to a rule, however firm and strong it is. And if it appeared that the situation required it, then France would not hesitate to join those who would like to intervene in order to assist those that are in danger."[28]

A fifth way to justify military action without an express Security Council authorization was simpler still: to minimize the very importance of a resolution by the Security Council. As U.S. defense secretary William Cohen said, referring to such a U.N. mandate, "The United States does not feel it's imperative. It's desirable, not imperative."[29] For the United States and other Western governments, *all* the United Nations could provide was "legitimacy." NATO, which could do much more besides, might "provide the desired multilateral cover, with less obstruction."[30] The deficiency of this line of thinking is that it suggests a utilitarian attitude toward international law, that it is valuable only so long as it is usable. In the event, if no external authorizing agency could be found, military action might be taken in total disregard of any requirements of legality, if such action were deemed to be necessary. Presumably this necessity would be based on grounds of national interest, viewed collectively, rather than on grounds of international law. A paper mandate would be no more than a fig leaf.

As allied officials explored these alternatives, three camps formed in what Ivo Daalder and Michael O'Hanlon have characterized as "a theological debate." First, there was a "Catholic" camp (France and Italy), which, while insisting on the need for an explicit U.N. mandate, recognized that "like sinning, this sacrosanct rule could be violated in exceptional circumstances." Second, and opposite, there was a "Lutheran" camp (including Britain and Germany), which sought to devise an alternative dogma, one based on recognition of a humanitarian crisis that was "both overwhelming in character and required an emergency response." The third camp (mainly the United States) was "agnostic" in that it considered the rule requiring a United Nations mandate to be "neither sacrosanct nor absolute."[31]

Faced with the dialectic of thought within the Alliance, NATO Secretary-general Javier Solana had to make what might be described as a "syncretistic" case, embracing a mixture of reasons, to justify the threat and use of force without an express Security Council authorization. The elements in his rationale, as summarized by Catherine Guicherd, included:

— the failure of Yugoslavia to fulfill the requirements set out by Resolutions 1160 and 1199;
— the imminent risk of a humanitarian catastrophe, as documented by the report of the U.N. Secretary-General Kofi Annan on September 4, 1998;
— the impossibility to obtain, in short order, a Security Council resolution mandating the use of force; and
— the fact that Resolution 1199 states that the deterioration of the situation in Kosovo constitutes a threat to peace and security in the region.[32]

By emphasizing these justifying motives, Solana placed NATO action within the context of the consideration of the Yugoslav problem by the United Nations, while maintaining the NATO members' prerogative to act without Security Council permission. The Secretary-General was obliged to do this by the urgency of the situation, by the responsibilities of his office, and by the lack of a shared legitimizing doctrine among the allies. He stated NATO's position himself and presented it as a consensus. This he did "admirably." On October 10, following some ten hours of debate in the North Atlantic Council, he gave a summing-up statement with the conclusion that there was a sufficient legal basis for moving forward with a threat of force and, if necessary, carrying it out.[33]

Launching Operation Allied Force

That opened the way for the NATO Council to approve an activation order (ACTORD), setting a date for the beginning of air strikes. To get final approval for such an order, all 19 member countries had to concur. In order to obtain unanimity, the reluctance of several NATO members (notably Germany and Italy, in the midst of government changes) had to be overcome. A "last-ditch" diplomatic effort therefore was made to persuade

Slobodan Milosevic to accept the United Nation's demands. After extracting from the Serb leader a key concession regarding a verification system for monitoring Yugoslavia's compliance with the U.N. demands, U.S. special envoy Richard Holbrooke returned to Brussels for a late-night briefing of the North Atlantic Council. In the early hours of October 13, the ambassadors approved ACTORDs for limited air strikes and a phased air campaign over Yugoslavia to begin in 96 hours. There was some hope that this would force Milosevic to negotiate.[34]

By noon that day Holbrooke announced an agreement with him. Their accord established a two-part verification system consisting of a ground element, the Kosovo Verification Mission (2,000 unarmed verifiers operating under OSCE auspices); and an aerial element, noncombatant aircraft flying over Kosovo (under NATO command). On October 24, in a new resolution, 1203, the U.N. Security Council welcomed these agreements and demanded of Yugoslavia "the full and prompt implementation" of its pledges in the Holbrooke-Milosevic agreement. No mention was made of measures that would be taken in the event of the Yugoslav government's noncompliance, after Russia and China took the bite out of the original draft of the resolution. This draft, prepared by France and Britain and endorsed by the United States, Japan, Germany, Italy, Sweden, and Portugal, authorized all "appropriate steps" to be taken should Yugoslavia fail to honor its obligations. When the final text of Resolution 1203, without any reference to "appropriate steps," was approved, both Russia and China abstained. To the Chinese delegate, Ambassador Qin Huasun, it was clear that the resolution did "not entail any authorization of using force or threatening to use force against the Federal Republic of Yugoslavia." At the same time, the United States, Britain, and France made it clear that they viewed that new resolution as permitting at least the enforcement of a ceasefire and as specifically opposing acts of aggression in Kosovo against unarmed observers or innocent civilians. Yet the need for legitimacy was still constraining. A senior European diplomat, speaking anonymously, said that he wondered whether the resolution was necessary if Western powers considered that they had the right to act militarily anyway. "If anything, it may have diluted the ability to move forcefully," he said of Resolution 1203.[35]

The Holbrooke-Milosevic agreement—achieved partly by the tactical use of a North Atlantic Council decision to approve ACTORDs that some NATO members might have believed would never actually have to be executed—did not work. At most, the agreement bought time. Yugoslav military operations not only against the Kosovo Liberation Army but also against the Muslim population of Kosovo continued. A turning point toward action was the appalling discovery in January 1999 of a massacre that occurred in the village of Racak. Subsequent negotiations at Rambouillet in France, regarding self-governance for Kosovo, did not produce the desired political settlement. A widespread conclusion was that Milosevic "only understands the language of force." On March 24, 1999, this finally was applied when NATO unleashed a series of air strikes against Serbia—Operation Allied Force.

Conclusion

NATO went to war—a term that NATO countries were reluctant to use—against Serbia without an explicit U.N. Security Council authorization. Yet its resort to force was not without legal foundation, which the Alliance recognized that it needed in order to be able to claim legitimacy for its military action. Fundamentally, these legal grounds for taking action were two. The first was that Yugoslavia's repression of its Kosovar Albanian population, which caused an outflow of refugees to neighboring countries, threatened regional stability and therefore constituted a threat to "international peace and security." This justified action by third parties, including NATO members, on the basis of Article 51 of the U.N. Charter recognizing the inherent right of individual and collective self-defense.[36] The second was that, under general international law and, in particular, international conventions pertaining to human rights, genocide, and protection of civilians in wartime, military intervention on behalf of the Kosovars was lawful on the basis of overwhelming humanitarian necessity.[37]

But was NATO right—did it act legitimately—in launching Operation Allied Force without at least *trying* to gain authorization from the U.N. Security Council? One cannot answer this question on a legal footing alone, for it entails a much broader historical and political analysis. Adam Roberts is right to point out that trying to get a resolution would have shown proper respect for the United Nations, and it would have exposed those who denied help to the victims of atrocities in Kosovo. He is also right to note, however, that a failed attempt to obtain a Security Council authorization would have jeopardized public support for military action and might have caused a rift amongst allies.[38] The actual choice, therefore, was between provoking a fight at the United Nations, conceivably even restarting the Cold War in that body, and evasively papering over deep disagreement, conceivably damaging even NATO in the long run by not allowing a full airing of differences regarding the wisdom of using force.

In a sense, the North Atlantic Council did substitute itself for the U.N. Security Council. However, it should not be forgotten, many of the same countries were involved in both settings, and the members are the ultimate source of authority in both organizations. The countries represented on both bodies were, in effect, shifting their decision-making from the one they preferred to believe in to the one they trusted would get things done. Though it is too early to say, as a historical judgment, this venue shift of October 1998 may have subtly changed the nature of the North Atlantic Council from the consultative chamber of a military alliance to something like the legislative, or rule-making, organ of a Euro-Atlantic security system.

Hitherto concentrated on the problem of collective defense, the North Atlantic Treaty Organization as a whole henceforth would have to focus on problems usually understood as those of collective security, ranging from peace enforcement to peacekeeping to postconflict peace building. Not only NATO members themselves, but also the members of the wider Euro-Atlantic Partnership Council (EAPC), as well as the OSCE and the European Union, are involved in these varied tasks. NATO, as the most effective instrument in the Atlantic world for taking forcible military action, is the *enabler* of the participation of others, including the United Nations Organization. This surely is a basis of the legitimacy of the action it took over Kosovo. NATO does not legitimize power. But it does give power to legitimacy.

Notes

1. *Charter of the United Nations and Statute of the International Court of Justice* (New York: United Nations Department of Public Information, 1991), p. 2.
2. See Articles 39, 41, and 42 of the U.N. Charter, Chapter VII.
3. David D. Caron, "The Legitimacy of the Collective Authority of the Security Council," *American Journal of International Law* 87 (October 1993): p. 552.
4. The subject of "legitimacy" at the international level is of increasing scholarly interest. See, for example: Thomas M. Franck, *The Power of Legitimacy Among Nations* (New York: Oxford University Press, 1990); Caron, "The Legitimacy of the Collective Authority of the Security Council"; and Ian Hurd, "Legitimacy and Authority in International Politics," *International Organization* 53 (spring 1999): pp. 379–408.
5. Article 2, paragraph 7, of the U.N. Charter states: "Nothing contained in the present Charter shall authorize the United Nations to intervene in matters which are essentially within the domestic jurisdiction of any state or shall require Members to submit such matters to settlement under the present Charter; but this principle shall not prejudice the application of enforcement measures under Chapter VII." *Charter of the United Nations*, p. 5.
6. Quoted in Sean Kay, "After Kosovo: NATO's Credibility Dilemma," *Strategic Dialogue* 31 (March 2000): p. 228.
7. Bruno Simma, "NATO, the U.N., and the Use of Force: Legal Aspects," paper presented at two policy roundtables organized by the United Nations Association of the United States of America in New York, March 11, 1999, and Washington, D.C., March 12, 1999.
8. Judith Miller, "Annan Takes Critical Stance on U.S. Actions in Kosovo," *New York Times,* May 19, 1999.

9. Kofi Annan, "Two Concepts of Sovereignty," *Economist,* September 18, 1999, pp. 49–50.
10. Arnold Wolfers, *Discord and Collaboration: Essays on International Politics* (Baltimore: The Johns Hopkins University Press, 1962), chap. 12.
11. Inis L. Claude, Jr., *Swords Into Plowshares: The Problems and Progress of International Organization* (New York: Random House, 1961), pp. 275–78.
12. Alan K. Henrikson, "The North Atlantic Alliance as a Form of World Order," in Alan K. Henrikson, ed., *Negotiating World Order: The Artisanship and Architecture of Global Diplomacy* (Wilmington, DE: Scholarly Resources, Inc., 1986), pp. 111–35; "NATO and the United Nations: Toward a Non-allergic Relationship," in *NATO in the Post–Cold War Era: Does It Have a Future?,* eds. S. Victor Papacosma and Mary Ann Heiss (New York: St. Martin's Press, 1995), pp. 95–112; "The United Nations and Regional Organizations: 'Kinglinks' of a 'Global Chain,'" *Duke Journal of Comparative and International Law* 7 (fall 1996): pp. 35–70.
13. For a perspective opposite to my own, see Lawrence S. Kaplan, "NATO and the U.N.: A Peculiar Relationship," *Contemporary European History* 7 (November 1998): pp. 329–42.
14. Inis L. Claude, Jr., *The Changing United Nations* (New York: Random House, 1967), chap. 4, "Collective Legitimization as a Political Function of the United Nations."
15. Ibid., p. 83.
16. The indictments made and, increasingly, the convictions produced by the International Criminal Tribunal for the Former Yugoslavia (ICTY) illustrate the reinforcing power that law can have for international actions in the political-military field such as Operation Allied Force.
17. Alan K. Henrikson, *Defining a New World Order: Toward a Practical Vision of Collective Action for International Peace and Security* (Medford, MA: The Fletcher School of Law and Diplomacy, Tufts University, 1991); Caron, "The Legitimacy of the Collective Authority of the Security Council."
18. Adam Roberts, "The United Nations and International Security," in *Ethnic Conflict and International Security,* ed. Michael E. Brown (Princeton: Princeton University Press, 1993), p. 218.
19. Ibid., pp. 218–19.
20. Thomas M. Franck, *Nation Against Nation: What Happened to the U.N. Dream and What the U.S. Can Do About It* (New York: Oxford University Press, 1985), pp. 39–40.
21. United Nations Resolution 1199 (1998), S/RES/1199, September 23, 1998, in *Winning Ugly: NATO's War to Save Kosovo,* Ivo H. Daalder and Michael E. O'Hanlon (Washington, D.C.: Brookings Institution Press, 2000), appendix C, pp. 247–51.
22. "Background Briefing: Under Secretary of Defense for Policy Walter B. Slocombe and Ambassador Vershbow" (Vilamoura, Portugal: U.S. Department of Defense, September 24, 1998), quoted in Daalder and O'Hanlon, *Winning Ugly,* p. 43.

23. Celestine Bohlen, "Russia Vows to Block the U.N. From Backing Attack on Serbs," *New York Times,* October 7, 1998.
24. Catherine Guicherd, "International Law and the War in Kosovo," *Survival* 41 (summer 1999): pp. 20–22.
25. Quoted in ibid., p. 27.
26. Daalder and O'Hanlon, *Winning Ugly,* appendix C, p. 251.
27. Ibid., pp. 27, 30.
28. Quoted in Guicherd, "International Law and the War in Kosovo," p. 28.
29. Craig R. Whitney, "NATO to Conduct Large Maneuvers to Warn Off Serbs," *New York Times,* June 12, 1998.
30. Jeffrey Laurenti, "The Policy Issue," paper prepared for "NATO, the U.N., and the Use of Force" policy roundtables, United Nations Association of the United States of America, New York, March 11, 1999, and Washington, D.C., March 12, 1999.
31. Daalder and O'Hanlon, *Winning Ugly,* p. 45.
32. Guicherd, "International Law and the War in Kosovo," pp. 27–28.
33. Daalder and O'Hanlon, *Winning Ugly,* p. 45.
34. Ibid., pp. 45, 47–48.
35. Youssef M. Ibrahim, "U.N. Measure Skirts Outright Threat of Force Against Milosevic," *New York Times,* October 25, 1998; Daalder and O'Hanlon, *Winning Ugly,* pp. 49, 288n.
36. See, for example, the suggestion by Italian defense minister Beniamino Andreatta that the Belgrade government's action might create "conditions for the application of Article 51." Guicherd, "International Law and the War in Kosovo," p. 28.
37. See, for example, a U.K. Foreign and Commonwealth Office note of October 1998 circulated to NATO allies, quoted in Adam Roberts, "NATO's 'Humanitarian' War Over Kosovo," *Survival* 41 (autumn 1999): p. 106.
38. Roberts, "NATO's 'Humanitarian War' Over Kosovo," p. 104.

CHAPTER FOUR

The European Union and NATO's War over Kosovo: Toward the Glass Ceiling?

Anne Deighton

Since the end of the Cold War, neither the EU, nor NATO, nor their leading member states have successfully crafted and executed a sustainable policy toward the former Yugoslavia.[1] The NATO air strikes over Kosovo between March 24 and June 7, 1999, marked yet one more stage in a grim Balkan conflict that has remained obstinately near the top of the Euro-Atlantic agenda for nearly ten years. Some aspects of the effects of this continuing conflict upon the EU form the substance of this chapter.

During the air strikes, the EU was indeed an ally for NATO. This chapter will first show how the EU, although it shared its civilian role with the G7-G8 during the conflict, played the role of handmaiden to the key state actors and to NATO as an institution. Despite tensions within the EU, supportive diplomatic initiatives were forthcoming, and EU cohesion was retained. Given that the air strikes did not receive equal support across the Union and that, in countries such as Italy and Greece, domestic opposition was very strongly articulated, this represented something of a triumph for EU solidarity. Further, the EU sought to play a major role in determining how postconflict policy toward Kosovo and the whole Balkan region should evolve, promoting plans for reconstruction and the political regeneration of both Kosovo and the wider Balkan region. Reconstruction planning for the region predated the war, but the human and physical devastation in Kosovo, a region that is outside but still very close to the EU border, spurred the EU states to seek to play a key role in postwar recovery. In this the European

Commission led the way, as did the Germans, who held the presidency of the Council of Ministers from January until the end of June 1999.[2]

The Kosovo air strikes also revealed deeper tensions between Europe's two leading international institutions. These tensions relate to the process of role definition and reinvigoration that has been continuing in both NATO and the EU since the end of the Cold War. The second part of this chapter will show how Kosovo has been a catalyst for change within the EU itself, although the initiation of these changes predates the air strikes. Longer-term proposals to develop a military capacity for the EU will be examined in particular, because the Kosovo air strikes exposed the capability weaknesses of the European NATO partners. Here, we find that these European defense proposals have taken the EU right up to the "glass ceiling," as, traditionally, the EU's competencies did not extend into the military sphere. Whether that glass ceiling is finally breached over the longer term will be a major test of EU change.[3]

An Ally in Force

To examine the role of the EU is a rather more diffuse task than the examination of one state's response to the air strikes.[4] It is impossible to talk about the EU as an autonomous player on the international chessboard during a period of armed conflict. All member states of the EU, except Ireland, Austria, Finland, and Sweden, are also members of NATO. The EU is not a war-fighting institution—indeed, given its original raison d'être, it is quite the opposite. The EU can act in the domain of foreign policy only with the unanimous consent of all members, where the supranational Commission acts as a nonvoting partner, which is not the case in areas of economic external relations and humanitarian aid. The role of the EU as an ally during the Kosovo conflict had therefore to be driven primarily by the political will and consent of all member states, using the instruments of foreign policy at its disposal. These instruments consisted of declarations and diplomatic initiatives, the capacity to impose sanctions, and planning for "postwar." Moreover, there were other European security institutions, notably the OSCE, which had also been given a role in the Balkans.

The outbreak of hostilities came at a time when the Union's own agenda was full and complex. Union politics were complicated because of the resignation of Jacques Santer, the Commission's president, and of his cabinet over allegations of mismanagement and corruption. European Parliament elections scheduled for June 13 made all member states more sensitive. The Amsterdam Treaty did not achieve final ratification until May 1, during the period of hostilities. But of more importance was the EU's own record in relation to the Balkans. The badly rushed recognition of parts of the former

Yugoslavia formed a part of the EC policy after pressure from Germany, and a series of U.N. and Community special representatives and envoys, working with other international organizations and the United States, had tirelessly sought to use personal and unarmed diplomacy in an effort to damp down the escalating levels of intercommunal violence. The Contact Group—a diplomatic coalition of the willing that included both the United States and Russia, as well as the EU, was essentially the driving diplomatic force behind Western policies, rather than the EU itself. By the time of the Dayton Accords of 1995, when the United States had been dragged back into a Western leadership position, the scars of the Balkans affected perceptions about the competence of the EU.

By early 1999, it was clear that the Western powers were in trouble again with the Serbian leader, Slobodan Milosevic. The British and French began to think in terms of troop deployments by the end of January, after the massacre at Racak, while the EU General Council now challenged both the Kosovar Albanian leadership and Milosevic to conform, and warned them both of the "severest consequences" of failure. It also indicated a readiness to organize a donors' conference for regional reconstruction, if Rambouillet succeeded.[5] The Contact Group was reconvened at Rambouillet in February to try and impose on Kosovo what was seen at the time as some kind of rerun of the Bosnia Dayton Accords. After the talks failed, military action of some sort seemed inevitable.[6] The EU now moved to support NATO's "war aims." Attention turned away from distributing exhortations to both Kosovars and Serbs to backing the anti-Milosevic rhetoric, securing the compliance of non-EU countries in east-central Europe, and looking for diplomatic ways forward for the West.[7] Plans for a partial oil embargo were implemented, and a ban on flights was also imposed, which added pressure on the Serbian leadership. These instruments represented the extent of Union competencies, but EU sanctions offered one important way forward that, given the legal status of the war and the lack of support from Russia and China, was denied to the United Nations.[8] The EU also gave special aid of 100 million euros to cope with the refugee problem.

At the end of May, on the suggestion of American secretary of state Madeleine Albright, a negotiating team consisting of the highly experienced Finnish president, Martti Ahtisaari, and Victor Chernomyrdin sought to open up channels of communication. Ahtisaari was the EU's representative, and thus the EU could exploit Finland's neutrality.[9] The appointment of Chernomyrdin was crucial: Russia's opposition to the air strikes weakened the diplomatic position of NATO and threatened relations with the EU, and the joint team was one way of involving the Russians in a much needed diplomatic initiative. Indeed, the German foreign minister Joschka Fischer, had explored the idea with the Russians of a bombing halt as early as

April 6; while France's concern to involve the United Nations from the start was partly driven by a desire not to isolate the Russians completely.[10]

At the same time, the EU sponsored longer-term plans for aid and reconstruction and for the revival of the Balkans.[11] The immediate reason for this initiative was an increasing concern that the air strikes would not alone be successful, and that the so-called frontline states might, in time, be called upon to support the considerable weight both of the continuing exodus of refugees and of a ground war.[12] But, now acting as a partner rather than simply an ally of NATO, the EU was also reviving earlier plans for the stability of the region that dated back to the early 1990s. The idea was to create a general stability pact and, within this, to open up the possibility of NATO and EU membership to frontline states in the long-term future, whilst specifically excluding Yugoslavia in the short term and rejecting the idea of Kosovar independence.

By the end of May the EU Commission, building on its own regional approach of 1996, established a stabilization and association process.[13] This gave the elements of the region—Bosnia-Herzegovina, Croatia, the Federal Republic of Yugoslavia, the Former Yugoslav Republic of Macedonia, and Albania—the perspective, in principle, of "full integration" into the structures of the EU. This would occur through a new kind of contractual relationship constructed with each country based upon conditionality and established procedures and working through established EU legislation. Clearly, FYROM and Albania were considered to have progressed much further than Croatia or Bosnia-Herzegovina or FRY itself.[14]

Although vague in many respects, including the sums involved, the Stability Pact of June then set out a framework for cooperation principally between the EU, the United States, Russia, Japan, and the Balkan countries themselves. It proposed an administrative structure to manage a series of bilateral and multilateral pacts, and economic and democratic reforms, thereby claiming a leading role in the recovery of the region through this firm European anchorage that the pact would bring. It was argued, however, that ultimately it was the states in the region that had to make the Stability Pact work. The pact also stated that the regional signatories saw the pact as reinforcing any efforts they might make to join Euro-Atlantic organizations. It even held out the prospect of membership to what was left of Yugoslavia itself, "following the political settlement of the Kosovo crisis on the basis of the principles agreed by G8 Foreign Ministers and taking into account the need for respect by all participants for the principles and objectives of this Pact," whilst also—and no doubt provocatively to Milosevic—opening up the possibility of special treatment for Montenegro. The administration would consist of a South Eastern Europe Regional Round Table, which was to act as the steering committee, backed by a European Reconstruction

Agency and supplementary Working Tables, under the control of an EU-appointed coordinator, in agreement with the OSCE, who would then work under the latter's auspices.[15] The decisions over the future of Kosovo were developed through the United Nations (UNMIK); however, the EU was to get a role in the reconstruction aspects of this agreement, and the Security Council resolution specifically welcomed the efforts to create a comprehensive approach to the region.[16]

So the EU did act as a diplomatic ally to NATO, with the support of the Contact Group and the G8. But of most importance was the informal group, the so-called Quint, which was essentially a secret transatlantic steering group of the United States, the United Kingdom, France, Germany, and Italy. At the level of political directors, this was where day-to-day Western decision-making lay: Meeting privately, with no secretariat, it was a light and flexible tool whose members worked by daily telephone conference calls. At key moments, especially after the unexpected surrender of Milosevic, this group was effectively making Western policy on the hoof.

This crucial ad hoc administrative response to the difficulties posed by Russian membership of the Contact Group, and the obvious flaws in NATO's own decision-making structures, shaped the Western diplomatic response, set the EU's own diplomatic agenda, and was decisive in sustaining EU support in the uncharted waters in which NATO was operating. There were considerable disagreements even among these four EU members about the bombardments and the prosecution of the military campaign. National views were very mixed: Britain was the self-appointed leader of the European NATO allies, while France, traditionally ambivalent about NATO, sought to work more closely within the U.N. framework. Germany, which held the EU presidency of the Council of Ministers and participated militarily in an unprecedented way, had a delicate domestic environment to sustain, given the Red-Green coalition. Meanwhile, in Italy, Premier Massimo D'Alema, a former Communist, faced strong domestic opposition even within his own coalition.

The Quint led and facilitated the delicate work of sustaining an EU consensus, and it is inconceivable that the NATO action could have continued had the EU taken a publicly hostile position. The focus on postwar reconstruction, and the need to keep the Russians involved in the broader plans for Balkan reconstruction, also meant that the EU position was not merely a passive one. As Fischer told the European Parliament, Kosovo had also become "a productive incentive for the achievement of further integration. The reason for this lies in the fact that with the war in Kosovo it became clear again what the core objective is in the process of European integration, i.e. the establishment of a lasting peaceful order on our continent. This insight relativized individual national interest and there was a willingness throughout Europe to move a crucial step forward in the historical task of completing the process of European integration. As such the crisis became an accelerator of history."[17]

The EU thus hung together and managed to provide continuous support for the first sustained NATO offensive military action. It carved out for itself the role as a lead power in trying to put together a package of postwar measures that might bring a chance of peace to the region. In these, it wove in a stronger commitment to enlarging the EU toward the region in the very long term. Whether in practice the multiplicity of institutions involved in the reconstruction process will act as a brake upon speedy decision-making (Who now owns the Balkan policy of the West?) remains to be seen.

EU and NATO: Forced to Change?

Kosovo has also brought a new dimension to the EU-NATO relationship. This is because of the proposal for an autonomous EU force that was refined during the air war between March and June 1999. To understand the impact that the use of force by NATO over Kosovo has had upon their institutional balance, a little history is required.

Since its creation in 1957, one defining characteristic of the EEC has been that it is a purely civilian power. It has developed in this way in part because of a scarring attempt to build a West European military force within the NATO framework that foundered in 1954, despite four years of agonizing diplomacy.[18] It then seemed clear that defense would remain well outside the remit of the EEC, although external trade matters were dealt with within the Treaty base. Indeed, it was not until the early 1970s that a mechanism to coordinate foreign policy positions was created. This was strictly informal, outside the Treaty base, and had no brief for defense issues, even when, in the Single European Act of 1987, this informal procedure was given a small secretariat. The convention had therefore been well established that defense issues were dealt with through NATO, or nationally. The European dimension to NATO was the Western European Union, which effectively had no military competencies and whose membership was conterminous neither with the EU nor with NATO. In what has turned out to be a richly innovative idea, in 1992, the WEU established non-Article 5 tasks for which it then felt itself to be suited. These so-called Petersberg Tasks consisted of humanitarian and rescue tasks, peacekeeping, crisis management, and peace enforcement.[19]

With the end of the Cold War, both NATO and the EU were inevitably forced to reexamine their roles and raisons d'être.[20] A competitive energy between the EU and NATO appeared during these years, whose resilience has been examined by institutionalist analysts. NATO defined its new Strategic Concept; proposed an outreach policy to east-central Europe through the North Atlantic Cooperation Council and the Partnership for Peace program; discussed the establishment of Combined Joint Task Forces, in which coalitions of the willing could perform Petersberg-type tasks without involving the whole NATO machinery; and finally enlarged itself to Poland, Hungary, and the Czech Republic by early 1999. At the same time, the Americans' Revolution in Military Affairs, with its prospect of capabilities and requirement assessment restructuring, provoked a certain amount of handwringing on the other side of the Atlantic, with fears of a two-speed Alliance, as the deficiencies in the European contribution were already being assessed.[21]

Within the EC, the process of adaptation was different, as member states first wanted to consolidate their existing policy program, including the European Monetary Union. The framers of the Maastricht and then the Amsterdam Treaties were also concerned to strengthen and to give European foreign policy a clearer remit, which was achieved by creating in the Maastricht Treaty the Common Foreign and Security Policy as an intergovernmental pillar. The Maastricht Treaty also allowed for requests to be made by the European Council to the WEU for military action. In the Amsterdam Treaty, this provision was fleshed out by reference to the Petersberg Tasks, which have proved to be a benchmark for what military work the Europeans might wish to undertake. The potential for European defense was included in the treaties, and the Amsterdam Treaty referred to "the possibility of the integration of the WEU into the Union, should the European Council so decide," although it also confirmed existing obligations to the common defense secured within NATO.[22] The question of a direct EU military capability was not addressed.

Then, in the autumn and winter of 1998, the Europeans made firmer declarations on this issue. On December 8, 1998, at a bilateral summit in Saint-Malo, British prime minister Tony Blair and French president Jacques Chirac dropped what might in time turn out to be a diplomatic bombshell. The Saint-Malo Declaration said: "The European Union needs to be in a position to play its full role on the international stage. This means making a reality of the Treaty of Amsterdam which will provide the essential basis for action by the Union. […] To this end, the Union must have the capacity for autonomous action, backed by credible, military forces, the means to decide to use them, and a readiness to do so, in order to respond to international crises […] acting in conformity with our respective obligations to NATO."[23] The initiative came from the British, not least because Prime Minister Blair had been concerned about the apparent impotence of the WEU and the failings of the Europeans to play an effective role in Bosnia.[24]

Less than four months later, the air strikes over Kosovo began. American planes carried out more than 80 percent of the air raids, although the Europeans had over 6,000 fast jets. When it came to putting together the peacekeeping force, Europe struggled to provide 40,000 troops, even though this figure was roughly one-fiftieth of its armed forces. The European partners in the Alliance were found to be unable to play a role commensurate with that of the United States. As the then British defense minister George Robertson put it: "You had to sweat and strain all your resources to get a deployable 2 percent of the totality. That will not be tolerable in the future [...] we clearly need more of those paper troops to be deployable, flexible, survivable, sustainable."[25] This was the more alarming given that since the Strategic Concept of 1991, NATO had recognized that the nature of conflict envisaged during the Cold War was now out of date, but that it was only with great difficulty that NATO could actually deploy the range of forces and hardware that it did. As an ally in force, the NATO European partners who were members of the EU were tested and found wanting.

During the air strikes, two important meetings were held, both of which gave shape to a potentially important change in EU-NATO relations, as they confirmed the possibility of the EU developing an autonomous military capacity. The first of these was the NATO Washington summit, held in April 1999, and the second was the Cologne European summit of the heads of state of the European Union, held even as the air strikes ended, in June 1999. No European standing army was proposed; but rather a force numbering around 50,000, which could be raised and deployed for Petersberg—non-Article 5—Tasks, was agreed to. Such a force would act on the instructions of the EU's supreme body, the European Council, and these tasks would be performed with the agreement of NATO and, if necessary, with the use of NATO assets. At the same time, the Defence Capabilities Initiative proposed adaptations to conform to the new Strategic Concept (also launched in Washington), looking particularly at command and control, information systems, interoperability and standardization, deployability, and the military capability of European allies.[26] On the back of the Defence Capabilities Initiative, it was thus possible to repackage the earlier European initiative in the context of capabilities rather than a European defense identity.

At Cologne, it was now also agreed that the WEU should indeed be folded into the EU and that a new, autonomous, rapid reaction force should be introduced that confirmed the thrust of the Amsterdam Treaty (which had been finally ratified only in May 1999). A new decision-making structure was now proposed that would include the involvement of ministers of defense within the Union to take forward the Anglo-French project proposed at Saint-Malo. A new post was created, to coordinate the work of the Common Foreign and Security Policy. The appointment of Javier Solana, former secretary-general of NATO, as the first holder of this post was to confirm the NATO orientation of the project.[27]

Washington and Cologne thus built upon earlier proposals, the fulfillment of which was sharpened and no doubt speeded up because the Kosovo air strikes had shown a need to reexamine both military structure and military capability. During the Cold War, NATO was the "glass ceiling" through which European collective defense efforts were not to go. This was understood and favored by the Europeans, and indeed it created a comfortable situation that actually suited Europeans and their Atlantic partners very well, despite occasional spats. Since the end of the Cold War, the so-called ratchet of European defense has been tightening, as the changes in the Maastricht and Amsterdam Treaties have shown. The Kosovo conflict acted as the spur, not the cause, of the possible rebalancing of European-American relations in the military sector. By the time the air strikes had ended, however, the EU had taken the quantum leap to give itself the potential to embrace a military role, albeit only of a rapid reaction force dealing with Petersberg Tasks. The sanctity of the Union's civilian role had ended. In this it had secured a NATO blessing.

Conclusion

The EU and NATO were allies in force during the Kosovo air strikes. The EU performed an important diplomatic backup role and ensured that it did not defect from a position of support for NATO during the action, which could have fatally undermined military efforts. It also asserted a leading role in trying to carve out a reconstruction program through the Stability Pact, the Stabilization and Association Agreements, and its role in UNMIK. However, despite being partners in force, the EU and NATO now find themselves immersed in a debate about military force that may well turn out to have significant long-term consequences. The roots of these changes stretch back both into the original structure and role of the Union itself and into the longer debate since 1989, but they have been highlighted by the Yugoslav crisis.

But the Kosovo air strikes also reflected the failure of a variety of European policies toward the region since the end of the Cold War: allied consensus and "allied" behavior was not a foregone conclusion. There was also a realization amongst the Europeans of the weakness of the measures available to the EU to intervene against a country that was not merely just beyond its borders but that could potentially become a member of the Union itself, and which had one of the "softest" regimes in the region during the Cold War. In 1995, the United States had taken control of policy toward Bosnia as events there deteriorated. In 1999, once again, the EU proved itself unequal to the task of dealing with the disintegrating Yugoslavia. During the bombing campaign, although there was widespread revulsion about the nature of what was going on within the region, there was also grave disquiet about the way in which the campaign was being conducted. Collateral damage caused by allied bombing often seemed excessive; the policy of flying high may have led to a death-free campaign for the pilots, but its effect was undoubtedly to cause greater indiscriminate harm than was intended. Further, the bitter row that broke out over the use or nonuse of ground troops to make a nonpermissive entry into Kosovo caused splits both between European allies and within the Alliance more generally. The unrelenting "demonization" of Milosevic and the comparisons made in the media to Hitler's policies of genocide rested very uncomfortably with the reluctance to risk the lives of NATO forces in a more purposeful campaign. There were considerable doubts about the functioning of the Alliance in time of conflict.

Reactions to Kosovo can be grouped around three interrelated problems. The first is why it was necessary for NATO to fight an offensive war in the Balkans. For the Europeans, proximity to the region and the fear of a spillover of destabilization there, meant that it was never possible not to try to have a policy for the region, however weak the policy instruments were. But previous efforts had failed. For the United States, however, the war raised the question of how far fighting in the Balkans and participating in the expensive and long-term postwar reconstruction there was in its own national interest. For all members of NATO, the debate about the human rights dimension of the action reflected an appreciation that NATO was in reality fighting an offensive campaign, based on dubious legal standing.

The second problem surrounds what operationalizing NATO revealed about its decision-making structure and its capabilities. Both EU and non-EU members of the Alliance were confronted with the first war in the 50 years of NATO's existence, with all the decision-making and capabilities problems that this presented. Kosovo became the link between war and the third problem, that of the long-term institutional relationship between the EU and NATO that the possibility of an autonomous reaction force had raised but which could not now be ignored. The United States had long been arguing that the Europeans did not carry their share of defense burdens and defense expenditure. Given the weaknesses exposed by Yugoslavia, these clearly had to be addressed. But there is a deeper question about the role of the United States as the sole world superpower; its post–Cold War national interests, unilateralism, and its relationship to the United Nations; its role within NATO, and how far in this latter role it should continue to act as a European power. United States reactions to the European initiatives since Saint-Malo have not been unreservedly enthusiastic about a European-inspired change, which might alter the institutional balance between the EU and NATO. Madeleine Albright's stern letter to the *Financial Times* the day after the Saint-Malo Declaration, in which she warned of duplication (of resources), discrimination (against non-EU members of NATO), and decoupling (between the EU and the United States) was only the beginning. A revealing article at the time of the NATO Summit said that the references to the European initiative at the summit were driven by the American desire to put an Alliance stamp on Saint-Malo, alluding to a determination "to make sure that things evolved along the right lines"—for example, using the American planning system—and "that they were not interested in a separate European defense."[28] There are also passages in the NATO communiqué that point to a reluctance to let European initiatives go too far: "The Alliance and the European Union share common strategic interests. Our respective efforts in building peace in the former Yugoslavia are complementary. Both organizations make decisive contributions to peace and stability on the European continent. Cooperation between the two organizations on topics of common concern, to be decided on a case-by-case basis, could be developed when it enhances the effectiveness of action by NATO and the EU."[29] The United States further expresses fears about the development of European conglomerates in the defense industrial sector, seeing them as a threat to United States production, and as a means for "Europeanizing" the armaments industry. The desire for leadership thus seems to remain, despite what John Kenneth Galbraith called the culture of contentment and despite a reluctance to risk American lives, which has a grip upon the public rhetoric of American politicians.[30]

Reactions in Europe, too, have been mixed. An autonomous EU rapid reaction force could spell the end of the particular quality of the European integration project, which has rested upon a belief in the force of a purely civilian power, deploying nonmilitary levers in the pursuit of European interests, although, of course, largely under the umbrella of NATO protection and retaining national defense forces. Such an interpretation implies to some that the European force may be the beginning of a rather different kind of EU, which, by embracing a military dimension, may in time acquire more traditional statelike qualities. Others argue that this is all little more than role specialization in the area of security, and that the Petersberg Tasks framework will act as a brake against the key NATO-EU countries ever wishing to dispense with the Article 5 protection that NATO offers. Whether we will emerge with the Europeans providing the manpower—the gurkhas of Europe—and gendarmerie-type operations in the Euro-Atlantic area, autonomously from but under the benevolent eye of NATO, while the heavy defense, backed up by very high-tech equipment and the decision-making high ground that this implies is left to the United States, or whether this is the beginning of a more comprehensive institutional rebalancing is as yet unclear.

The impact of institutional pressures upon reform is one that has exercised scholars since international institutions became key players in international politics. There is an argument that if there are strong enough supporters for change within an institution, they, and other actors, can generate change. It is not yet clear how strong the institutional pressures of finally being able to operate an effective CFSP and the pressure for a European reaction force are, although neofunctionalist arguments about the spillover of competencies to the Commission over the longer period may well be pertinent. Yet the remarks by the president of the European Commission, Romano Prodi, on May 10 about his long-term ambition to see the creation of a European army may, on the other hand, have been counterproductive, not only to those who know of the four years of agony that the European Defence Community debate produced between 1950 and 1954, but also to those who fear overt federalism, rather than covert confederalism.

Political will in Europe to develop the project will be shaped by an interpretation of what this means to individual states, to the Union, and to the Alliance. The neutrals in the Union—Ireland, Austria, Sweden, and Finland—naturally seek to ensure that the consequences of the initiative will not be to bring NATO closer to the Union by allowing the Union to remain too dependent upon NATO (United States) assets, or by giving NATO the "first refusal" on participation in any operation. Britain and France, the key players in the initiative, have very different rationales and aims. For the British, the prospect of leadership in an area of traditional British strength, as long as they can continue to cleave to American power, is coupled by its fear that the EMU project threatens to sideline them with every day that passes. The British are committed to ensuring that the Americans do not feel threatened by developments, and agree that NATO should retain some kind of *droit de regard*. France is more concerned to push forward on the "autonomy" of any new rapid reaction force, and is, for obvious reasons, and at least in public, less inclined to support a strong NATO framework for operations. The Germans, emerging through their involvement in Yugoslavia from their traditionally nonmilitary stance, now have a difficult balancing role, being part of the Franco-German couple that drives much Union progress and at the same time an enthusiastic member of NATO.[31] Germany is also undergoing a massive restructuring of its armed forces and has recently cut its defense budget. And it is upon finance as well as political will that the way forward will be determined over time. The defense climate has, since the end of the Cold War, been one of cuts in defense expenditure. If the Europeans are not prepared to spend more or to reduce expenditure in other parts of their national military budgets, the project may well prove to be something of a cul-de-sac and to evaporate over time.

So whether there now remains a natural Euro-Atlantic security community after the Cold War is a question that is being hotly debated by politicians and political scientists alike. Overlapping membership and interests, ideological convergence, institutional resilience, and a "Euro-Atlantic reflex" shaped by the Cold War experience point to continuity. The Europeans will need considerable political will, financial expenditure, and a preparedness to change EU institutional structures if there is to be a fundamental reworking of EU-NATO relations. They need to assess how much institutional change the EU can undertake without irreparably disturbing the roots of the EU-NATO and EU-U.S., relationships. Further, the United States' perceptions of its own interests and its role in world affairs will remain a determining factor. Thus the Balkan conflict, and Bosnia and Kosovo in particular, has brought to the surface a longer-term ambiguity about the roles of the EU and NATO in the post–Cold War world, and about whether their relationship and their different roles still constitute a natural partnership, or a forced one. But the effect of this initiative must, over time, alter the structural relationship between the EU and NATO. If it succeeds, it could open the way to new perspectives about the EU's international role. If it fails or withers on the vine, however, then the relationship between the two institutions will still require recalibration, now that the question has been laid on the table.

However, there is an irony here that takes us back to Kosovo. How and where any European Union rapid reaction force may operate is not yet defined. Although the 50,000-strong force will be made available for Petersberg Tasks, in theory the areas in which it may be deployed are, at least in the short term, very few. But there is one zone of conflict into which an EU force of 50,000 may well, in time and with the support of NATO, be deployed. And that is Kosovo.

Notes

1. I am grateful to officials from the FCO, MoD, European Commission, NATO, WEU, and WEUISS for confidential advice and information for this chapter. The European Union (EU) came into being in 1993, with the ratification of the Maastricht Treaty. Between its creation, in 1957, and 1967, it was entitled the European Economic Community (EEC). With the Merger Treaty of 1967, the Coal and Steel Community, the EEC, and Euratom were renamed the European Communities (EC). What has essentially been the same international organization has therefore had three names.
2. The six-month rotating presidency was then taken over by Finland, a neutral member state. Finland had joined the EU in 1995, and this was its first presidency.

3. The term "glass ceiling" is used by feminists, and it implies that although in theory the opportunities for women are boundless, in reality women are held back by constraints that are not easily visible.
4. See the chapters on France, Germany, Britain, and Italy in this volume. EU states that are NATO members are Britain, Germany, Italy, Spain, Portugal, Greece, the Netherlands, Belgium, Luxembourg, and Denmark. France withdrew from the military command structure in 1966 but fought as a part of the NATO operation over Kosovo.
5. General Affairs Council, meeting 2,161, Luxembourg, February 21–22, 1999; General Affairs Council, meeting 2,158, Brussels, January 25, 1999. At the same time, NAC authorized planning for air strikes.
6. Milosevic did not attend Rambouillet, and it was later asserted that his presence in Dayton had been decisive. One reason for this was his fear of traveling outside his country, given the experience of General Pinochet in the United Kingdom. One of the negotiators there remarked that his B, if not his C, team had been sent; based on confidential interviews. On Rambouillet, see Marc Weller, "The Rambouillet Conference on Kosovo," *International Affairs* 75 (April 1999): pp. 211–51.
7. Statement by the European Council on Kosovo, March 23, 1999, CFSP presidency statement, 8278/99, May 12, 1999.
8. European Commission, IP/99/319, May 11, 1999; the embargo was declared on April 23, 1999. Confidential interviews.
9. Declaration of the EU on Kosovo, PESC/99/53, May 31, 1999.
10. *Le Monde*, June 5, 1999; *Wall Street Journal Europe*, April 23, 1999. This was a good example of the French working toward institutional balancing and was in tune with their frequent and public demands for a genuinely multipolar world, and not one dominated by one superpower.
11. *Wall Street Journal Europe*, April 6, 1999, article by Westendorp, high representative of the international community for the civil implementation of the Dayton Peace Accords. Solutions—such as bargaining Kosovo against Republika Srpska—were aired but rejected.
12. Luxembourg General Affairs Council, April 9, 1999; *Guardian*, April 9, 1999; General Affairs Council, April 8, 1999; statement by the EU presidency, April 8, 1999. The Commission's aid package was 160 million euro, taken from reserves and existing budgets. There were also very ambitious and startling remarks made about the need to expand both the EU and NATO.
13. COM(99)235, May 1999. The regional approach was reinforced through the common strategy agreed upon at the Vienna European Council of December 1998.
14. Cologne European Council presidency conclusions, June 3–4, 1999, paragraphs 3 and 4, pp. 62–77; confirmed in the Stability Pact for South Eastern Europe, June 10, 1999, paragraph 20.
15. The signatories were the foreign ministers of the member states of the European Union; the European Commission; the foreign ministers of Albania, Bosnia-Herzegovina, Bulgaria, Croatia, Hungary, Romania, the Russian Federation, Slovenia, the Former Yugoslav Republic of Macedonia, Turkey, and the United States of America; the OSCE chairman-in-office and the

representative of the Council of Europe; the foreign ministers of Canada and Japan; representatives of the United Nations, UNHCR, NATO, OECD, WEU, the International Monetary Fund, the World Bank, the European Investment Bank, and the European Bank for Reconstruction and Development; representatives of the Royaumont process, BSEC, CEI, SECI, and SEECP; June 10, 1999. They welcomed the fact that the EU and the United States made support for the Stability Pact a priority in their New Transatlantic Agenda, as well as the fact that the EU and the Russian Federation made the Stability Pact a priority in their political dialogue.

16. The U.N. Security Council Resolution 1244 gave roles to the UNHCR, the United Nations, and the OSCE as well. U.N. Security Council Resolution S/RES/1244, June 10, 1999. The EU also contributed through its Obnova reconstruction program.
17. Joschka Fischer to the European Parliament, July 21, 1999.
18. On the European Defence Community failure, see Renata Dwan, *An Uncommon Community: France and the European Defence Community, 1950–1954*, unpublished D.Phil. thesis, University of Oxford, 1996.
19. The procedure was called European Political Cooperation. Decisions were essentially declaratory, and the Commission was not directly involved as a decision-maker in European Political Cooperation. On the WEU, see Anne Deighton, ed., *Defence, Security, Integration: Western European Union, 1954–1997* (Oxford: EIRU, 1997). Full membership of WEU was reserved for NATO members; however, not all NATO members were able or willing to be full members of the WEU (Denmark, Turkey, and Iceland). Some EU members (Finland, Sweden, Ireland, Austria) were not able to be full members of the WEU as they were not members of NATO.
20. For a discussion of the theoretical implications of this change, see the chapters by David Haglund and Stephen Walt in this volume.
21. See, for example, an article by George Robertson, who was then the British minister of defense, in *RUSI Journal* (April–May 1999). He was speaking before hostilities broke out over Kosovo.
22. Title V, paragraph 1, Amsterdam Treaty, 1997, Petersberg paragraph 2.
23. Joint Declaration on European Defence, British-French summit, Saint-Malo, December 3–4, 1999. Article J.7, Treaty of Amsterdam, signed 1997.
24. Confidential interviews.
25. *Financial Times*, September 15, 1999. Fighting capacity was actually closer to 3,000 than 6,000 jets: confidential interviews.
26. NATO Summit, Washington, April 23–25, 1999, "Defence Capabilities Initiative; Final Communiqué."
27. Whilst NATO remained the key to collective security, it said that "the EU should have at its disposal the appropriate capabilities and structures for effective decision-making in crisis management with the scope of the Petersberg tasks," and "the capacity for autonomous action backed up by credible military capabilities and appropriate decision-making bodies, to allow the Council to take decisions on the whole range of political, economic and military instruments at its disposal when responding to crisis situations."

28. *International Herald Tribune*, April 30–May 2, 1999.
29. "Defence Capabilities Initiative; Final Communiqué," NATO Summit, April 1999.
30. Alarm about concurrence, or military overstretch, in which the United States might find itself engaged in too many fields of operations at the same time, may also be the reason for a perceived lack of willingness to engage militarily. Or, as George Kennan put it, notwithstanding an obligation to Europe and Yugoslavia as part of the European-American civilization, "what we ought to do at this point is to try to cut ourselves down to size in the dreams and aspirations we direct to our possibilities for world leadership." *New York Review of Books*, Kennan interviewed by Richard Ullman, June 1999.
31. The startling Franco-German proposal of November 1999 to use the Eurocorps in Kosovo is evidence of this balancing act.

PART TWO

National Perspectives on Operation Allied Force

CHAPTER FIVE

Kosovo and the Future of U.S. Engagement in Europe: Continued Hegemony or Impending Retrenchment?

Charles A. Kupchan

The events of the 1990s suggest that the United States will remain Europe's chief protector and peacemaker long into this new century. Washington took the lead in expanding NATO and setting a new course for the Atlantic security order. The United States was also critical to bringing peace to the Balkans. American forces led NATO into battle over Kosovo, with Washington effectively running the war and U.S. aircraft flying most of the missions. NATO's intervention in Yugoslavia demonstrated that, in President Clinton's words, America is "the indispensable nation," and that American power and purpose are alive and well in Europe.

Beneath the surface, however, a very different picture is emerging. The United States has indeed taken the lead in expanding NATO and building a new European order that will include the Continent's new and aspiring democracies. But the foundation is increasingly shaky, built on an American polity that has a dwindling interest in footing the bill for construction and upkeep. America's commitments in Europe are expanding rapidly at the same time that the political appetite for robust internationalism is shrinking at an equal pace.

Now that the first wave of NATO enlargement has been completed, enthusiasm for further enlargement is rapidly dissipating. Successive waves of enlargement are by no means assured. The battle for Kosovo, while it did demonstrate U.S. willingness to fight for European stability, also made clear that America's dominant strategic role in Europe enjoys increasingly tenuous political support in the United States. America came to Europe's assistance to prevent a wider war in the Balkans. But the operation also revealed that Europe's strategic dependence upon the United States is becoming politically unsustainable. America's political class supported the war only reluctantly, and the operation was restricted to air power to avoid American casualties. Despite the success of the air campaign and the absence of a single NATO combat casualty, the U.S. Senate's main reaction was to pass unanimously a resolution bemoaning the "glaring shortcomings" in European defense capabilities, and urging the European Union to rectify the "overall imbalance" within the Alliance.[1]

In this essay, I examine the extent to which NATO's war for Kosovo exposed the fissures in the post–World War II consensus in the United States about European security. The debate over U.S. engagement and the conduct of the war itself made clear that the continuation of America's role as Europe's protector of last resort can by no means be taken for granted. I then put the prospect of waning internationalism in the United States in a broader context by discussing why America's unipolar moment is likely to come to an end as this new century proceeds. Finally, I turn to the implications of an American retrenchment for the Atlantic Alliance, and argue that Europe should redouble its efforts to build a common defense policy and capability and become more self-reliant. A stronger and more self-confident Europe would strengthen the Atlantic link and ensure that Europe would not be left in the lurch were the United States to pass the next time military conflict emerges in Europe's periphery.[2]

The Legacy of NATO's Battle for Kosovo

NATO's successful battle to drive Serb forces from Kosovo seems, at least at face value, to confirm that the United States is prepared to remain Europe's strategic guarantor. With stability in southern Europe threatened by ethnic conflict in the Balkans, the United States rose to the occasion and took the lead in orchestrating NATO action. The United States effectively ran the war, kept recalcitrant allies in line, and contributed the lion's share of military assets to the bombing campaign.

The bigger picture, however, suggests anything but a new era of U.S.-led crusades to protect Europe from ethnic and civil conflict. America's effort in the Balkans was at best half-hearted and enjoyed only razor-thin political support. From the outset, President Clinton blocked the use of ground forces, severely constraining the military operation and weakening NATO's hand in coercive diplomacy. Even after weeks of an air war that only exacerbated the humanitarian crisis NATO was supposed to resolve and increased the probability of a southward spread of the war, President Clinton maintained his veto. Moreover, he insisted that allied aircraft bomb from no lower than 15,000 feet to avoid being shot down.

Congressional opposition to the conflict only made matters worse. A month into a war that had not produced a single U.S. casualty, the House nevertheless expressed grave misgivings, voting 290–139 to refuse funding for sending U.S. ground troops to Yugoslavia without congressional approval. On the air war, the House was only a shade more adventuresome, with a tie vote (213–213) on a resolution endorsing the bombing campaign. Congress's behavior hardly represented a resounding confirmation of America's commitment to stability in the heart of Europe.

The battle for Kosovo thus underscored the growing mismatch between America's external policies and its internal politics. Clinton knew that a failure to confront Milosevic over Kosovo would likely jeopardize Macedonia and, with it, the entire Balkan peninsula. Doing nothing was therefore out of the question. At the same time, even before the conflict began, centrists from both main U.S. political parties argued passionately that Kosovo did not involve America's vital interests and that Europe should assume responsibility for its own troubles. Former Secretary of State Henry Kissinger, hardly an isolationist, argued before the bombing campaign began that "the proposed deployment [of U.S. troops] in Kosovo does not deal with any threat to American security as traditionally conceived [...]. If Kosovo presents a security problem, it is to Europe."[3]

Clinton responded by taking the middle road, authorizing an air campaign but nothing more. Coercion from the air did succeed in reining in Milosevic and compelling him to withdraw his troops from Kosovo. Nonetheless, the conflict should hardly be seen as a precedent for the future. NATO aircraft were able to do heavy damage to the Yugoslav army only after a KLA offensive on the ground forced the Yugoslav army to concentrate in defensive and exposed positions. And throughout the conflict, Milosevic could easily have taken advantage of NATO's weakness on the ground to widen the war to Macedonia or Montenegro. NATO would then have been in a precarious position and grievously exposed.

Press reports published after the end of the conflict indicate that NATO would have eventually moved to a ground campaign had Milosevic not backed down. In order to ensure the return of Albanian refugees prior to the onset of winter, NATO had begun initial preparations for a ground invasion of Kosovo even before Milosevic's capitulation. But it was only when NATO leaders realized that the Alliance could well lose its battle with Milosevic that they were prepared to move to a ground campaign and assume the associated risks. Embarking on a massive air campaign without first putting a serious ground force in the region was not just short-sighted, but also irresponsible.

Rather than forcing American policymakers and voters to confront the gap between increasing commitments and decreasing internationalism, NATO's war for Kosovo served only to reinforce the illusion that the United States could preserve global stability on the cheap. Clinton pursued a very activist defense policy, repeatedly sending U.S. forces into action in Haiti, Iraq, and the Balkans. But the absence of casualties has left America's appetite for war untested. Somalia, the only case in which U.S. soldiers were killed in combat, does not provide cause for optimism. After the loss of 18 Americans, the United States packed its bags and headed for home.

American behavior since the end of the conflict over Kosovo gives further indication of Washington's clear intent to limit the scope of U.S. commitments in the Balkans. European forces have picked up the bulk of peacekeeping responsibilities in Kosovo, and the EU is taking the lead on economic reconstruction. Even before the end of fighting, President Clinton promised Americans in his Memorial Day address that "when the peacekeeping force goes in there [Kosovo], the overwhelming majority of people will be European; and that when the reconstruction begins, the overwhelming amount of investment will be European."[4] As mentioned above, the U.S. Senate's main response to the crisis in Kosovo has been to pass a resolution calling on Europe to carry much more of its own defense burden. And many of the candidates in the presidential race criticized the activist bent in Clinton's foreign policy, promising a more restrained and less interventionist approach.

Despite the facade of unity within NATO, America's deep ambivalence about the war and its aversion to casualties did not go unnoticed in Europe. It is no coincidence that in the aftermath of Kosovo, the European Union has redoubled its efforts to forge a collective defense policy and a military force capable of operating independently of the United States. Europeans have been acting on the recognition that they may well be on their own when the next military crisis emerges on the Continent. As British prime minister Tony Blair asserted in justifying the initiative, "We Europeans should not expect the United States to have to play a part in every disorder in our own back yard."[5]

Europe's renewed effort to forge a collective defense capability stems not just from fear of U.S. disengagement. Many European politicians and military leaders had their confidence in U.S. leadership shaken by the war over Kosovo. Despite the positive outcome of the war, the British and French in particular were critical of America's conduct of the war and especially its unwillingness to countenance casualties. As one British defense expert complained, "Clinton's public dismissal of a ground option was inexcusable, as was the absence of alternative strategies for prevailing if Milosevic failed to back down."[6]

The war over Kosovo thus sent an ominous signal about America's dissipating willingness to be Europe's chief peacemaker and its protector of last resort. If the United States had close to zero tolerance for casualties in a region considered key to stability in southeastern Europe, it will have no appetite whatsoever for engagements farther afield. America fought the right war in Kosovo, and fortunately prevailed. But the sobering message left behind is that such a war is very unlikely to happen again.

The Waning of Unipolarity

America's behavior in Kosovo was indicative of a broader retrenchment in U.S. foreign policy that will become more pronounced in the years ahead. This retrenchment has structural roots—the disappearance of bipolarity in the wake of the Soviet Union's collapse, and the transition from unipolarity to multipolarity that looms on the horizon. As America's unipolar moment comes to an end, so too will its willingness to be the global guarantor of last resort.

Contemporary systemic change is likely to occur through different mechanisms than in the past. Most analysts of international politics trace change in the distribution of power to two sources: the secular diffusion over time and space of productive capabilities and material resources; and balancing against concentrations of power motivated by the search for security and prestige. Today's great powers will become tomorrow's has-beens as nodes of innovation and efficiency move from the core to the periphery of the international system. In addition, reigning hegemons threaten rising secondary states and thereby provoke the formation of countervailing coalitions. Taken together, these dynamics drive the cyclical pattern of the rise and fall of great powers.[7]

In contrast to this historical pattern, neither the diffusion of power nor balancing against the United States will be an important factor driving the coming transition in the international system. It will be decades before any single state can match the United States in terms of either military or economic capability. Current power asymmetries are by historical standards extreme. The United States spends more on defense than all other great powers combined and more on defense research and development than the rest of the world combined. Its gross economic output dwarfs that of most other countries, and its expenditure on research and development points to a growing qualitative edge in a global economy increasingly dominated by high-technology sectors.[8]

Nor is balancing against American power likely to provoke a countervailing coalition. The United States is separated from both Europe and Asia by large expanses of water, making American power less threatening. Furthermore, it is hard to imagine that the United States would engage in behavior sufficiently aggressive to provoke opposing alliances. Even in the wake of NATO's air campaign against Yugoslavia, U.S. forces are for the most part welcomed by local powers in Europe and East Asia. Despite sporadic comments from French, Russian, and Chinese officials about America's overbearing behavior, the United States is generally viewed as a benign power, not as a predatory hegemon.[9]

The waning of unipolarity is therefore likely to stem from two novel sources: regional amalgamation in Europe and shrinking internationalism in the United States. Europe is in the midst of a long-term process of political and economic integration that is gradually eliminating the importance of borders and centralizing authority and resources. To be sure, the EU is not yet an amalgamated polity with a single center of authority. Nor does Europe have a military capability commensurate with its economic resources.

But trend lines do indicate that Europe is heading in the direction of becoming a new pole of power. Now that its single market has been accompanied by a single currency, Europe has a collective weight on matters of trade and finance rivaling that of the United States. The aggregate wealth of the EU's 15 members is already roughly equal to America's, and the coming entry of a host of new members will tilt the balance in Europe's favor. In addition, Europe has recently embarked on efforts to forge a common defense policy and to acquire the military wherewithal to operate independently of U.S. forces. It will be decades, if ever, before the EU becomes a unitary state, especially in light of its impending enlargement to the east. But as its resources grow and its decision-making becomes more centralized, power and influence will become more equally distributed between the two sides of the Atlantic.

The continuing rise of Europe and its leveling effect on the global distribution of power will occur gradually. Of more immediate impact will be a diminishing appetite for robust internationalism in the United States. Today's unipolar landscape is a function not just of America's preponderant resources, but also of its willingness to use them to underwrite international order. Accordingly, should the will of the body politic to bear the costs and risks of international leadership decline, so too will America's position of global primacy.

As mentioned above, the appetite of the American polity for robust internationalism has ostensibly diminished little, if at all, since the collapse of the Soviet Union. Both the Bush and Clinton administrations pursued ambitious and activist foreign policies. The United States has taken the lead in building an open international economy and promoting financial stability, and it has repeatedly deployed its forces to trouble spots around the globe. But American internationalism is now at a high-water mark, and for four compelling reasons, it will be dissipating in the years ahead.

First, the scope of America's commitments in Europe is not in equilibrium with the Continent's new strategic landscape. The demise of the Soviet Union and the disappearance of the threat that gave rise to NATO should have lightened America's load in Europe. Instead, America's strategic commitments on the European continent have increased markedly over the course of the past decade. NATO admitted Poland, Hungary, and the Czech Republic last year, extending American defense guarantees into central Europe. In addition, Bosnia, Kosovo, Macedonia, and Albania have effectively become NATO protectorates, and Slovenia, Croatia, Romania, and Bulgaria are now readying themselves to qualify for NATO membership. The prospect of these new commitments will force the United States to reconsider its strategic position in Europe. And absent a transcendent threat, the United States is likely to gravitate toward a strategic role in Europe that is less onerous and ambitious than during the Cold War. An American internationalism that is sustainable over the long term will entail fewer, not more, commitments. From this geopolitical perspective, the 1990s promise to be an aberration, not a precedent for the future.

Second, the internationalism of the 1990s has been sustained by a period of unprecedented economic growth in the United States. A booming stock market, an expanding economy, and substantial budget surpluses have created a political atmosphere conducive to trade liberalization, expenditure on the military, and repeated engagement in solving problems in less fortunate parts of the globe. And even under these auspicious conditions, the internationalist agenda has shown signs of faltering. Congress, for example, has mustered only a fickle enthusiasm for free trade, approving NAFTA in 1993 and the Uruguay Round in 1994, but then denying President Clinton fast-track negotiating authority in 1997. Congress has also been skeptical of America's interventions in Bosnia and Kosovo, tolerating them, but little more. When the stock market sputters and growth stalls (a matter of when, not if), these inward-looking currents will grow much stronger. The little support for free trade that still exists will dwindle. And such stinginess is likely to spread into the security realm, intensifying the domestic debate over burden sharing and calls within Congress for America's regional partners to shoulder increased defense responsibilities.

Third, although the United States pursued a very activist defense policy during the 1990s, it did so on the cheap. Bill Clinton repeatedly authorized the use of force in the Balkans and in the Middle East. But he relied almost exclusively on air power, successfully avoiding the casualties likely to accompany the introduction of ground troops into combat. The illusion that internationalism can be maintained with no or minimal loss of life will likely come back to haunt the United States in the years ahead, limiting its ability to use force in the appropriate manner when necessary.

Fourth, generational change is likely to take a toll on the character and scope of U.S. engagement abroad. The younger Americans already rising to positions of influence in the public and private sectors have not lived through the formative experiences—World War II and the rebuilding of Europe—that serve as historical anchors of internationalism. Individuals schooled in the 1990s and now entering the workforce will not even have firsthand experience of the Cold War. These Americans will not necessarily be isolationist, but they will certainly be less interested in and knowledgeable about foreign affairs than their older colleagues—a pattern already becoming apparent in Congress. In the absence of a manifest threat to American national security, making the case for engagement and sacrifice abroad thus promises to grow increasingly difficult with time. Trend lines clearly point to a turning inward and a nation tiring of carrying the burdens of global leadership. As the United States seeks to lighten its load in the years ahead, Europe's success in spreading democracy and stability (especially in comparison with East Asia) will make it a likely candidate for a diminishing U.S. role.

Europe Without its American Pacifier?

The prospect of a diminishing American role in managing European security is already causing concern in Europe. The central issue is not, as in the past, who will balance against Russia, but how the European project will fare if it can no longer rely on the United States as its strategic guarantor. In his 1986 article in *Foreign Policy,* "Europe's American Pacifier," Josef Joffe wrote that America's presence in Europe is central to preventing the return of national rivalries to Europe. Many contemporary analysts believe that Joffe's analysis still holds and that the viability of European integration continues to depend on America's continental commitment.[10]

If the above analysis is correct, however, Europe cannot rely indefinitely on America's protective umbrella to ensure its security and preempt intra-European competition. As they look to the future, prudence thus necessitates that NATO members forge a vision of European security that is less Atlantic and more European than in the past. Europe is in fact further along in developing such a self-sustaining regional order than is commonly recognized, especially in the United States. American power and purpose unquestionably made possible European integration. American guarantees enabled West Europeans to be comfortable with German recovery and rearmament.

And NATO effectively took the weightiest security issues off the European agenda, allowing the European project to focus almost exclusively on economic and political integration.

But Europe is now to a significant extent running on its own steam, making the prospect of less reliance on its American pacifier far less worrisome. The success of the European project stems from the fact that Europe integrated itself internally at the same time that it was integrated into the Atlantic community of capitalist democracies. Germany dealt with its past and made peace with its neighbors, paving the way for a collective process of integration that has produced dramatic results: the European Union. Europe stands in stark contrast to Asia, where Japan and other countries were integrated into the community of capitalist democracies, but the region failed to take advantage of American guarantees to pursue its own political integration. Unlike Germany, Japan neither confronted its past nor sought reconciliation with the victims of its aggression. This historical difference today leaves East Asia with a far more fragile and dangerous security environment than Europe.

The durability of the European polity stems in large part from the geopolitical transformation that has resulted from decades of integration. The Franco-German coalition has established itself as Europe's benign power center, with smaller states arraying themselves in concentric circles around this core. The centripetal force of effective regional unipolarity has replaced the destructive jockeying that plagued Europe during its long decades of multipolarity. In addition, through a host of institutions and practices—a European parliament, a common market, a single currency—EU members have gradually pooled their sovereignties, enabling the national state to exist comfortably alongside a supranational union. That most of Europe's new democracies are now waiting impatiently for entry into the EU makes clear the appeal of this construction. And the prospect of entry in turn provides impetus behind reform and the resolution of disputes in central and eastern Europe.[11]

Nor is Europe oblivious to the fact that it must begin to shoulder more responsibility in security matters. EU members have for years agreed on the need for a common foreign and defense policy—but have failed to follow through with concrete steps. The tide appears to be turning. British prime minister Tony Blair has made a top priority the creation of a more robust European defense capability. Javier Solana, the former secretary-general of NATO, is now the EU's first-ever defense chief. He is overseeing a host of defense reforms, including establishing a European rapid reaction force capable of deploying without U.S. assistance, and developing a policy planning unit within the EU. The main impetus behind these initiatives is not, as some U.S. critics charge, to undermine American influence in Europe.

Rather, Europeans are becoming increasingly aware that their strategic dependence on the United States is untenable over the long term.

Despite good reasons to be optimistic about the European project, it is also clear that the EU has much hard work ahead. Blair's noble intentions aside, formidable obstacles stand in the way of a more coherent foreign and defense policy.[12] Only a few years ago, Europe failed miserably when it tried to stop on its own the bloodshed in the Balkans. On the economic front, structural rigidities and an overextended state sector continue to produce low growth and high unemployment. Economic stagnation and political stalemate, if they continue, will take a toll on the EU's coherence. So too does generational change pose a potential problem. For younger generations who have lived through neither the horrors of World War II nor the formidable task of rebuilding Europe, escaping the past will no longer serve as a sufficient rationale for the European project. Elites will have to generate new arguments to ensure the integrity of the Franco-German coalition and the broader European polity.

As they build a stable Atlantic community for the future, both Americans and Europeans thus need to pay far more attention to locking in a European construction that will withstand the potential retrenchment of American power. At the same time that the United States shapes the evolution of NATO, it must also do what it can to strengthen the EU as an independent and durable center of power. Even if it comes at the expense of U.S. influence in Europe or trade across the Atlantic, a stronger and self-sustaining European polity is in America's long-term interests.

Washington can help strengthen Europe's core by dealing with Germany and France collectively. (Britain should be included in this troika down the road if Blair continues to move his country closer to Europe.) The United States should encourage, rather than look with suspicion at, efforts to strengthen Europe's own defense capabilities and initiatives such as the joint visit of Helmut Kohl and Jacques Chirac to Moscow in 1998. The notion that NATO should be turned into a vehicle for global military operations, which was commonly advocated by members of the Clinton Administration and by several outside analysts in recent years, should also be abandoned.[13] Rather than press European forces to join their U.S. counterparts in battling common threats wherever they emerge, Washington should encourage Europe to shoulder more of the burden in its own neighborhood. Europeans must consolidate peace on the Continent before they can afford to focus their primary attention elsewhere.

Washington can do only so much, however; it is primarily up to the Europeans themselves to prepare for a more balanced Atlantic relationship. Locking in the Franco-German coalition, especially as a new generation of leaders rises to power, is a top priority. The new German government must make unequivocal its commitment to solidarity with France, especially as all of Europe watches carefully the implications of the move of Germany's capital from Bonn to Berlin. France and Germany must not just ensure the smooth implementation of monetary union and other aspects of economic and political integration. They must also begin to address in earnest how to move forward on the defense front.

Reallocating defense spending is a top priority. Europe spends roughly 60 percent of what America does on defense, but maintains 50 percent more soldiers under arms. Europe's troops are organized primarily for territorial defense, the duty of the past, not for the projection of force, the challenge of today and tomorrow. Europe must trade a large but hollow army for a smaller force with more capability and flexibility.

Over time, Europe will also have to increase its defense spending to buy air and sea lift, build lighter but potent forces capable of rapid deployment, and improve the technological sophistication of its hardware. If U.S. and European forces are to operate together in Europe or elsewhere, Europe has to do a much better job of keeping pace with the revolution in military technology. The United States launched 80 percent of the precision-guided munitions and 95 percent of the cruise missiles used in the Kosovo war because of inadequate and outdated European arsenals. Some European pilots participating in the air campaign did not even have secure communication systems enabling them to speak to one another safely when in combat.

A true European defense force will also be limited in size and political weight unless Germany joins Great Britain and France as an equal military partner. Although Germany's willingness to bear security burdens outside of its borders has increased considerably since 1991, a full commitment to European defense will require strong political leadership by a new generation of German politicians.

The European Union and the United States should work together closely as Europe's defense efforts move ahead. NATO should remain the key forum for decision-making, and U.S. and European militaries should ensure that they can operate together. At the same time, Europe must develop the ability to act on its own if the United States chooses not to engage. Managing the emergence of a more confident Europe will require improved institutional linkages between NATO and the EU and more European representation in NATO commands.

U.S.-European Rivalry?

American engagement in Europe remains vital to the stability of the Continent. U.S. leadership is needed to draw Russia into Western institutions.

And the European Union still lacks both the political will and the military capability to take the lead on security matters. At least for now, the United States must remain Europe's strategic guarantor.

At the same time, the vision I am laying out is one in which Europe over the course of the next decade becomes a much more influential and independent actor. The United States does not exit the scene, but it no longer plays the role of pacifier and protector. This evolution of the transatlantic relationship is both desirable and inevitable. It is desirable because Europe's current level of strategic dependence on the United States is simply unsustainable over the long term; Americans will not indefinitely foot the bill for European stability. Europe therefore had better get its house in order. It is inevitable because as Europe deepens its collective governance and becomes a more formidable economic entity, it will aspire to a level of influence commensurate with its power.

The critical question for the future is thus not whether Europe will rise as an independent power center, but what effect a self-possessed Europe will have on the character of relations across the Atlantic. History suggests that a more equal distribution of power and influence between Europe and the United States will bring with it renewed geopolitical competition. The emergence of rivalry among poles of power is, after all, one of the few recurring truths of international politics.

Whether relative parity will indeed trigger rivalry between Europe and the United States depends in large part on what it is that now keeps the Atlantic relationship in such good shape. If, on the one hand, it is American preponderance that now holds competition in abeyance, then the rise of Europe promises to trigger geopolitical competition. From this perspective, Europe is following America's lead because it does not have the power to do otherwise. When the power asymmetry comes to an end, so will European acquiescence. If, on the other hand, a shared commitment to democratic values and a common vision of an open, multilateral order are the foundation of the transatlantic community, then the West should easily weather a more equal distribution of power across the Atlantic. From this perspective, democratic norms and multilateral institutions will overwhelm the incentives on both sides of the Atlantic to engage in power balancing.[14]

My own assessment is that power asymmetry and shared norms and institutions are working together to produce the current durability and cohesiveness of the transatlantic community. Europe has been following America's lead in part because of U.S. preponderance, but also because it welcomes the particular brand of international order that the United States has crafted. As Europe matures and its aspirations broaden, more competition with the United States will follow. But this competition is likely to be muted and restricted largely to the economic realm. Such optimism that geopolitical rivalry between North America and Europe is not on the horizon stems from the following considerations.

The Atlantic democracies are far more than allies of convenience. They have succeeded in carving out a unique political space in which the rules of anarchic competition no longer apply. These states enjoy unprecedented levels of trust and reciprocity. It is hard to imagine that their interests would diverge sufficiently to trigger strategic rivalry. Indeed, armed conflict among the members of the Atlantic community has become unthinkable. These attributes of the Atlantic community are deeply rooted in the democratic character of its members and in the thick network of institutions they have erected to regulate their relations. The benign quality of the relationship between North America and Europe is very unlikely to be threatened even by a quantitative shift in the balance of power.

The character of the emerging European polity also minimizes the potential for security competition between Europe and the United States. The European Union is primarily an instrument for managing the power of its member states, not for amassing and projecting it. Furthermore, even as integration proceeds, cultural and linguistic barriers are likely to prevent Europe from amalgamating into a single pole of power under a central authority. The decentralized nature of the emerging Europe will limit its willingness and ability to project power externally, further diminishing the risk of geopolitical competition with the United States.[15]

Despite the low probability that Europe's rise will lead to estrangement from the United States, some preventive measures are in order. Washington should ensure that it makes room for and encourages a stronger and more independent Europe. American efforts to resist Europe's ascent as a power center would only alienate Europeans and increase the chances of balancing and geopolitical rivalry. The United States and its European partners should also strengthen multilateral practices and institutions. When Washington is no longer able to call the shots, it will have no choice but to rely more heavily on consensual governance and multilateral institutions to manage international order.

Conclusion

My analysis should not be interpreted as a warning of America's impending departure from Europe. On the contrary, the United States is likely to remain engaged in managing European security well into the next century. At the same time, the current scope of America's preponderance—and the reliance of virtually every quarter of the globe on that preponderance—will not last. While they have the luxury of doing so, the United States and its main regional partners should begin to imagine life after *Pax Americana*.

This perspective necessitates both a short-term and a long-term strategy for the Atlantic community. In the short term, the United States should continue to guide NATO's evolution and buy more time for the EU to develop a common security policy and the requisite military forces. Over the long term, the United States and its NATO allies should take steps to facilitate the gradual devolution of increasing responsibility to the European Union. A more balanced relationship between the United States and Europe, and a European security order that is more European and less Atlantic, holds out the best hope for preserving a cohesive transatlantic community. As the twenty-first century progresses, America must become Europe's partner, no longer its pacifier.

Notes

1. Senate Resolution 175, August 5, 1999.
2. The analysis presented in this chapter draws on three previously published articles: "The Balkans: Fractured U.S. Resolve and the Paradox in Limited U.S. Involvement," *Washington Post,* June 13, 1997; "Life After Pax Americana," *World Policy Journal* 16 (fall 1999): pp. 20–27; and "Rethinking Europe," *The National Interest* 56 (summer 1999): pp. 73–80.
3. See Steven Erlanger, "NATO Was Closer to Ground War in Kosovo than Is Widely Realized," *New York Times,* November 7, 1999.
4. "Remarks by the President at Memorial Day Service, Arlington National Cemetery," May 31, 1999 (http://ofcn.org/cyber.serv/teledem/pb/1999/may/pr19990531a).
5. Speech at the Royal United Services Institute, March 8, 1999.
6. Confidential interview.
7. See Robert Gilpin, *War and Change in World Politics* (Cambridge: Cambridge University Press, 1981); Paul Kennedy, *The Rise and Fall of the Great Powers* (New York: Random House, 1987); and Christopher Layne, "The Unipolar Illusion: Why New Great Powers Will Rise," *International Security* 17 (spring 1993): pp. 5–51.
8. William C. Wohlforth, "The Stability of a Unipolar World," *International Security* 24 (summer 1999): pp. 10–22.
9. On the concept of benign power, see Charles Kupchan, "After Pax Americana: Benign Power, Regional Integration, and the Sources of a Stable Multipolarity," *International Security* 23 (fall 1998): pp. 40–79.
10. See Joseph Joffe, "Europe's American Pacifier," *Foreign Policy* 54 (spring 1984): pp. 64–82; and Robert Art, "Why Western Europe Needs the United States and NATO," *Political Science Quarterly* 111 (spring 1996): pp. 1–39.
11. For further discussion of the long-term implications of integration for European security and the transformation from multipolarity to unipolarity, see Ole Waever, "Integration as Security," in Charles Kupchan, ed., *Atlantic Security: Contending Visions* (New York: Council on Foreign Relations, 1998); and Kupchan, "After Pax Americana."

12. See Philip Gordon, "Europe's Uncommon Foreign Policy," *International Security* 22 (winter 1997–98): pp. 74–100.
13. On the policy of the Clinton administration, see "New Visions for NATO," *New York Times,* December 7, 1998, p. A26. See also Robert Blackwill, *The Future of Transatlantic Relations* (New York: Council on Foreign Relations, 1999).
14. See John Ikenberry, "Institutions, Strategic Restraint, and the Persistence of American Postwar Order," *International Security* 23 (winter 1998–99): pp. 43–78.
15. Fareed Zakaria has shown that centralization and a strong state were necessary conditions for ambitious external policies in the United States. See *From Wealth to Power: The Unusual Origins of America's World Role* (Princeton: Princeton University Press, 1998).

CHAPTER SIX

Allied Force or Forced Allies? The Allies' Perspective

David G. Haglund

In an interview published in the Madrid daily *El País* shortly after the ending of the war with Serbia, French anthropologist Emmanuel Todd drew an analogy between NATO and the Delian League.[1] This Athenian-led alliance, constructed for the initial purpose of amassing Greek power against the Persian empire, grew over time into an Athenian empire, which ultimately went to war (in 431 B.C.) against rival Greek states led by Sparta.[2] The war against Serbia, Todd suggested, revealed how much NATO had come to resemble the Delian League. America has become the new Athens, the imperial protector of lesser allies, from whom little may be required or expected militarily, yet much is demanded politically and economically. This arrangement, to Todd, poses an obvious threat to the other allies, however much they may think their display of unity against Slobodan Milosevic has advanced their interests.[3]

It is, to be sure, hardly unusual for a French intellectual to speculate upon the dangers—real or imagined—of unchecked American power; after all, was it not the French foreign minister, Hubert Védrine, who popularized the label "hyperpower" to express the problems thought to be associated with the current imbalance in global and transatlantic power?[4] Nor is such speculation anything new for French policymakers or analysts: alone among the Western allies, France has for some time been most concerned about "balance" within the Alliance.[5]

Theorizing about the *necessary* implications of unbalanced power has been a staple for at least one school of international relations thinkers, namely the predominantly U.S.-based "structural realists," who can outdo even the French in prophesying the somber prospects that must ensue from the inevitable tendency of "power" to grow until checked by other power. This group of theorists, though perhaps not putting it exactly as does Todd, tends to go even further. The West, they argue, will eventually fall apart, and whether or not the fate of the Greek city-states awaits the current allies (structural realists are divided on this question), the least that needs to be said is that the same cause that triggered Greco-Greek rivalry (the "excessive" growth of one state's power) will generate counterbalancing forces even within NATO.[6]

Clearly, the Todd thesis would be compatible with the view that Kosovo only represents only the most recent iteration of the spectacle of "forced allies." Yet there is another way of regarding NATO, one that is more suggestive of this book's title: "allied force." Instead of NATO being the vehicle *par excellence* for the projection of American interests pure and simple, it can be better interpreted as the means of allowing allies, whatever their size, to advance their own interests. Moreover, in doing the latter, NATO might be regarded as offering them a degree of penetration into—even influence upon—American foreign policy debates. As I argue below, the Alliance can be conceived as a mechanism for helping to codetermine the American "national interest," with the result being that the latter resembles a collective (Western) interest that is constituted from a collective Western "identity" and set of shared values.

According to this ambitious construe of NATO as a "democratic alliance," there is no reason why the "empire" (if it is an empire) must eventually disintegrate in the absence of the erstwhile threat, for inside a "zone of peace" where power and its balancing matters little, there is likewise no reason why America's robust military profile need threaten the security interest of any democratic state. Quite the contrary. Through skillful diplomacy, these smaller allies might even avail themselves of American power to such an extent that, in advancing their own (as well as the general) interest, they are in effect "taxing" the American public and not their own populations. For these smaller allies, America's military thus becomes an inexpensive "force multiplier."

Now, it is a staple of isolationist thinking in America that this is exactly what cunning smaller allies have been doing to the United States well before Kosovo: "free riding" on its prowess without paying the price that such military might would normally entail.[7] Needless to say, it is not only isolationists who would redress the "burden" of Alliance defense: "burden sharing" has been an American concern for almost as long as there has been a NATO, and lately even the western Europeans are coming to accept that the quid pro quo for Europe's getting more of a say in the management of transatlantic security is that it contributes more to the military capability of the Alliance. Nonetheless, American isolationists have made burden sharing a somewhat sinister issue, one representing nothing so much as the ripping off of the U.S. taxpayer by smallish ingrates with the cheek to call themselves friends and "allies."

What "Allied" Perspective?

In a nutshell, the preceding section presents two contrasting alternatives for contemplating the Alliance. For Emmanuel Todd, the allies are little more than pawns from whom economic and political tribute is exacted by their imperial master. American isolationists regard them as useless appendages, deviously managing to drag America into their incessant quarrels—and, to add injury to insult, requiring it to do most of the paying, and the fighting, in resolution of those quarrels! Different as Todd's may be from that of the isolationists, both conceptualizations of NATO hold it to be a nettlesome contrivance.

It would be tempting to suggest that this dichotomy constitutes the most fruitful means of framing the notion of an "allies' perspective." On one assessment, we find huddled together the wretched, hapless allies, whose fate becomes worse as their power lessens. On another we gasp in outrage at the coterie of sinister countries, content to nourish themselves on the vital juices of their noble, benevolent, yet slightly dimwitted, protector, while frustrating that protector's purposes.[8] Depending on one's view of things, if it were a movie, Bela Lugosi could play either part, America's or the allies'.

However much it might make for good theater, such a dichotomous portrayal of NATO would be fallacious. There were during the previous decade conceptual faultlines running through the Alliance (there always have been), but they tended to be located not on a transoceanic basis but rather on an intra-European one. More importantly, the divergences within the Alliance did not seem, between the Dayton Accords in 1995 and the Kosovo crisis of 1998–99, to be primarily of a transatlantic nature, at least not the way they were in the early part of the 1990s.[9]

Simply put, there was no allies' perspective, nor was there a discernible "widening" of the Atlantic *during* the run-up to, and fighting of, the war with Serbia. It is true that *since* that war a rift appears to be taking form between Washington and some of the leading western European powers, but during the crisis and the war itself, as the various chapters in this volume explain, such a cleavage was hardly apparent. It is also true that one of the supposed "lessons" of the war is that the European allies have become fortified in their desire to construct a more unified and coherent security and defense capability (ESDI), and this—were it to be taken seriously— would seem to suggest, first, that the Europeans are all tuned to the same strategic frequency and, second, that somehow Europe's transatlantic allies must be negatively affected by such a development, notwithstanding all the polite supportive rhetoric from North Americans in recent years.[10]

Yes, the European states that are also in the European Union have indicated for some time that they need to form a more coherent ensemble to further their common security interests. What Kosovo did was to highlight the discrepancy between Europe's strategic reach and its grasp. What the crisis has not done is to generate significant new commitments to spending for the common defense; in the short term, if defense budgets in Germany and elsewhere in the EU are to be taken as evidence of anything, it might even be remarked that member states are moving away from, not toward, the goal of a "Europe of defense." In this regard, Pascal Boniface's comments remain as appropriate after Kosovo as they were before the crisis:

> Europe, like France, is at a crossroads. It can become a power in its own right with genuine autonomy from the United States, capable of acting on the strategic level in total independence. [...] To do so it must forget all about peace dividends, and maintain—nay, increase—its defence spending. Or it can decide that the security of Europe's own frontiers is assured, that there really is no threat today, and that more pressing problems than the construction of a Europe of defence should command the attention of its governments.
>
> Both options are clear, and each possesses its own logic and advantages; but a choice needs to be made. For the time being, and this is hardly satisfying, all that has been done is to proclaim the first option, but to put the other into practice. It is a gentle illusion that will lead straight to some cruel disillusionment.[11]

It is not just that the European allies differ as to the degree to which they are willing to spend for the sake of their mooted security and defense policy (ESDP); they also differ on the meaning of the Alliance to them (and this, of course, can affect their willingness to spend on a European defense entity). To date, notwithstanding the numerous attestations that Kosovo really *has* energized the ESDI/ESDP project,[12] the war with Serbia has had little short-term impact upon the manner in which the Alliance is perceived. This may change, however.

To understand why it has yet to do so, it is necessary to sample some allied perceptions of the NATO/American leadership issue. Doing this requires at least a modest resort to theory, for how one theorizes goes a long way toward explaining how one "perceives." Ultimately, the "allies' perspective" becomes a matter of the allies' theoretical understanding of the Western alliance.

The analysis that follows is divided into three sections. The first approaches the Alliance and the American role from the point of view of constructivist theory, and makes the claim that at least some European states tend to regard NATO as approximating (maybe even representing) a "democratic alliance." The second section approaches the Alliance and the American role from the perspective of a "theoretically informed narrative,"[13] and seeks to provide context to the issue under examination by demonstrating the change in "fissiparous" tendencies over the past ten years. The third section looks at how the actions of so-called smaller allies during the Kosovo crisis might contribute to our piecing together the puzzle labeled "the allies' perspective." I take the cases of Canada and Spain, on the basis that if any of the allies were "forced," it should have been these middle-ranking states that had, withal, something to bring to the battlefield (there being no purpose in trying to "force" a Luxembourg or an Iceland to contribute to the Alliance's combat capability).

Is NATO a "Democratic Alliance," and Would It Matter if It Were?

Whatever else Kosovo represented, it surely demonstrated the amazing spectacle of center-left governments given over to a vigorous venting of outraged indignation. If NATO's action was not the "aggression" its critics charged, then the least that can be said is that the Alliance was "aggressive" in showing its determination to halt Serbian ethnic cleansing and to trammel upon Serbian "sovereignty" (within the limits, of course, of what postmodern Western states consider to be acceptable casualties among *their own* forces).[14]

It has been widely observed that NATO, for the first time in its history, went to war; less remarked is that the Alliance that prosecuted Operation Allied Force was not the familiar NATO of the Cold War. Collective defense still received due deference as the charter mandate of the group, but none of the allies really was threatened by Belgrade. NATO obviously was an organization with a broader security writ than heretofore; perhaps the term "democratic alliance" best captures the sense of that writ.

With the new NATO has come a "new Atlanticism." At least this is the perspective of allies on the center left, and could even be said to approximate the Clinton administration's conception. Significantly, most allied governments in 1999 were center left in orientation, and even Spain's "conservative" government departed minimally from the norm. In short, NATO and the West were being imagined as a grouping of liberal democratic states that not only had forged among themselves a "security community," but had demonstrated a heretofore unknown *goût* for using military means to project political values.

Karsten Voigt, an adviser in the German foreign ministry and former member of the Bundestag from the Social Democratic Party (SPD), provides insight, both in his personal career pattern and in his recent policy advocacy, into the manner in which NATO has evolved—at least in perceptions. Like so many of the "generation of 1968" now in power in Europe, Voigt had once been both anti-NATO and rather "ambivalent" (this is a euphemism) about America: as he explains, his generation may have been culturally "Americanized," but politically they were anti-American, while the conservative German governments of the 1950s and early 1960s were culturally anti-American yet politically pro-American.[15] Over time, he insists, *pace* the conventional wisdom, the Atlantic has been narrowing, with the result being that a convergence of interests (some say values) has been a marked feature of transatlantic relations of late.[16]

Thus the amazing solidarity that Germans could show in the early stages of the air war (which received the approval of 95 percent of the Bundestag members and nearly that high a percentage of the public) owed nothing to their being "forced" into a bellicose line, and much to a perception that NATO's actions really did express German preferences. Voigt's image of the NATO of 1999 looks like nothing so much as the model "democratic alliance."

Among some Alliance watchers, this "new NATO" of the late 1990s had for several years been in the process of so transforming itself that it had even overstepped the traditional boundary between international organization and domestic institutions. As a result, suggested Michael Brenner, NATO "should be viewed as an evolving civic community whose pacific relations are the institutionalized norm rather than the calculated preference of states."[17] Put differently, NATO was contributing to the shaping of a collective identity among Western policy elites (and presumably their publics).

"Collective identity" is a relatively new addition to the vocabulary of international security. In Alexander Wendt's words, it refers to "positive identification with the welfare of another, such that the other is seen as a cognitive extension of the Self rather than as independent."[18] No longer just a clearinghouse of national interests and a valued forum for consultation and coordination (as institutionalists and "neoclassical realists" would have it),[19] the Alliance is regarded by constructivists as something truly new under the international security sun.

To Wendt, who pushed this argument furthest, NATO could be the first, and best, example of post-Westphalian governance by means of the "international state," i.e., a transnational structure able and willing to assume certain traditional functions heretofore only fulfilled, if fulfilled at all, by the territorial state.[20] Among those functions, Wendt argued, none was as basal as the providing of security, which is what he said NATO did, by dint of its being a "collective security system" characterized by its "joint control of organized violence potential in a transnational space."[21]

What is significant about the recent interpretation of NATO within the context of collective identity is not the misleading claim that the Alliance had become a "collective security" organization. Rather, the significance inhered in the theorists' insistence that we should not take for granted that state action must always be self-interested and egoistic, or as Wendt put it, that state interests must be considered to be "exogenous to interaction."[22] Instead, interests and the identities that subtend them are "constructed" through social interaction, in this case within the Alliance, through what is sometimes inelegantly referred to as "intersubjective" discourse.

For those who see "social constructivism" as a promising alternative to "rationalist" theories of alliances, it is necessary to go beyond the confines of the systemic level of analysis, as inhabited by either the structural realists or the institutionalists, and descend to the "second image" consisting of the state and society. There we encounter the theory of the democratic alliance. For one of its leading exponents, Thomas Risse, not only do democracies not fight each other, but "democratic allies form democratic alliances."[23] This latter contention is not the tautology it might seem at first glance, for what Risse is saying is that democratic states form a grouping whose constituent elements share so many values and are influenced by so many common norms that their citizens and leaders increasingly can be said to have developed a common (or "collective") identity. Moreover, this identity is strong enough even to shape the group's perception of security threat, on the basis of distinctions drawn between it (the "in-group") and others (the "out-group").

As Risse explains it, the "collective identity of actors in democratic systems defines both the in-group of friends and the out-group of potential foes."[24] Identity, not power relations, becomes fundamental to the recognition of adversaries, and thus can spawn alliances, at least among the democratic states (hence the "democratic," or threat-independent, alliance). Not only does such a theory account for NATO's robust opposition to Slobodan Milosevic (archetype of the nondemocratic, illiberal "out-group"), but it also explains why the Delian League is such an inappropriate analogy.

Moreover, it turns on its head the traditional realist conception of alliance formation, which holds that states feeling imperiled by a powerful foe will band together in self-protection, perhaps even discovering in the process that they have, outside of the defense and security realm, some interests and even values in common with their new allies.[25] For Risse, this puts the cart before the horse: states first feel a sense of kinship with others of their ilk, then they develop (or mutually "constitute") a collective identity that undergirds the sense of community, and, in turn, that "sense of community, by delimiting the boundaries of who belonged to 'us,' also defined 'them.' [...] In other words, the collective identity led to the threat perception, not the other way around."[26]

Democratic peace theory, says Risse, may reflect the reality that democracies do not tend to fight each other, but the theory is mute on the reason for this happy outcome unless it is modified by social constructivism: "[E]nmity as well as friendship in the international system [result neither] from some inherent features of the international distribution of power, as realists would assume, nor from the domestic structures of states as such, as [...] liberals argue. Rather, [they are] socially constructed."[27]

According to this view, NATO is more than a marriage of security convenience based on the partners' interests; it is a community of shared values, the foremost of which are human rights, the rule of law, and, especially, democratic governance. As such, it can be expected to persist.[28] Moreover, even if U.S. leadership might attenuate, there is still no cause for despair if we assume that Western allies have internalized these values.[29] What is striking about the recent literature on NATO as a community of values is the uniform claim that neither an enemy nor a boss is required to keep the allies allied. Their norms and values inform their interests, and the latter in turn become ever more congruent, to the point that one can speak of them not as a summed (and negotiable) set, but rather as a single collective interest emerging from a single collective identity.[30]

It would be churlish, and almost certainly wrongheaded, to dismiss the democratic peace, but it may be suggested that the emphasis upon collective identity could ultimately distract our attention from something else that warrants analysis, namely the congruence of various individual (otherwise known as national) interests, so that peace results—or at least the Alliance persists—because its members wish it to. In short, NATO may endure because self-interested (albeit "enlightened") cooperation continues to make sense to those who seek to do well for themselves and, in doing so, also do good for the wider community.[31]

Although structural realists may see little future in long-term security cooperation, many neoclassical realists, who stress *raison d'état* and not anarchy as their key concept, should have little difficulty comprehending the Atlantic Alliance's ability to survive as a social institution of major significance. These realists need not (though some clearly do) dismiss the existence of a collective identity in the West; it may be conceded in the abstract that appeals to collective identity cannot harm, and might even help, the cause of the Alliance's cohesion in the absence of a powerful adversary.

But what the neoclassical realist would not concede is the conflation of discrete states (and their preferences) within a collective will that is different from, or more than, the sum of its parts. Sovereignty matters to the neoclassical realist, for whom security cooperation depends on convergence less of norms and values and more of those essentially contested concepts known as interests, which the neoclassical realist insists must in the first instance owe more to "exogenous" factors than the constructivist is prepared to concede.

Thus, to obtain further gain on the "allies' perspective," it is worth probing whether Western interests have been increasingly divergent or convergent. If the former, then it would seem "forced allies" would be the proper descriptor for their "unity" on Kosovo; if the latter, "allied force" would be more accurate. Given that the springtime of 1999 not only found NATO at war but also observing its fiftieth anniversary, I focus in the following section on the issues that were said to be most divisive within the Alliance at the time of its previous major birthday celebration in 1989.

Is NATO a Fractious Alliance?

As NATO was approaching its fortieth anniversary in the late 1980s, it was common to observe that it seemed mired in conflict—not so much with its adversaries as with itself. One academic, who subsequently became U.S. ambassador to NATO, noted then that the Alliance "had had about as many crises as birthdays," a comment that reflected the query of another American some years before, who wondered, apropos the disarray of transatlantic security affairs, "When has NATO ever been in array?"[32] The point of these citations is to remind readers of what should never be forgotten: NATO has always been a disputatious family. But is it disputatious to the point of fracturing?

During the Cold War, it was believed (not without reason) that NATO's internal disputes could always be held in check by the existence of the Soviet threat, and with the disappearance of that threat, many observers have been quick to pronounce the impending extinction of the Alliance as a viable security organization (even if it does not actually disappear from the Brussels phone book). I begin by reviewing the source of intra-Alliance disunity *during* the Cold War, as debated by pundits. I then review some of the recent theoretical claims and counterclaims regarding the Alliance's ability to exist as more than a phone number and a postal address in the early twenty-first century.

NATO's Cold War Travails

When NATO turned forty, scholars from a variety of alliance countries were bending their efforts in quest of knowledge regarding the current state and future prospects of NATO. And what were they worrying about? Some issues of concern have simply disappeared, while others have retained a redoubtable staying power.

The most impressive changes have occurred, not surprisingly, in the area of nuclear arsenals and strategy. It is sometimes imagined, and has been argued in both German and Canadian governmental circles, that NATO should rethink its commitment, some say addiction, to the nuclear status quo.[33] In fact, the nuclear status quo of the late Cold War era no longer exists, even if the nuclear elements of the Alliance's new Strategic Concept reflected little change from its 1991 Strategic Concept.[34]

Whereas today nearly everyone regards NATO's nuclear arsenal to be a "political" force (whatever that may mean), and hardly anyone can identify the theater-based components of that arsenal (now restricted to dual-capable aircraft), a decade ago the Alliance was emerging from a long struggle over the credibility and mechanisms of "extended deterrence"—a struggle that engendered an enormous amount of ill-feeling among publics on both sides of the Atlantic, associated with criticisms made by Americans and Europeans alike that nuclear arrangements were more likely to jeopardize than to preserve their security.

A decade ago, nearly everyone seemed to be concerned about NATO's nuclear arsenal, but today such worries sound archaic; whatever else the Alliance may have done in the 1990s, it shed its image as an organization dedicated *exclusively* (or even primarily) to the collective defense of its members. That collective-defense function, to be sure, remains at the charter core of the Alliance, but one would have to be very inattentive to escape noticing that NATO has been reconfiguring itself as a conflict-management if not conflict-resolution agency for the southeastern periphery of Europe. In this new NATO, the old "coupling" woes centering on short-range nuclear successors to the intermediate-range nuclear forces are long forgotten.[35]

This does not mean all is or shall be bliss in Brussels, even though the war against Serbia was resolved more or less on NATO's, not Belgrade's, terms. A decade ago the West was emerging from a second trough of despondency, associated with the conviction that the Atlantic was "widening" due to America's becoming more "American" and Europe's more "European," presumably on political, sociological, and regional-economic grounds.[36] One implication of this multifaceted divergence was that, should the threat ever disappear, the tendency would be for centrifugal forces, already strong during the Cold War, to tear the Alliance apart in its aftermath.[37] This fear was given special poignancy by the belief of many that America was in economic "decline" while western Europe was marching from one economic victory to another as it grew more integrated. Added to this was the assumption that as North America became less "European" ethnically and demographically, attachment to the value structure known as Atlanticism would be bound to weaken.

Again, there is something old-fashioned if not downright incorrect about such assumptions. The United States, after some tergiversations (over

Bosnia) in 1994, reaffirmed that its interests were very much linked to Europe. Canada has shown an even greater tendency to jettison a prior inclination to distance itself from the old Continent. Whatever else may have been implied by the presence of American and Canadian warplanes in Serbian skies, it surely was not the strategic "widening" of the Atlantic.

Among theorists, many have not had problems explaining why the Alliance retains its pride of place in transatlantic security in the absence of a great-power adversary.[38] We have already examined the claims of constructivists on the matter of NATO's ability to ride out the absence of a strategic foe. Opposing the optimism of the constructivists is the pessimism of the structural realists, who insist that an alliance without an enemy is an oxymoron: to them, in the pithy words of Kenneth Waltz (written in 1993), "NATO's days are not numbered, but its years are."[39] This prediction might well prove true over the long term (how can it be denied that *any* entity's years are numbered if one waits long enough?). But if Waltz turns out to be right in the short to medium term, it will likely be for reasons other than the one he and other structural realists adduce, namely that alliances cannot survive the disappearance of a "worthy opponent."[40]

Indeed, a recent structural-realist prophecy of demise holds just the opposite: if the Alliance never *had* to do anything, it probably could endure. But in light of NATO's territorial and conceptual enlargements, the likelihood grows of greater risks and costs having to be incurred in the pursuit of European security. And, to Stephen Walt, such an escalation is bound to exacerbate preexisting strains within the Alliance, precisely because a more isolationist American public will eventually prevail over the country's internationalist elites and force a reduced commitment to the security of a Europe seen as an economic rival rather than a partner. Walt concludes that while the process may be delayed, it cannot be prevented, for "a powerful set of domestic and international forces is pulling the transatlantic alliance apart." NATO may seem to be in good shape, but it is really "beginning to resemble Oscar Wilde's Dorian Gray, appearing youthful and robust as it grows older—but becoming ever more infirm."[41]

The injection of economic competition into the contemplation of transatlantic prospects is hardly new; unlike the concerns of a decade ago over nuclear arsenals and doctrines, or over a "widening Atlantic" stemming from sociopolitical divergence, the economic dimension has been relatively (not totally) invariant as a generator of expectations regarding intra-alliance discord. It has done so for the generic reasons identified by Walt and others; and it has done so for more specific reasons, stemming from the economics of defense production and trade.

Those who detect in economic competition the source of the Alliance's most profound internal challenge hail from a variety of theoretical and ideological perspectives. On the left, it has long been an article of faith that the naturally competitive capitalist countries would face an impossible task limiting their competition to the economic sphere.[42] Writers of a more conservative kidney, including not a few enamored of "hegemonic stability theory," echo the perspective of those of the left, *mutatis mutandis*. Indeed, the conservative assessment of competition's consequences can sometimes sound more somber than the leftist one. For example, in 1990, Edward Luttwak warned that the ending of the Cold War would usher in a new era of strife between the quondam allies.[43] For Luttwak, the Soviet threat had been the West's "strategic safety net." Take it away, and the fall could be hard indeed. "It is worth recalling," he wrote in 1989, "that during the 1920s—the last 'threatless' era—commercial competition quickly deteriorated into economic warfare."[44]

Other writers have been evincing concern lately about the tendency of economic strife to generate conflict. Michael Mastanduno believes that America has adopted a grand strategy for the post–Cold War era, that it is the strategy of "primacy," and that it normally predisposes Washington *not* to unilateralism but rather to multilateralism, on the grounds that this is required to provide the needed legitimacy to American attempts at hegemonic leadership. However, he and others detect a worrisome tendency on the part of the same administration that is willing to adopt conciliatory approaches toward allies on political-strategic matters, an unwillingness to be similarly solicitous when it comes to *economic* matters.[45] In effect, Mastanduno writes, Washington has been "trying simultaneously to play 'economic hardball' and 'security softball.'"[46] Although the tension is strongest in America's relationship with Japan, a recurring problem area with implications for the Atlantic Alliance is the aforementioned one of "burden sharing."

Is there evidence to support the claim that economic hardball is taking a toll on political relations? Space does not permit a thorough investigation of the question here; suffice it to note simply that while the allies were bombing, in solidarity, Slobodan Milosevic, they were also engaging in commercial fisticuffs with each other.[47] In other words, their frequent trade spats did not seem to have inhibited their ability to rally together to pursue a common security cause in the Balkans.

How, then, can we account for "allied force"? Might it be that the allies, whatever their size and irrespective of their economic difficulties with fellow allies, had a set of individual interests that could best—some say only—be pursued within the context of an alliance in which they were, for varying reasons, prepared to continue to invest resources? In the next section I look at two allies, neither huge nor tiny, who participated actively in the air war and do not appear to have done so either reluctantly or because they were "forced" to do so by the United States. Moreover, these are allies who not only have had an ongoing set of economic tiffs with America, but also with each other, and had come to the brink of a shooting (not just shouting) match, in the "Turbot War" of 1995. I refer, of course, to Canada and Spain.

"Forced Allies"? Ottawa and Madrid in Serbian Skies

As did the other allies, small or otherwise, Canada saw the war very much as a humanitarian conflict. And like the other allies, it also had some strategic (if unstated) interests at stake, associated with the need to preserve the credibility of the Alliance. Traditionally, ever since 1949, NATO was held by Canadian policymakers to be a device by and through which Canadian purposes might be furthered by American power. At the same time, NATO was seen as a means of *containing* American power, thereby making the bilateral relationship more comfortable, from Ottawa's perspective. This second function for NATO, in Ottawa's reckoning, used to depend upon the European allies being invoked as a "counterweight," to use the metaphor of choice.[48]

More recently, Canadian policymakers have seen in the "new" NATO a tool that promises to fulfill some of the loftier purposes once associated more exclusively with the United Nations. Notably, the Alliance is conceptualized as a most useful means of furthering "human-security" ends.[49] Not surprisingly, therefore, in Ottawa as in other allied capitals, policymakers and opinion shapers stressed the humanitarian aspects of the war. Indeed, Canada and its foreign minister, Lloyd Axworthy, figured among the vanguard of the "humanitarian hawks," and for some weeks during the war's initial phase, Canada was out in front of the United States and alongside Britain in suggesting that a ground offensive might yet be necessary.[50]

Canada began the twentieth century as an eager participant in international security relations through the British empire, and was ending it as an equally engaged participant in the U.N. peacekeeping regime. The cover of a recent book on Canadian grand strategy, which featured Queen Victoria sporting a U.N. blue beret, brilliantly captured the two foci of Canadian strategy: "empire" and "umpire."[51]

Though apt for the early 1990s, today the symbolism seems misplaced. Whereas at the start of the 1990s the United Nations was embarking on a period of activism in international security, one in which Canada figured largely indeed, by the end of that decade the world body seemed once more to be stuck in the quagmire of Security Council disunity. And Canada, which has so prided itself on contributions to U.N. peacekeeping, would increasingly send its soldiers on peace-related missions under NATO, not U.N., operational auspices. Even before the war against Serbia, some 90 percent of Canadian peace-related deployments were coming under

NATO control, albeit (in the case of Bosnia) with general U.N. blessing. For the initial stage of involvement with Serbia (i.e., the air war), such "blessing" could not be obtained, and while the lack of sanction did occasion an agonizing debate within the Department of Foreign Affairs and International Trade, Ottawa nevertheless opted to give humanitarian concerns priority over the felt need to work through the Security Council. The decision reflected an assumption that the latter was hardly going to be able to authorize forcible means of reversing ethnic cleansing in Kosovo.[52]

Canada would clearly like to see a United Nations that is capable of overcoming some of its recent problems, so that it might once again demonstrate the promise of the early post–Cold War years. At the same time, the Canadian rapprochement with the "new" NATO cannot be denied and may even be expected to continue, for the Alliance's recent emphasis upon cooperative security—and even more to the point, upon "human security"—did occasion a "return" to the Alliance bosom, from which Canada had indeed been getting progressively estranged during the closing years of the Cold War. Notwithstanding the numerous claims made in the early 1990s about Canadian policy inexorably drifting away from the security arrangements of the Atlantic world, Canada has undeniably refocused upon NATO during the past few years.

The prodigal son may be settling down in the Alliance home once more, but only because it wants to return to Atlanticism (embodied in what is regarded as the "human-security alliance"), not to prodigality. Can the benefits of the new NATO continue to be enjoyed without Canada's having to absorb an unwelcome share of that new alliance burden? The evidence of the war against Serbia, though mixed, is that they can be—or at least that they have been, so far. Canada managed in the spring of 1999 to do what many would have thought impossible: make a significant military contribution without at the same time suffering the consequences of "umpire's overstretch"—consequences that seemed to be so starkly on display earlier in the 1990s during the height of U.N. peacekeeping involvement.[53]

If the military dues of NATO membership in an era characterized by the "revolution in military affairs" involve some demonstrable competency in high-technology warfare, then Canada has been able to capitalize on past investment in fighter aircraft and precision-guided munitions to stake a defensible claim that it more than "did its part" in stopping ethnic cleansing in Kosovo. On the other hand, real concern does remain regarding the ability of the ground forces to sustain a robust presence in Balkans peacekeeping operations, and it is fair to say that the army units deployed to Bosnia, Kosovo, and Macedonia—some 2,650 personnel by August 1999—represent the limits of a permanently sustainable force given current funding realities.[54]

Canada was able to avoid "overstretch" during the air war because it had what most of the other (non-U.S.) allied air forces lacked: precision-guided missiles (PGMs) capable of being unleashed from Canada's 18 CF-18 fighter-bombers deployed in theater. NATO flew more than 27,000 sorties (strike and otherwise) during Operation Allied Force; of that total, Canadian aircraft accounted for 678 (in what Canada termed Operation Echo). Although the number of aircraft Canada contributed was roughly comparable to that supplied by several other allies (including France, the United Kingdom, Germany, and Turkey), operationally Canada was much more important than most, with the obvious exception of the U.S. Air Force. The latter supplied 715 of Operation Allied Force's 912 aircraft, and flew the lion's share of the sorties. But Canada's pilots, because they had the PGMs—but also because of their high level of training and their unsurpassed ability to be interoperable with the USAF—flew nearly 10 percent of all strike sorties during Operation Allied Force. As well, the overwhelming number of strike "packages" sent over Serbian skies were led by either Americans or Canadians.[55]

If Canada's participation in the air war must cast some doubt on the utility of its classification among the "smaller" allies, then Spain's own military involvement raises similar questions. On the one hand, Spain's population ranks it much closer to the European "big" powers than to the "small" ones; more to the point, perhaps, is that Spain was among the very few allied countries whose air forces possessed PGMs and thus who could strike at night with accuracy.[56]

Kosovo affected Spain as it did the other "smaller" allies. Madrid saw in the crisis a humanitarian challenge that simply had to be addressed—all the more so if the vision of a more coherent "Europe of defense" was ever to become a reality. But Spaniards proved more reluctant than their leaders—and than the public in Canada—to back the air war. In fact, Spain was among the allies in which public opinion waxed least enthusiastic about bombing Serbs. Partly this has to do with the country's lugubrious military history, from the civil war of the 1930s to the long period of rule by General Franco. Partly it may have something to do with Spain's own internal political difficulties, which have made it sensitive to allegations of "terrorism" by separatist groups. As late as two months before the air war, Spanish officials were joining with their Yugoslav counterparts to denounce Albanian separatist violence in Kosovo and Metohija.[57]

Though Spanish leaders preferred to stress the country's generous contributions to the refugee crisis, Spanish bombs were dropped nonetheless. The country's F-18s were in on the first wave of attacks on March 24, 1999, and had flown, by early June, some 200 sorties, of which 160 were strike sorties, with the remaining 40 being air-to-air "caps." The strike sorties resulted in actual attacks (with GBU-16 laser-guided bombs) being made against some

70 Serb targets.[58] Militarily, with an armed force some three times the size of Canada's, Spain seems to have refined the art of "burden sharing" in a fairly cost-effective manner, doing more than Portugal and Belgium but less than Canada; it committed eight of its F-18s to Operation Allied Force, and also allowed U.S. military aircraft on the way to Serbia to use bases on Spanish soil. While only a third of Spaniards supported the air war, and nearly half thought that it would not bring peace in the Balkans, some 40 percent still believed their country needed to take military measures as a means of fulfilling Spain's obligations to NATO.[59]

On the ground, Spain did its part, contributing 1,200 soldiers to KFOR, in which they have been integrated into a multinational brigade under Italian commandment.[60] Spanish forces had also taken part in earlier peace operations in the Balkans, first in UNPROFOR, later in IFOR/SFOR. It is hard to escape the conclusion that it was Spain's NATO "membership dues," along with its humanitarian sensibilities, that led it to military involvement in the war against Serbia. It was both a war for values and a war for a seat at the table. There does not seem to be any evidence that Spain was "forced" (by others) to participate in the air war.

Madrid was hardly operating as a free agent, but the source of strategic constraint clearly was internal, and very much related to a desire to build "Europe" and to enhance Spain's standing. In this regard, the decision of the government of José Maria Aznar in 1996 to integrate the country's armed forces fully into the Alliance, coupled with Madrid's determination to leverage its membership in prominent Western institutions to advance its claim to rank among Europe's "first division" states,[61] simply made it impossible for Spain to abstain from military participation against Serbia, however distasteful such participation must have been to many Spaniards.

For his own part, Prime Minister Aznar sounded every bit as enthusiastic as the Alliance's humanitarian hawks, or at least could so sound when sharing the podium with one of the most prominent hawks, British prime minister Tony Blair. During the early weeks of the air campaign, the two leaders held a joint press conference at Chequers in which they affirmed the need to maintain NATO unity on Kosovo. From what Aznar said, it was difficult to distinguish him from Blair: "I have to say that everything Tony Blair has said is exact from the political point of view. We share, concerning Kosovo, the same goals, the same values and the same firm resolve for our objectives to prevail."[62]

Conclusion

This chapter has advanced two claims. There was no "allied" perspective per se on the eve of the war with Serbia; and whatever else the allies were doing by going to war, it was not because they were bowing to American ukase. The Delian League seems to be an inappropriate analogy in this respect. Nevertheless, while it may be comforting (to some) to imagine that a collective identity among Western states (and, more to the point, nations) is responsible for the current trend toward humanitarian interventionism, there are a number of more traditional, "interest"-based explanations at hand to account for allied unity during the 1999 war.

True, it was a war for "values"; but it was also a war for NATO, whose preservation member states could agree, for a variety of reasons, made sense to them, because it served their interests. There was a surprising degree of unity—at least by NATO standards and in stark contrast to earlier crises in the Balkans—and while it undoubtedly took the management skills of someone to have brought this about, the notion of "forced allies" seems extremely far-fetched, as the cases of such midsized allies as Canada and Spain appear to demonstrate. The notion seems even more far-fetched than does that of any particular ally's being *the* "indispensable nation."

Notes

1. Portions of this introductory section are based upon material in a chapter I coauthored with Allen Sens, "The (Not So) Free Riders," in *Kosovo and the Challenge of Humanitarian Intervention: Selective Indignation, Collective Action, and International Citizenship,* ed. Albrecht Schnabel and Ramesh Thakur (Tokyo: United Nations University Press, 2000).
2. F. S. Northedge, *The International Political System* (London: Faber & Faber, 1976), pp. 43–45; Adda B. Bozeman, *Politics and Culture in International History* (Princeton: Princeton University Press, 1960), pp. 80–82.
3. Octavi Martí, "No existe una conciencia común europea," *El País* (Madrid), August 11, 1999.
4. John Vinocur, "France Has a Hard Sell to Rein in U.S. Power," *International Herald Tribune,* February 6–7, 1999, p. 2. On the origins and significance of this contest between Paris and Washington, see David G. Haglund, ed., *The France-U.S. Leadership Race: Closely Watched Allies* (Kingston, Ont.: Queen's Quarterly Press, 2000).
5. Crane Brinton, *The Americans and the French* (Cambridge: Harvard University Press, 1968); Frank Costigliola, *France and the United States: The Cold Alliance Since World War II* (New York: Twayne, 1992).
6. Christopher Layne, "Rethinking American Grand Strategy: Hegemony or Balance of Power in the Twenty-First Century?" *World Policy Journal* 15 (summer 1998): 8–28.
7. By "isolationist" I do *not* mean to suggest a disposition to withdraw from the strategic, political, and economic affairs of the world; that is a caricatured use of a political label that never did reflect reality, not even in the interwar period. What I *do* mean to suggest by the label is a propensity for unilateralism over

multilateralism; sometimes it can be unilateralism in pursuit of action, sometimes unilateralism in support of inaction. In the case of the former, the important distinction to be drawn is between acting alone and acting with others (especially allies). See David G. Haglund, *Latin America and the Transformation of U.S. Strategic Thought, 1936–1940* (Albuquerque: University of New Mexico Press, 1984), pp. 18–22; and Walter A. McDougall, *Promised Land, Crusader State: The American Encounter with the World Since 1776* (Boston: Houghton Mifflin, 1997), chap. 2: "Unilateralism, or Isolationism (So Called)."

8. Witness the tempest over whether a British general, Sir Michael Jackson, was "insubordinate" in refusing to carry out orders from NATO's supreme commander, General Wesley Clark, to use force to seize the Pristina airport prior to the arrival of Russian troops in June 1999. Joseph Fitchett, "Disobeying Orders: NATO Veil Lifted," *International Herald Tribune,* September 11–12, 1999, pp. 1, 4.

9. For a differing assessment, one stressing how pronounced the cleavages are in the transatlantic world, cf. Christopher Coker, *Twilight of the West* (Boulder: Westview, 1998).

10. On the general trend toward building the ESDI within the Alliance, see Paul Cornish, "European Security: The End of Architecture and the New NATO," *International Affairs* 72 (October 1996): pp. 751–69. Whether this can be accomplished is argued from optimistic and pessimistic perspectives by, respectively, Hugh De Santis, "Mutualism: An American Strategy for the Next Century," *World Policy Journal* 15 (winter 1998–99): pp. 41–52; and Alexander Moens, "NATO's Dilemma and the Elusive European Defence Identity," *Security Dialogue* 29 (December 1998): pp. 463–75.

11. Pascal Boniface, *The Will to Powerlessness: Reflections on Our Global Age* (Kingston: Queen's Quarterly Press, 1999), p. 131.

12. For one such claim that Europe is now doing more for its own defense, see Owen Harries, "Three Rules for a Superpower to Live By," *New York Times,* August 23, 1999, p. A19. Also see Flora Lewis, "Like It or Fear It, a United Europe Is on the Way," *International Herald Tribune,* June 30, 2000, p. 8.

13. The "theoretically informed narrative," as Gideon Rose so felicitously phrases it, is a preference of neoclassical realists, who might be situated at midpoint between structural realists and constructivists. See Rose, "Neoclassical Realism and Theories of Foreign Policy," *World Politics* 51 (October 1998): pp. 144–72.

14. The limits are thought to be rather constraining, not just for the United States, but for all the Western allies; see Lawrence Freedman, "The Changing Forms of Military Conflict," *Survival* 40 (winter 1998–99): pp. 39–56.

15. Presentation to fourteenth Annual German-Canadian Atlantik-Brücke Conference, Freiberg, Germany, July 12, 1999.

16. Address to the conference "NATO—The First Fifty Years: From 'Security of the West' to 'Securing Peace in Europe,'" Bonn, May 20, 1999.

17. Michael Brenner, "The Multilateral Moment," in *Multilateralism and Western Strategy,* ed. Michael Brenner (New York: St. Martin's Press, 1995), p. 8. Also see Jaap de Wilde, "Reversal in the International System? The Long Peace

Debate in the Present," *Working Papers 21/1994* (Copenhagen: Centre for Peace and Conflict Research, 1994), pp. 8–9; and John S. Duffield, "NATO's Functions after the Cold War," *Political Science Quarterly* 109 (winter 1994–95): p. 777.
18. Alexander Wendt, "Identity and Structural Change in International Politics," in *The Return of Culture and Identity in IR Theory*, ed. Yosef Lapid and Friedrich Kratochwil (Boulder: Lynne Rienner, 1997), p. 52.
19. See John W. Holmes, "Fearful Symmetry: The Dilemmas of Consultation and Coordination in the North Atlantic Treaty Organization," *International Organization* 22 (autumn 1968): pp. 821–40.
20. Wendt borrows this concept from Robert W. Cox, *Power, Production, and World Order* (New York: Columbia University Press, 1987), pp. 253–65.
21. Alexander E. Wendt, "Collective Identity Formation and the International State," *American Political Science Review* 88 (June 1994): p. 392. Also see John Gerard Ruggie, "Territoriality and Beyond: Problematizing Modernity in International Relations," *International Organization* 47 (winter 1993): pp. 139–74.
22. Wendt, "Collective Identity Formation," pp. 384–85. He elaborates upon this contention in "Anarchy Is What States Make of It: The Social Construction of Power Politics," *International Organization* 46 (spring 1992): pp. 391–425.
23. Thomas Risse-Kappen, *Cooperation Among Democracies: The European Influence on U.S. Foreign Policy* (Princeton: Princeton University Press, 1995), p. 204. Since the publication of this book, the author shortened his surname.
24. Thomas Risse, "Transatlantic Identity and the Future of Canada-UK Relations," in *Transatlantic Identity? Canada, the United Kingdom and International Order*, ed. Robert Wolfe (Kingston, Ont.: Queen's University School of Policy Studies, 1997), pp. 27–29.
25. See Stephen M. Walt, "Why Alliances Endure or Collapse," *Survival* 39 (spring 1997): pp. 156–79.
26. Risse-Kappen, *Cooperation Among Democracies*, p. 32.
27. Thomas Risse-Kappen, "Democratic Peace—Warlike Democracies? A Social Constructivist Interpretation of the Liberal Argument," *European Journal of International Relations* 1 (December 1995): p. 503.
28. Risse-Kappen, *Cooperation Among Democracies*, pp. 194–95. Note the perhaps unintentional equating of "alliance" with "security community." The terms should not be used synonymously, for security community does not have to lead to alliance, nor should the particular alliance under discussion, NATO, be called a security community so long as two of its members, Greece and Turkey, continue to threaten each other with organized violence.
29. Mark A. Boyer, *International Cooperation and Public Goods: Opportunities for the Western Alliance* (Baltimore: Johns Hopkins University Press, 1993), p. 121.
30. Risse-Kappen, "Democratic Peace—Warlike Democracies?" p. 511.
31. For valuable insight into why the "national interest" continues to possess meaning and how it may contribute to the maintenance of a rule-based international order, see Friedrich Kratochwil, "On the Notion of 'Interest' in International Relations," *International Organization* 36 (winter 1982): pp. 1–30. For a useful attempt to synthesize realist theory with democratic peace (or "liberal") theory,

see John M. Owen, "How Liberalism Produces Democratic Peace," in *Debating the Democratic Peace*, ed. Michael E. Brown, Sean M. Lynn-Jones, and Steven E. Miller (Cambridge: MIT Press, 1996), pp. 151–52.

32. The former comment is from Robert Hunter, "Will the United States Remain a European Power?" *Survival* 30 (May–June 1988): p. 210; the latter is quoted in François Heisbourg, "Europe/États-Unis: le couplage stratégique menacé," *Politique étrangère* 52 (spring 1987): pp. 111–12. Although Heisbourg did not name the American official, it is believed the remark can be attributed to Harold Brown, secretary of defense during the Carter administration.

33. See David G. Haglund, ed., *Pondering NATO's Nuclear Options: Gambits for a Post–Westphalian World* (Kingston: Queen's Quarterly Press, 1999).

34. The relevant portions of the 1991 document appertaining to nuclear weapons are paragraphs 55–57 in "The Alliance's Strategic Concept, Agreed by the Heads of State and Government participating in the meeting of the North Atlantic Council in Rome on 7–8 November 1991," *NATO Handbook* (Brussels: NATO Office of Information and Press, 1995), pp. 247–48. For the most recent iteration, see "The Alliance's Strategic Concept," Press Release NAC-S(99)65, April 24, 1999, http://www.nato.int/docu/pr/1999/p99-065e.htm.

35. "Coupling" angst, however, is hard to eliminate completely, as attested by the current debate over the implications for transatlantic security of America's mooted National Missile Defense.

36. This was the thesis of Ralf Dahrendorf, "The Europeanization of Europe," in *A Widening Atlantic? Domestic Change and Foreign Policy*, ed. Andrew J. Pierre (New York: Council on Foreign Relations, 1986), pp. 5–56.

37. Richard K. Betts, "NATO's Mid-Life Crisis," *Foreign Affairs* 68 (spring 1989): p. 38.

38. For an enumeration of theory-based predictions of a long life for NATO, see David G. Haglund, "Must NATO Fail? Theories, Myths, and Policy Dilemmas," *International Journal* 50 (autumn 1995): pp. 651–74; Gunther Hellmann and Reinhard Wolf, "Neorealism, Neoliberal Institutionalism, and the Future of NATO," *Security Studies* 3 (autumn 1993): pp. 3–43; and Lars Skålnes, "From the Outside In, From the Inside Out: NATO Expansion and International Relations Theory," *Security Studies* 7 (summer 1998): pp. 44–87.

39. Kenneth N. Waltz, "The Emerging Structure of International Politics," *International Security* 18 (fall 1993): p. 75.

40. Ibid. One writer has put the same thought into different words when he observed that "if you take away its enemy, you will begin to see an alliance looking like a plant without water." Josef Joffe, "Die NATO und Nostradamus," *Süddeutsche Zeitung*, February 6, 1995, p. 4.

41. Stephen Walt, "The Ties That Fray: Why Europe and America Are Drifting Apart," *National Interest* 54 (winter 1998–99): pp. 10–11. See also Walt's contribution to this volume. The latest survey study by the Chicago Council on Foreign Relations can be interpreted as giving support to Walt's claim. See John E. Rielly, "Americans and the World: A Survey at Century's End," *Foreign Policy* 114 (spring 1999): pp. 97–114.

42. See Mary Kaldor, *The Disintegrating West* (New York: Hill and Wang, 1978); and John Palmer, *Europe Without America? The Crisis in Atlantic Relations* (Oxford: Oxford University Press, 1987).
43. See Edward N. Luttwak, "From Geopolitics to Geo-Economics: Logic of Conflict, Grammar of Commerce," *National Interest* 20 (summer 1990): pp. 17–23; and Luttwak, "War by Other Means," *Report on Business Magazine* 15 (April 1999): pp. 111–14.
44. Edward N. Luttwak, "The Alliance, Without an Enemy," *New York Times*, February 3, 1989, p. 21.
45. For similar criticisms, see James Schlesinger, "Fragmentation and Hubris: A Shaky Basis for American Leadership," *National Interest* 49 (fall 1997): pp. 3–9; and Garry Wills, "Bully of the Free World," *Foreign Affairs* 78 (March–April 1999): pp. 50–59.
46. Michael Mastanduno, "Preserving the Unipolar Moment: Realist Theories and U.S. Grand Strategy after the Cold War," in *America's Strategic Choices*, ed. Michael E. Brown et al. (Cambridge: MIT Press, 1997), p. 126.
47. "When the Snarling's Over," *Economist*, March 13, 1999, pp. 17–18; and David E. Sanger, "Trade Ruling: A Notable U.S. Victory," *International Herald Tribune*, April 8, 1999, pp. 1–2.
48. See Tom Keating and Larry Pratt, *Canada, NATO and the Bomb: The Western Alliance in Crisis* (Edmonton: Hurtig, 1988). Much more recently, one author has argued that Ottawa's bid to find a balance within the Alliance has not succeeded; see Roy Rempel, *Counterweights: The Failure of Canada's German and European Policy, 1955–1995* (Montréal and Kingston: McGill-Queen's University Press, 1996). I discuss the counterweight metaphor in my *The North Atlantic Triangle Revisited: Canadian Grand Strategy at Century's End*, no. 4 in the *Contemporary Affairs* series (Toronto: Irwin/CIIA, 2000).
49. See Paul Heinbecker, "Human Security," *Behind the Headlines* 56 (winter 1999): pp. 4–9; and Lloyd Axworthy, "NATO's New Security Vocation," *NATO Review* 47 (winter 1999): pp. 8–11.
50. Jeff Sallot, "Canada's Tone Turning Dovish," *Globe and Mail* (Toronto), May 20, 1999, p. A16.
51. Norman Hillmer and J. L. Granatstein, *From Empire to Umpire: Canada and the World to the 1990s* (Toronto: Copp Clark Longman, 1994).
52. See David M. Law, "With the U.N. Whenever Possible, Without When Necessary," in *New NATO, New Century: Canada, the United States, and the Future of the Atlantic Alliance*, ed. David G. Haglund (Kingston, Ont.: Queen's University Centre for International Relations, in cooperation with the Canadian Institute of Strategic Studies, 2000), pp. 27–42.
53. This is not to suggest that it was easy for Canada to deploy 18 CF-18 aircraft in theater, only that it was *possible* for it to do so. There were, needless to say, costs associated with its contribution to the air war. See, for instance, Paul Koring, "Air Force Racked by Poor Gear, 'Burnout,'" *Globe and Mail* (Toronto), June 6, 2000, pp. A1, A9; and David Bashow et al., "Mission Ready: Canada's Role in the Kosovo Air Campaign," *Canadian Military Journal* 1 (spring 2000): pp. 55–61.

54. Jeff Sallot, "Baril Fears Troop Burnout," *Globe and Mail* (Toronto), May 28, 1999, pp. A1, A4.
55. Of the 678 CF-18 sorties of Op Echo, 558 were air-to-ground, with the remaining 120 being air-to-air "caps" (or, combat air patrols). Of the 558 air-to-ground sorties, 224 resulted in weapons being dropped. Of the latter sorties, 158 resulted in successful hits.
56. Others possessing this capability were the United States, Britain, and Canada.
57. Serbian Unity Congress, "Spain, Yugoslavia Condemn Terrorism," January 15, 1999, http://www.suc.org/news/yds/b150199_e.html#N2. This is a report of a press conference held in Madrid by the foreign ministers of Yugoslavia and Spain, respectively Zivadin Jovanovic and Abel Matutes.
58. Lucas Bertomeu Gras, "Operaciones aéreas en Yugoslavia," *Revista de Aeronáutica y Astronáutica* 685 (July–August 1999): pp. 569–70.
59. "Wary Spaniards," *Economist*, April 17, 1999, p. 54.
60. Víctor Hernández and Elisa Beni Uzábal, "España, en la Fuerza de Seguridad para Kosovo," *Revista Española de Defensa* 12 (June 1999): pp. 14–16.
61. "Spain: In Transit," *Economist*, December 14, 1996, pp. 3–18. Also see "Spanish Parliament OKs Full Participation in NATO," *New York Times*, November 15, 1996, http://www.mtholyoke.edu/acad/intrel/spain.htm.
62. Foreign and Commonwealth Office, London, "Anglo-Spanish Bilateral Talks," April 10, 1999.

CHAPTER SEVEN

France: Kosovo and the Emergence of a New European Security

Alex Macleod

For many observers France represents the consummate realist state, with its emphasis on a narrow view of national interest, a seeming obsession with autonomy in foreign and defense policy (especially from the United States), and its insistence on being viewed as a great power. This chapter will challenge this assessment, at least as it characterizes current French foreign and security policy. It will be argued that since the end of the Cold War, international institutions have had an increasing impact on how French decision-makers formulate national interests, and that these institutions have become a crucial component of France's foreign and security policy. The Kosovo crisis showed just how far France has gone on the road to multilateralism. It will also be claimed, in conclusion, that French involvement in the NATO operations against Serbia has led to further French thinking about Europe's security structures and in particular about the aim of establishing a true European Security and Defense Identity.

The French Road to Multilateralism

Most students of French foreign policy emphasize its conception of a particular international role for France. Usually expressed in terms of "French exceptionalism" or de Gaulle's famous "certain idea of France," this image, which is shared across the political spectrum, can be summed up in what one French political scientist has called a "dual idea: France embodies universal values and has as its mission to spread them across the world."[1] Pushing this view even further, an American analyst recently observed that, because of their belief that French greatness conditions the world to look to France for inspiration, the French have a strong tendency to view their national interest in general or systemic terms. What makes France great is its universality.[2]

At the heart of French foreign policy lies the pursuit of France's place among the major players of the international system, or its *rang* (rank). This objective involves not only seeking prestige as an end in itself,[3] but also affirming France's presence and influence on the international stage.

When a state is convinced that the world needs it and that its international standing represents a vital part of its influence, then any change in the international system that threatens to redistribute power is likely to produce a crisis over this state's sense of identity. The end of the Second World War, the Suez crisis, and the end of the Cold War have been three defining moments for French foreign policy. Each of these events led to calls for a reassessment of France's place in the world, and each was followed by some form of French international assertiveness. In 1945, France struggled to regain recognition on the part of the "Big Three" of its great-power status by adopting obstructive positions over allied policy toward West Germany. After the Suez disaster of 1956, France, like Britain, was forced to realize that it was no longer in the same league as the two superpowers. This event was followed by a gradual estrangement from the United States that culminated in Charles de Gaulle's reformulation of French foreign policy. On each of these two occasions, France had to accept the idea that it had become a "middle-rank" power on the world stage, even if it was still one of the great European powers. It came to terms with this new situation by defining itself as a medium-sized power with worldwide responsibilities, which enjoyed a quasi-sphere of influence in French-speaking Africa and a presence in the Pacific. However, the end of the Cold War created probably the deepest crisis in French foreign policy, whose effects were still being felt ten years later.

Since the fall of the Berlin Wall, France has been searching for ways to reassert itself internationally. Important parts of the foundations of its foreign policy have disappeared or have been under attack. It can no longer navigate between the two superpowers. It has been, to say the least, ambivalent about Germany's challenge to its leadership in Europe. Its permanent seat on the U.N. Security Council has been questioned. Even its dominant role in French-speaking Africa is no longer uncontested, especially since the events in Rwanda in 1994.

Foreign Minister Hubert Védrine summed up his countrymen's dilemmas as they have sought to cope with these changes when he talked of

> [...] a sort of wavering in the French mind between what we proclaim, our universal role, our voice, our rank, our principles, our values and the exact

opposite, which is a sort of melancholy when we see that it is not working and that we are not the center of the world.[4]

This statement suggests a deep identity crisis that has led to attempts to redefine French roles in the international system. The 1994 *Livre blanc sur la défense* (White Paper on Defense), endorsed by the government, provides a good insight into how French policymakers have tried to reconstruct their country's identity in the post–Cold War era. Going beyond the realist view of power, it defined *rang* as:

> [...] a particular combination of factors of not only economic but also military, diplomatic, or even scientific and cultural power. It takes into account the influence exercised through *la Francophonie* as well as immaterial elements, linked to the strength of ideas and a certain vocation for the universal.[5]

France still equates its interests with its responsibilities, created by "its obligations as a permanent member of the Security Council, its history, its particular vocation."[6] French leaders also like to remind everyone that their country is the "planet's fourth commercial power."[7] And so, thanks to its international standing, France "belongs to the few countries that can influence stability in the world."[8]

French decision-makers have come to the conclusion that foreign policy can no longer be confined to interstate diplomacy. It now goes through institutions, in particular the European Union and the United Nations, a body that has become, in the words of a former foreign minister, "a fundamental axis of our foreign policy."[9] As for the EU, the white paper went so far as to decree that maintaining France's *rang* "will be largely linked to its ability to influence the construction of Europe and the coming developments of Europe."[10] Clearly, in French foreign policy, international institutions are no longer seen as *constraints* but rather as *facilitators* and as *initiators*.

Of course, French leaders still see institutions in terms of the opportunity they might offer them to extend their country's influence, but they also accept the need for a multilateral approach to international relations and the logical consequences of this position. Such an approach involves acting through institutions not simply to coordinate policies between states or to reflect a lowest common denominator, but to formulate policies and common behaviors that express the collective will of members, and which will be considered binding. As John Ruggie puts it, "multilateralism is an institutional form that coordinates relations among three or more states on the basis of generalized principles of conduct."[11]

Exercising influence under multilateralism supposes the capacity to elaborate, and to get other major players to accept, the norms and principles that shape behavior. It is here that France places much of its claim to its *rang* or status as an important power. In particular, it has attempted to feature among the "norm entrepreneurs" of the world.[12] Thanks to the leading role played by the Franco-German tandem in developing European integration from the beginning, France has had the opportunity to act as a norm entrepreneur within the European Union. Until recently, French aloofness made that role more difficult to play in the United Nations. The end of the Cold War and the easing of tensions between the United States and Russia have broadened the scope for action by lesser states bent on influencing the course of international affairs.

Going beyond the obvious security and commercial interests that every state promotes and defends, the main characteristics of French identity in the post–Cold War world have contributed to the construction of less tangible interests that have tended to shape its foreign policy's long-term objectives and its more immediate practice. First among these interests is still the need to maintain French influence. Second, France aims for a world in which decisions involving peace and security must be clearly authorized by multilateral institutions.[13] Third, this new emphasis on multilateralism has brought changes to the practice of one of the central values of traditional Gaullist foreign policy, that of national independence and autonomous foreign policy. Reference is still made to this notion, but the practice of French policy indicates a shift toward exercising influence through institutions, rather than acting alone. Fourth, it continues to see itself as the leader of *la Francophonie*, both as a concept and as a formal group of international institutions. Fifth, in keeping with its role as a norm entrepreneur, those norms that it has convinced others to adopt will act as a constant point of reference both for its own conduct and for that of other states. Sixth, and finally, France must defend the various components of its identity and ensure that they are recognized by the other major powers, in particular the United States.

The Lessons of Kosovo

Of all the major international crises in which France has been involved since the end of the Cold War, the conflict in Kosovo is the one that has allowed it to develop most fully a strategy of achieving security through international institutions. During the Gulf War, for example, France had to content itself with playing a fairly minor role behind the United States, and found little room to influence events. It certainly took a leading part in the war in Bosnia, but could not consider the way the situation developed as very satisfactory for the future of European security for several reasons. To begin with, there was too much confusion about the exact role of the two major security institutions involved, NATO and the United Nations, and the division of authority between them. Second, European institutions, notably the European Union and the Western European Union (WEU), were denied any effective place during operations and were excluded from the final settlement. Third, the Dayton Agreement, which put an end to the fighting, became possible only because of American intervention, and showed once again that European security without a U.S. presence remained an illusion.

When NATO launched its first air raids on March 24, 1999, France was much more ready to treat the ensuing conflict as a major test of European security through international institutions. It had already taken a lead in the search for a durable solution to the crisis in Kosovo, first by convincing the Americans to back UNSC Resolution 1199, adopted in September 1998, which was later used to justify military measures against Belgrade, and then by cohosting with Britain the talks at Rambouillet, the failure of which precipitated the conflict.[14] Above all, European security arrangements had progressed since the war in Bosnia. NATO had begun to give greater recognition to the notion of a European Security and Defense Identity. The European Union, especially since the signing of the Amsterdam Treaty in 1997, appeared better equipped to be involved in security matters. Finally two informal institutions, the Contact Group, created in 1994 at the height of the war in Bosnia, and the G7/G8, existed as forums where the major players could continue to talk. These two bodies facilitated a solution to the conflict by ensuring Russian involvement, a necessary prelude to any UNSC resolution.

Through the five international institutions involved in Kosovo—the UNSC, NATO, the EU, the Contact Group, and the G8—France was able to develop its security strategy of using institutions to maintain and expand its influence, whilst accepting that these institutions also limited its freedom of action as a state. Thus, the bodies it favored most were all essentially intergovernmental, i.e., they allowed France to exercise a veto and to maintain some control over events in Kosovo, with undoubted success. They also participated in shaping the development of the institutions involved. They drew their own lessons from the conflict for the future of European security, in particular the need for Europe to be responsible for its own defense, independently from the United States, for what they dubbed *l'Europe de la défense,* by which they meant not only a made-in-Europe defense policy but also a truly European military capability.

From the very beginning, the French government justified the war by arguing that it was a battle for a certain conception of Europe and European values,[15] for human rights,[16] even for European civilization[17] or, more simply, a defense of European security and regional stability.[18] Nonetheless, from the French point of view, it was necessary to establish the legality and legitimacy of this action against a sovereign state. This was achieved by referring specifically to the three UNSC resolutions on Kosovo adopted in 1998 (Resolutions 1160, 1199, and 1203) and by defending recourse to NATO as the only possible response to the urgency of the situation, since the Security Council was in no position to play its role of maintaining peace and security.[19]

Throughout the conflict French leaders felt uncomfortable with the decision to bypass the United Nations and took great pains to insist that NATO's intervention represented an exception that should never be construed as a precedent. In their view U.N. sanction for any final settlement remained absolutely indispensable. They dismissed the charge made by domestic critics, especially on the left, that they were simply bowing to American pressure. They insisted that NATO could act only with the support of all 19 members and declared that France was using its influence to control both the military actions and the general strategy of that organization. In doing so, they confirmed their country's traditional policy of solidarity toward NATO in a period of crisis, including full participation at the military level,[20] whilst maintaining a large degree of autonomy.

The Washington summit celebrating NATO's fiftieth anniversary in late April 1999 provided France with an excellent opportunity to set out its views on what direction NATO should take. According to official statements, France achieved four objectives in Washington: a clear definition of the geographic limits of NATO's military activities; NATO's recognition and acceptance of the notion of European defense; keeping the door open to future enlargement; and reaffirmation of NATO's respect for the U.N. Charter and the role of the Security Council, particularly in peacekeeping operations.[21] These claims probably overstated French success in Washington,[22] but they indicated a desire to convince opinion at home that France's continued participation in NATO in no way jeopardized its autonomy in the organization. This held despite France having enjoyed a difficult relationship with NATO since the days of de Gaulle. But the claims also suggested that France could not really conceive of European security without NATO, even if it sought to limit the extent and scope of its activities.

Though French decision-makers deemed that the urgency of the situation demanded rapid NATO military intervention, they declared that no international security operation could forgo authorization from the UNSC. This policy undoubtedly reflected French reservations about the U.S. role in European security and the need for a counterweight to American power. It also expressed a more general concern with maintaining the United Nations as the ultimate source of international law and legitimacy for the use of force. During the Kosovo crisis, France often clashed directly with the

United States over this question. In the words of Prime Minister Jospin, the United Nations had to regain its role and "to have a central action in the search for a settlement."[23] United Nations approval for NATO's actions and the need for the Security Council to take responsibility for the final settlement and peacekeeping within Kosovo became vital themes of French policy.

President Chirac revealed the extent of differences over these issues during the Washington summit, when he talked of French disagreement with the position of some of "our allies and notably our American friends" who advocated freeing NATO from U.N. authority.[24] This was not just a quarrel about the conduct of this particular conflict. As the French saw it, it was the "whole international order put in place after the Second World War that was being questioned in this discussion. It was also our vision of the world that was in some ways being discussed, even threatened." After the conflict, the French president felt he could claim that his country's diplomacy had scored a decisive victory by ensuring that the United Nations had found again "the role and the place it must have in a world organized with a rule of international law."[25]

The French "vision of the world" included reserving an important place in European security for Russia. France's policymakers insisted frequently on the impossibility of obtaining any meaningful solution to the conflict without Russia. To a large extent, they continued to see their country as the bridge between the former superpower and the West, and claimed credit for convincing the other allies to include Russia in any negotiations on a settlement. The French were persistent in maintaining contact with the Russians, both bilaterally and within international institutions. Since the UNSC could not act without Russian support, it was vital to prepare the ground beforehand. The G8 provided the necessary forum in which agreement could be reached between the major powers, including four of the five permanent members of the Security Council. The document adopted by the G8 on May 6, 1999, became the basis for the UNSC resolution on a settlement voted a month later. The French congratulated themselves on having played a major part, with Russia, in bringing about this result and in having obtained a meeting that "not everyone desired."[26]

If the French pushed hard for a prominent U.N. role in the conflict, they also saw it as an opportunity to define the place of the European Union as a security institution. The conditions for greater EU participation were certainly much more favorable than in the war in Bosnia, from which this body had been effectively excluded. In the first place, with three new members, all traditionally neutral, and at least four states from eastern Europe in line for accession, the EU had strengthened its claim as the main spokesman for post–Cold War Europe. Secondly, France had begun to clarify its relationship with NATO and had succeeded in obtaining recognition of the concept of ESDI, even if its actual content remained vague. A European defense policy was no longer perceived as a direct challenge to the Alliance. Thirdly, Britain had elected a more pro-European government, with a comfortable majority, which had expressed its desire for closer defense ties among Europeans by signing a joint defense agreement with France at Saint-Malo in December 1998. Finally, the Treaty of Amsterdam, which made specific reference to progress toward a common defense policy, came officially into force on May 1, 1999.

At all stages of the conflict French leaders stressed the need for the EU to play a full role. For Foreign Minister Védrine, this meant that it should act as a "designer and a leader" and not just as a "counter for distributing subsidies for reconstruction."[27] France attempted to translate these sentiments into a series of immediate, medium-term, and long-term policies to be enacted through the European Union.

In the short run, the allies agreed that one of the most important measures for hastening the conclusion of the conflict was oil sanctions against Yugoslavia. French policymakers argued, successfully, that there existed no legal basis for an oil blockade within the NATO framework. Moreover, they claimed that the type of embargo envisioned by certain NATO members, which would have involved boarding ships from third countries and blocking access to the ports of Montenegro, constituted an act of war, and, as such, needed authorization from the UNSC. At a mid-April meeting of the European Council, France proposed, and obtained unanimous backing for, a policy of oil sanctions against Yugoslavia, which became binding on all EU members. It also included a call for associate EU members to respect this decision. After some wrangling at the Washington summit, NATO also agreed to abide by the same rules.

As a medium-term measure, France advocated that the EU should assume full responsibility for civil administration over Kosovo after a settlement. Even before the conflict was over, however, it softened its position on that issue. Foreign Minister Védrine acknowledged that the decision was up to the UNSC, adding that the EU was "in a way a candidate for this mission in liaison with the OSCE."[28] As for NATO, France was determined to limit it to a strictly military role with absolutely no part in running civil affairs. Though it gained unanimous EU support for its position, it had to bow to the decision to create a U.N.-administered Kosovo. France did not give up the fight entirely, however, and it called for this administration to be headed by an EU personality. President Chirac then lobbied successfully for his country's own candidate, Health Minister Bernard Kouchner.[29]

Like all the NATO allies, France was aware of the need for a durable solution to ethnic and national tensions in the Balkans. At the behest of

Germany, which presided over the Union at the time, the EU put forward its principal plan for regional security, the Stability Pact for South Eastern Europe. The debate around this ambitious idea throws some light on the French view of the EU. Publicly the government welcomed this plan, whilst trying to play down its significance. A Foreign Affairs spokeswoman explained that it was not really a plan, but rather some "German ideas," which President Chirac had already suggested could be interesting but which "largely covered the ideas of other allies."[30] As for Foreign Minister Védrine, he damned the project with faint praise, calling it a "good working basis for a great European Union policy."[31] A major concern lay behind the lack of enthusiasm for a proposal that, as Védrine rightly pointed out, simply followed on from the Stability Pact for Central Europe put forward by France in 1993 and adopted by the OSCE in 1994.[32] French decision-makers harbored fundamental doubts about the effects of the pact on the future of the Union itself. The Germans had used this opportunity to raise the unsettled issue of further EU eastward enlargement. Such a plan would obviously postpone indefinitely French aims of a more integrated European Union. As one French diplomat expressed it, either "Germany has partly abandoned the shape of Europe for which it has militated for forty years, or it wants to reshape it differently."[33] Despite these objections, France had little choice but to go along with a plan that obviously enjoyed wide international support.

French leaders were much more positive about the project of a European defense policy. They considered that recognition of efforts to formulate a truly European security and defense policy constituted one of the most important gains from the NATO Summit in Washington. They acknowledged that the Kosovo conflict had revealed the real weaknesses of a united European defense, but they saw reasons for optimism. The 1998 Saint-Malo Declaration had indicated a radical change in the British attitude, even if that document still viewed NATO as an important player in European security. The operations in Kosovo underlined how indispensable the Franco-British axis had become to any meaningful European defense policy in French eyes.

Just when the end of the conflict was in sight, the European Council, meeting in Cologne, adopted the outlines of a common defense and security policy. Despite President Chirac's claim that this resolution represented "an important moment in the construction of a European defense identity,"[34] his more cautious foreign minister, Hubert Védrine, warned that there was no reason to think that either a European defense policy or a common European foreign policy would emerge "fully armed" from the Kosovo crisis.[35] He also noted that the conflict had demonstrated that only NATO possessed the military means for a large-scale operation.[36] Finally, it was reiterated in Cologne that a European defense policy would be intergovernmental, a decision that Defense Minister Alain Richard welcomed with obvious satisfaction.[37]

At every stage of the conflict, France attempted to exert its influence within the institutions involved and took full advantage of its potential veto power. Not only did French decision-makers insist on seeking general U.N. authority for the operation, and on giving the EU a leading role, they also claimed that the allies had "recognized the importance of [France's] role" in NATO.[38] President Chirac boasted after the conflict that "there was not one single target that was not agreed upon by France beforehand."[39] Throughout the war, France intervened within the Alliance to halt attacks on Yugoslav civil installations. It also took credit for steering air raids toward Yugoslav forces deployed in Kosovo itself, for sparing Montenegro as much as possible, and for preventing NATO from proceeding to stage 3 of its operations, which would have entailed intensifying and extending air raids.[40] Prime Minister Jospin also claimed that NATO's five conditions for ending its operations were based on "French proposals."[41]

On one important issue—whether or not to send in ground forces to hasten the end of the war—the evidence is unclear. Most public declarations would suggest that France strongly opposed this measure. There seemed to be a great deal of internal debate, however. For example, Prime Minister Jospin refused to rule out the possibility of a ground offensive just one week after the beginning of hostilities, despite a claim to the contrary by Foreign Minister Védrine the day before, and then one week later announced that the question was "completely premature."[42] A few days later, Health Minister Bernard Kouchner declared his support for the use of ground troops without being called to task, at least not publicly.[43] Less than a week afterward, in an apparent reference to the use of ground forces, President Chirac talked of the need to use "additional means" in an address to the nation, though, according to French officials, such a move depended on a mandate from the Security Council.[44] After having joined forces with the British to urge the Americans to consider sending ground troops into Kosovo, the French once again came out against this change in strategy.

President Chirac appeared to be rewriting history when he claimed, after the conflict, that he had never thought this option either "serious or reasonable" and that he had strongly disagreed with British prime minister Tony Blair on this issue.[45] In fact, as late as the end of May, the British, French, German, Italian, and American defense ministers, meeting in Bonn, gave careful consideration to a ground assault, which, according to some sources, was to have taken place in late June or early July.[46] However, there can be no doubt that the question of a ground invasion created problems for the French government. At home, it had to contend with opposition from within its own ranks, especially from Communists. Abroad, as President Chirac freely admitted, it had to be rejected, "notably because of the reactions it would not have failed [...] to provoke from our Russian friends."[47] At the same time, the French prevented any quarrel with the more militant British by muting their opposition.

Unlike the British government, which enjoyed a huge majority and could depend on the two major opposition parties to support at least the principles of the NATO intervention, the French executive faced possible division at two levels: between the president and the government and within the government coalition. No such divisions opened. As in the two previous situations in which the presidency and the government were of different political stripes, a president from the right and a Socialist prime minister continued to speak with one voice on foreign policy. This well-publicized agreement certainly had a positive effect on public support for the war.[48]

Within the government, the potential for division seemed enormous. Aside from Socialists, the cabinet also contained Communists, Greens, and members of the small but influential left-wing Citizens' Movement (MDC—Mouvement des Citoyens). Any defection could have weakened the government and harmed the image of the "plural majority" of the left. In 1991, MDC leader Jean-Pierre Chevènement had resigned as François Mitterrand's defense minister in opposition to French involvement in the Gulf War, and he did not support French participation in the bombing of Serbia. In 1999, he held the key post of minister of the Interior, and the government could not afford to lose him. Chevènement, however, did not seem anxious to quit the government. His only gesture was to distribute a text opposing the NATO operation at the end of a cabinet meeting in early April.[49] The Communists opposed the bombings throughout, denounced them vehemently in *L'Humanité,* and participated in demonstrations, but they stopped short of breaking with the government. As for the Greens, after some initial misgivings, they decided to support the war, and even called for bringing in ground troops if necessary.[50]

The main debate over France's role in the Kosovo conflict took place within the parties and amongst intellectuals. As expected, open opposition was found in the far-right National Front and among small groups on the far left. Divisions over the war in mainstream parties tended to reflect a deeper split between so-called sovereigntists, jealous of maintaining France's autonomy in international affairs, and those who could best be described as internationalists, much more open to international institutions. The latter formed the majority opinion within the Socialist Party, the parties of the center right, and the Gaullist RPR (Rassemblement pour la République), whilst the Communists, the MDC, and certain traditional Gaullists all espoused the sovereigntist position, which was also supported by the rightist fringe of the parliamentary opposition. The forces of sovereigntism within both the government and the opposition never mustered enough strength to seriously challenge the policies adopted by President Chirac or by the Jospin government.

Amongst intellectuals, the debate tended to be an affair of the left. Left-leaning papers such as *Le Monde* and *Libération* supported the government, as did the weekly *Nouvel Observateur*, though they all made room for dissenting views. *Le Monde diplomatique* and the new weekly *Marianne* condemned the operation. Ostensibly, the debate within the left was about the merits of joining forces with the rest of NATO to attack a sovereign state. In reality, as a commentator astutely pointed out, it was yet another episode, albeit one of the most virulent in recent memory, of the ongoing battle between the moral "rightist left" and the republican "radical left," with its strong anti-American bias.[51] In many ways, this division reflected the sovereigntist-internationalist cleavage between and within political parties. Despite the passion that accompanied this debate, French decision-makers were much more concerned with shoring up support from public opinion.

The authors of the first government report on the lessons of the Kosovo conflict claimed it "confirmed that public opinion plays a decisive role in the conduct of operations."[52] This document also concluded that public opinion gave massive support for the NATO operation, though it conceded that people were "disturbed by the humanitarian crisis and hesitant about the hypothesis of an engagement of ground forces." As usual, published polls have to be treated with caution, but most of them appear to bear out this assessment of public support for French participation in the bombing campaign. According to Ipsos surveys taken between March 26 and May 22, support for the NATO operation fluctuated from 57 percent at the beginning of the war to a high of 72 percent in the second week of April and fell to 63 percent in the third week of May. Surprisingly, support for French participation was slightly higher (59, 73, and 67 percent).[53] The same polls also indicated fairly consistent support for a ground invasion, if "air strikes should prove insufficient to solve the crisis," ranging from a low of 55 percent in the third week of May to a high of 65 percent in the second week of April. On the other hand, a poll taken by another firm, BVA, in mid-May suggested that opponents of a ground war outnumbered supporters by 47 percent to 43 percent.[54] These figures tend to corroborate the view of several commentators that support for the conflict was not as solid as it might appear.

Backing for NATO action appeared to be emotional, inspired by the news and pictures of massacres and the stream of refugees, rather than political.[55] If French public opinion seemed clear about its views of Serbian treatment of the Kosovar population, it appeared unaware of the aims of the allied strikes against Yugoslavia.[56] Furthermore, even while it declared itself massively in favor of NATO action, the French population grew gradually more pessimistic about the chances of it actually leading to a successful outcome.[57] Less than a month into the war, it already began to favor opening negotiations with Milosevic and halting the bombing.[58]

These findings indicate that, at best, French support for the war was fragile and confused. Without making a direct link between public opinion and foreign policy, it becomes easier to understand why the French leadership could not take it for granted that it would automatically be followed if it adopted the sort of aggressive stance that Britain's Tony Blair felt authorized to take. Opinion certainly did not decide policy, but it did lay down some of its limits.

Conclusion: The Emerging New European Security

However much French decision-makers might celebrate this collective victory over Yugoslavia and proclaim that it would not have been possible without the intervention of international security institutions, they were forced to admit not only that European security still depended on a continued U.S. presence, but also that the EU contribution left much to be desired. As Foreign Minister Védrine acknowledged, Europe's preponderant role in solving the crisis was due above all to the coordination between "the four great European diplomatic powers," and not to "Europe as such, as the European Union."[59] Clearly, French foreign policy in general, and its European security policy in particular, found itself caught between the claims of realism, with its emphasis on state policies guided by national interest, and the post–Cold War evolution toward international security through collective action within institutions.

The conflict in Kosovo represents an important stage in the French perception of Europe's security arrangements. The objective of a European Security and Defense Identity built around the WEU as an arm of the EU seems as far off as ever. It has not been totally abandoned, but clearly the French have come to recognize that, at least for the time being, it can be achieved only through and within NATO. On the other hand, the French feel that progress toward a made-in-Europe defense policy has been made, especially thanks to a more cooperative approach on the part of the British, which was largely confirmed in the months following the conflict. The operations in Kosovo also brought to the fore the institutions that, in France's estimation, are the most useful for ensuring a broadly based security structure in Europe, and suggested the principles on which the latter should be based.

First, the conflict emphasized the need for a security policy that goes far beyond defense policy. With the end of the Cold War, European security must be concerned with such issues as regional stability and the respect for human rights. Second, this security can no longer remain the monopoly of military alliances such as NATO, whose mandate has been significantly reformulated. It must now reserve an important place for the European Union, which has access to the resources needed to ensure long-term regional stability. The war has also confirmed those norms and rules of behavior, the so-called Copenhagen criteria, which any aspiring member must conform to and which act as a strong incentive to keeping the peace and abiding by the values of liberal democracy, which underlie the European conception of security. Last, it is evident that European security needs the involvement of both former superpowers: NATO's power to intervene obviously rested on a U.S. commitment to European security, but no settlement could have been reached without Russian participation.

In terms of institutions, especially in times of crisis, as far as France is concerned, European security can be assured only by those who have the capacity to act effectively. At the present time, this capacity is still restricted to NATO, the EU, and the UNSC. The one pan-European security institution that should be playing an important role in European security, the OSCE, remains blocked by the rule of unanimity. True, such informal bodies as the Contact Group and the G8 played an important role throughout the conflict, but in the final analysis they proved useful mainly as a means for keeping contact between the Western allies and Russia, and thus as an antechamber for agreements leading to legally binding decisions from the U.N. Security Council.

Notes

1. Marcel Merle, *Sociologie des relations internationales,* 3rd edition (Paris: Dalloz, 1988), p. 292.
2. Philip Gordon, *A Certain Idea of France: French Security Policy and the Gaullist Legacy* (Princeton: Princeton University Press, 1993), p. 16.
3. Alfred Grosser, "Le rôle et le rang," in André Lewin, ed., *La France et l'ONU depuis 1945* (Condé-sur-Noireau: Arléa-Corlet, 1995), p. 64.
4. "Entretien du ministre des Affaires étrangères, M. Hubert Védrine, avec la presse anglo-saxonne," October 7, 1997. All references to speeches and interviews of French decision-makers have been taken from the French Ministry of Foreign Affairs web site at http://www.france.diplomatie.fr, unless otherwise indicated (author's translation). The dates refer to the days on which the statements were made.
5. *Livre blanc sur la défense 1994* (Paris, Union générale d'Éditions, 1994), p. 51 (author's italics).

6. Ibid., p. 50.
7. "Allocation du Président de la République, M. Jacques Chirac, à l'occasion du dîner d'État offert en l'honneur du Président des États-Unis du Mexique, M. Ernesto Zedillo," October 6, 1997.
8. *Livre blanc,* p. 51.
9. "Vœux du ministre des Affaires étrangères, M. Alain Juppé, aux agents du Département," January 6, 1995. For French post–Cold War diplomacy through institutions, see Stanley Hoffmann, "French Dilemmas and Strategies in the New Europe," in *After the Cold War: International Institutions and State Strategies in Europe, 1989–1991,* ed. Robert O. Keohane et al. (Cambridge: Harvard University Press, 1993), pp. 142–45.
10. *Livre blanc,* p. 52.
11. John Gerard Ruggie, "Multilateralism: The Anatomy of an Institution," in *Multilateralism Matters: The Theory and Praxis of an Institutional Form,* ed. John Gerard Ruggie (New York: Columbia University Press, 1993), p. 11.
12. Ann Florini, "The Evolution of International Norms," *International Studies Quarterly* 40 (September 1996): p. 375.
13. The *Livre blanc* identifies the UNSC as "the only international authority with the right to decide coercive measures or the use of force against a state, outside actions of legitimate individual or collective defense under article 51 of the Charter." As a permanent member of the Council, France must aim at "strengthening its [France's] influence, at allowing it to meet greater responsibilities. […]" *Livre blanc,* p. 72.
14. For the French role in the events leading up to the conflict, see Claire Tréan, "La diplomatie européenne aux commandes," *Le Monde,* June 5, 1999.
15. "Intervention du Premier ministre, M. Lionel Jospin, à l'Assemblée nationale," March 26, 1999.
16. "Déclaration du Président de la République, M. Jacques Chirac," March 24, 1999.
17. "Remise du prix Charlemagne au Premier ministre de Grande-Bretagne, Tony Blair. Allocution du Premier ministre, Lionel Jospin," May 13, 1999.
18. "Entretien du Ministre des Affaires étrangères, M. Hubert Védrine, avec le 'Club de la presse' sur 'Europe 1,'" March 29, 1999.
19. "Intervention du Premier ministre, M. Lionel Jospin, à l'Assemblée nationale," March 26, 1999.
20. For example, France was the greatest European contributor of aircraft to NATO's raids against Yugoslavia—in number of planes if not by the success of their raids. See John Laurenson, "French pilots fly for NATO," http://news.bbc.co.uk.
21. Ministry of Foreign Affairs, *Point de presse,* April 26, 1999.
22. In an editorial, *Le Monde* pointed out that reference to the United Nations was made in a "vague and fuzzy way"; "La nouvelle OTAN," *Le Monde,* April 27, 1999; and underlined the weakness of European support for France's positions: Patrice de Beer and Luc Rosenzweig, "Le nouveau 'concept stratégique' de l'organisation atlantique," *Le Monde,* April 27, 1999. American diplomats appeared to share this narrower view of French "success"; see John F. Harris, "Clinton Coaxes Allies to Fragile Consensus," *Washington Post,* April 26, 1999.

23. "Interview du Premier ministre au Journal de 20h sur 'France 2,'" April 8, 1999.
24. "Sommet de l'OTAN. Conférence de presse du Président de la République, M. Jacques Chirac," April 24, 1999.
25. "Entretien du Président de la République, M. Jacques Chirac, avec 'TF1,'" June 10, 1999.
26. "Visite en Russie. Conférence de presse du Président de la République, Jacques Chirac," May 13, 1999. President Chirac presumably was referring to Britain and the United States, since the Ministry of Foreign Affairs had earlier complained that these two countries were stalling further meetings of G8 foreign ministers on Kosovo; Ministry of Foreign Affairs, "Déclarations conjointes des porte-parole du ministère des Affaires étrangères et du ministère de la Défense," May 5, 1999.
27. "Entretien avec le ministre des Affaires étrangères, M. Hubert Védrine," *Le Figaro,* April 21, 1999.
28. "Visite en Russie. Conférence de presse conjointe du ministre des Affaires étrangères, M. Hubert Védrine, et du ministre russe des Affaires étrangères, M. Igor Ivanov—propos du ministre," May 11, 1999.
29. Judith Miller, "French Aide Named to Leading Rebuilding Effort," *New York Times,* July 3, 1999.
30. Ministry of Foreign Affairs, *Point de presse,* April 16, 1999.
31. "Entretien du ministre des Affaires étrangères, M. Hubert Védrine, avec le quotidien 'La Croix,'" May 21, 1999.
32. "Entretien avec le ministre des Affaires étrangères, M. Hubert Védrine," *Le Figaro,* April 21, 1999.
33. Philippe Lemaître, "Europe: 'Pacte de stabilité des Balkans' et intégration des pays de l'Est," *Le Monde,* July 30, 1999.
34. "Conseil européen de Cologne. Conférence de presse conjointe du Président de la République, M. Jacques Chirac, et du Premier ministre, Lionel Jospin," June 4, 1999.
35. "Entretien du ministre des Affaires étrangères, M. Hubert Védrine, avec 'L'Hebdo des socialistes,'" June 18, 1999.
36. "Entretien du ministre des Affaires étrangères, M. Hubert Védrine, avec le 'Club de la presse' sur 'Europe 1,'" June 20, 1999. President Chirac had made a similar observation a few days earlier. See "Entretien du Président de la République, M. Jacques Chirac, avec 'TF1,'" June 10, 1999.
37. Jean-Gabriel Frédet, "Alain Richard: ce que le Kosovo m'a appris," *Le Nouvel Observateur,* July 15–21, 1999, p. 32
38. Ministère de la Défense (Ministry of Defense), *Les enseignements du Kosovo,* November 1999. This was the first official assessment of the French role in Kosovo to be published after the conflict.
39. "Interview télévisée de Monsieur Jacques Chirac, Président de la République à l'occasion de la Fête nationale," July 14, 1999. A later account suggests that the NATO commander, General Wesley Clark, deliberately put the allies before a fait accompli. See the transcript of the BBC 2 program *Newsnight,* August 20, 1999, Mark Urban, "Nato's inner Kosovo conflict," http://news.bbc.co.uk.

40. These examples are all taken from official statements, speeches, and interviews made during the conflict. For a general presentation of French influence over NATO strategy, see Serge July, "La guerre, version elyséenne," *Libération*, April 17 and 18, 1999.
41. See Antoine Guiral, "Elysée-Matignon, le front uni," *Libération*, April 8, 1999.
42. For Jospin's position, see Jean-Michel Aphatie, Jean-Baptiste de Montvalon, and Michel Noblecourt, "Lionel Jospin refuse d'exclure l'hypothèse d'une action terrestre," *Le Monde*, April 1, 1999, and "Interview du Premier ministre au Journal de 20h sur 'France 2,'" April 8, 1999. For Védrine's declaration, see "Entretien du ministre des Affaires étrangères, M. Hubert Védrine, avec le 'Club de la presse' sur 'Europe 1,'" March 29, 1999.
43. Éric Favreau and Pierre Haski, "Kouchner réclame des troupes au sol pour arrêter le massacre," *Libération*, April 15, 1999.
44. "Intervention radiotélevisée du Président de la République, M. Jacques Chirac, sur l'évolution de la situation au Kosovo," April 21, 1999. For the view of French officials, see Michael R. Gordon and Craig Whitney, "2 NATO Allies Press U.S. to Weigh the Use of Ground Forces," *New York Times*, April 22, 1999.
45. "Entretien du Président de la République, M. Jacques Chirac, avec 'TF1,'" June 10, 1999.
46. Daniel Vernet, "La stratégie de l'Alliance pour faire céder Belgrade pèsera longtemps sur l'avenir de la province," *Le Monde*, June 25, 1999 ; and Vincent Jauvert, "Rien ne s'est passé comme prévu," *Le Nouvel Observateur*, July 1–6, 1999. According to a British newspaper, Britain and the United States, presumably with the support of France and other members of NATO, planned a "massive ground invasion in Kosovo" for early September; Patrick Wintour and Peter Beaumont, "Revealed: the secret plan to invade Kosovo," The *Observer*, July 18, 1999. These sources all suggest agreement among major NATO partners on the need for a ground attack if diplomacy failed.
47. "Visite en Russie. Conférence de presse du Président de la République, M. Jacques Chirac," May 13, 1999.
48. Pierre Giacometti and Eric Dupin, "Débat: Intervention de l'OTAN en Yougoslavie: les déterminants de l'opinion publique," Ipsos, http://www.canalipsos.com., April 19, 1999.
49. Jean-Michel Aphatie, "Le manifeste 'philosophique' de M. Chevènement contre la guerre," *Le Monde*, April 3, 1999.
50. Ariane Chemin, "La conversion des Verts au réalisme diplomatique," *Le Monde*, April 3, 1999.
51. Marie-France Etchegoin, "Intellectuels: le poison du Kosovo," *Le Nouvel Observateur*, June 3–9, 1999.
52. Ministry of Defense, *Les enseignements du Kosovo*, loc. cit.
53. For a summary, see Eric Dupin, "Otan: approbation fataliste des Français," Ipsos, loc. cit., May 26, 1999. When the polling firm CSA asked a question, early in the war, about bombing Serbia (as opposed to supporting NATO operations), opinion was relatively negative, with 40 percent for and 46 percent against; Eric Dupin, "Les raids contre la Serbie divisent l'opinion internationale," CSA, March 29, 1999.

54. BVA poll, taken May 17–19, 1999, (http://www.bva.fr/archives/kosovo9920.html).
55. Pierre Giacometti and Eric Dupin, "Débat: Intervention de l'OTAN en Yougoslavie," loc. cit.
56. Ibid.
57. See Eric Dupin, "Otan: l'approbation fataliste des Français," loc. cit. Between April 9–10 and April 17, the number of those who believed NATO was failing rose from 29 percent to 52 percent. They were also at 52 percent just over a month later.
58. A poll taken by CSA showed as early as the middle of April that 52 percent of those surveyed favored this position; see Dominique de Montvalon, "Les Français se posent des questions," *Le Parisien,* April 19, 1999
59. "Kosovo. Entretien du ministre des Affaires étrangères, M. Hubert Védrine, avec 'France Inter,'" June 4, 1999. See also Pierre Haski, "Kosovo: dans les coulisses du 'club des cinq,'" *Libération,* July 1, 1999.

CHAPTER EIGHT

Germany and the Kosovo Conflict*

Peter Rudolf

Only diehard American neorealists would have dared to predict what happened in the spring of 1999: "For the first time since 1945, German forces are taking offensive military operations against a sovereign state. The historic watershed is all the more remarkable because it is under the control of a 'Red-Green' coalition government, and without a clear U.N. mandate."[1] Although the war clearly was a watershed for German politics and foreign policy, the approach taken in the Kosovo conflict was consistent with the main features of Germany's political-military culture after 1945: its deeply ingrained antimilitarism, its almost instinctive multilateralism, and its human rights commitment.[2]

The central argument of this chapter is that Germany's "dual strategy" of supporting allied military pressure and pushing diplomatic initiatives can be interpreted as an attempt to reconcile and balance these basic foreign policy orientations. The challenge was to do so in a crisis situation in which the United States had taken over the requested leadership role but structured the process in a way that left German policymakers little room for choice. Germany did not want to bear the blame for the failure of a policy of coercive diplomacy it had agreed to in principle under the Kohl government. Moreover, American pressure to consent to a clear and credible military threat later came at a time in which the domestic constellation could not have been more susceptible to it.

In the fall of 1998, the newly elected Red-Green coalition government, which had strongly committed itself to human rights, was eager to avoid any impression that it would pursue a German *Sonderweg* (special path) setting Germany apart from its Western allies. When it became clear that coercive diplomacy finally meant war, German policymakers saw no alternative to participating in limited military strikes, apparently sharing NATO's basic assumption that, after a few days of air attacks, the Yugoslav leadership would give in to NATO's demands. Participation was seen as the precondition for preserving the multilateral framework in which the Federal Republic traditionally has smoothly exercised its influence. And it was the nature of the Kosovo conflict that made Germany willingly follow American leadership. If the war had not been fought for "moral values" but for traditional "national interests" such as oil or regional stability, domestic resistance to German military participation would have been much greater and politically more effective. Of course, the wider implications of the Kosovo conflict for regional stability and the influx of refugees from Kosovo affected German interests, but the prevailing perception in the German discourse was that the use of military force was the last resort to forestall a humanitarian catastrophe.

From Coercive Diplomacy to War

Confronted with the escalating Kosovo conflict in 1997, the German government under Chancellor Kohl avoided acting alone and firmly embedded its response into the existing multilateral frameworks: the Contact Group, the EU's Common Foreign and Security Policy, and NATO.[3] For example, when tensions in Kosovo were rising in the fall of 1997, Germany and France undertook a joint diplomatic initiative. In a letter to the Serbian president, German foreign minister Klaus Kinkel and his French colleague Hubert Védrine pressed for a negotiated solution, indicating that the EU might reciprocate with restoring trade preferences.[4] After the civil war–like conflict fully broke out in late February 1998, the German government was highly concerned, now sending out the message to Washington that American leadership was urgently needed.[5]

For the United States, the question arose whether the old threat to use force "in the event of conflict in Kosovo caused by Serbian action"—first made by the Bush administration in December 1992, and reiterated by then Secretary of State Warren Christopher in February and March 1993—was still on the table. Reportedly, Secretary of State Madeleine Albright, not wanting to repeat earlier American mistakes in the Bosnian conflict, paved the way for a policy of "coercive diplomacy" when stating on March 7, 1998, in Rome: "We are not going to stand by and watch the Serbian authorities do in Kosovo what they can no longer get away with doing in Bosnia."[6]

German foreign minister Klaus Kinkel supported a policy of threatening Milosevic, but insisted on a mandate given by the United Nations Security Council, a concern that was apparently not shared by Defense Minister

Volker Ruehe but that reflected domestic realities: Military strikes without a U.N. mandate would probably have led to severe conflict with the opposition parties, certainly with the Greens but also with the SPD. In both parties, the views on the use of military force differed to a great extent, but the basic party line was clear: If military force beyond collective defense under Article 5 of the NATO treaty is to be used at all, a U.N. mandate will be needed.[7] At the time of the evolving Kosovo crisis, only a few voices in the SPD dissented from this plank in the party platform, among them Rudolf Scharping.[8]

With the United States taking the lead in bringing about a negotiated solution through shuttle diplomacy between Pristina and Belgrade, Germany could make little input into this process. The German idea of a Dayton-style conclave did not resonate with the U.S. administration. German policy concentrated upon getting Moscow on board so that a United Nations resolution authorizing military force would not encounter a Russian veto. Unable to get Russian consent to military action and—as Foreign Minister Kinkel admitted—under "immense pressure"[9] from the United States to decide about German participation in military strikes, German foreign policymakers were confronted with a dilemma, at a time when the fall 1998 federal election ended the Kohl era:[10] either to act contrary to long-held beliefs about the legitimate use of military force or to undermine the credibility of NATO's military threat by refusing to participate in air strikes not authorized by the Security Council.

It is a matter of speculation whether Chancellor Kohl, with his established foreign policy credentials, would have been able or willing to resist American pressure. Reportedly, he had misgivings about the overall American approach in the Kosovo crisis. For the incoming Red-Green government, however, the dilemma was even worse. The designated Chancellor Schroeder wanted to avoid any impression that Germany under the new government would be an unreliable ally. Visiting Washington before assuming office, he assured President Clinton that Germany would support potential military action against Yugoslavia. The final decision about actual German military participation was to be taken after assuming office. But three days later on October 12, 1998, Clinton insisted that the decision about German military participation no longer be postponed. As Foreign Minister Fischer later recalled, he and Schroeder, while they were on their way to consult with Chancellor Kohl, had "fifteen minutes [left] to decide a question of war and peace."[11]

Why did the Clinton administration suddenly increase its pressure? According to press reports, then Defense Minister Volker Ruehe urged Washington to nail down the new government and to insist on a quick decision. Another explanation holds that Richard Holbrooke called Clinton, saying that Milosevic, realizing the "German gap," would not take NATO's threat seriously as long as Germany was not willing to act.[12] In the end, an incoming government, which in its coalition treaty had just promised to work toward the preservation of the "monopoly of force of the United Nations," consented to German participation in potential air strikes against Yugoslavia.

As Foreign Minister Fischer later was quoted as saying, the United States did not leave Germany any possibility to influence anything.[13] He and his party were faced with the question of whether the Red-Green government would fail even before it had taken office, since Gerhard Schroeder was determined to avoid any impression that a Social Democratic chancellor would prove to be an unreliable ally.[14] If Germany had refused to take part in threatened military strikes, Chancellor Schroeder later argued, it could have been blamed for the failure of Holbrooke's negotiating mission. This could have led to a tremendous loss of image and influence for Germany in international relations.[15] Gerhard Schroeder, it became clear from the beginning, did not want to taint his chancellorship with accusations of a German *Sonderweg*. Instead, Germany would move further ahead toward becoming a "normal" alliance partner, ready to shoulder military responsibilities commensurate with its "European interests."[16] Although Chancellor Schroeder later stressed that the decision in favor of German military participation was taken "voluntarily" (*aus freier Überzeugung*),[17] domestic and foreign policy interests did not leave much choice. And at least the timing of the decision clearly owed a lot to American pressure.

Thus, the Social Democrats and their junior partners in the coalition government supported the decision taken by the Kohl government on October 12, 1998, to authorize the activation order for NATO air strikes. When the Bundestag came together to decide about the participation of Tornado aircraft on October 16, NATO's coercive diplomacy had already produced results. In this situation, the vote in the Bundestag was not only about German reliability among its Western partners, it was also about whether the pressure on Milosevic to follow through on his promises would be maintained. Even most of the Green members of parliament authorized German participation in NATO air strikes to prevent a humanitarian catastrophe. All in all, 500 of 580 parliamentarians voted in favor of German participation, with the members of the East German-based Party of Democratic Socialism (PDS) representing the bulk of the 62 dissenting votes.[18]

The importance of this decision of the Bundestag, which provided the legal basis for German participation in Operation Allied Force, went well beyond the Kosovo case. Indeed it was a precedent in a constitutional gray area. The Federal Constitutional Court (*Bundesverfassungsgericht*) had stated in its 1994 decision about the participation of German forces in operations in Somalia and the former Yugoslavia that the use of the Bundeswehr for operations within a collective security system was constitutional and that alliances for collective defense can be understood as such systems of collective security as long as they are strictly committed to preserving peace. But the assumption seemed to be that—without a formal change of the North Atlantic Treaty—NATO structures would be used only for operations that were authorized by the Security Council.[19] Under pressure not to undermine NATO's coercive diplomacy and to forestall an acute humanitarian catastrophe, however, legal considerations were mostly set aside. Among the supporters of the decision, it was mainly then Foreign Minister Kinkel who clearly stated that the decision by NATO was not intended to create a "general license" (*Generalvollmacht*) for military intervention without authorization of the United Nations.

The issue of military intervention came up again after the massacre at Racak in mid-January 1999. Now the U.S. government put forward the idea to force Milosevic to accept the deployment of NATO troops in Kosovo, which would monitor the withdrawal of Yugoslav military forces. Although the convening of the Rambouillet conference was seen as a success of German policy, the actual negotiations were more and more run by the United States. With the United States taking the lead and the French and British governments eager to stake out special roles, Germany again was pushed to the sidelines, trying everything to avoid war but in the end having little influence.[20]

Wartime Politics

When the Rambouillet negotiations finally failed and NATO made good on its threat, German participation in the air strikes provoked surprisingly little domestic dissent. The fact that military intervention occurred under a coalition of Social Democrats and Greens certainly helped to contain domestic opposition.[21] Germany seemed to be drawing the moral lessons from its history, as it found itself fighting an allegedly unavoidable but moral war for human rights and against a "barbaric form of fascism."[22] In these conditions, the left would have had a hard time opposing a war not fought for selfish national interests but for moral values, a war not fought for oil but for human rights, a war that had to be fought to prevent future wars in the Balkans, a war that spelled the end of the futile "appeasement" of Milosevic—the latter being an argument mainly used by Foreign Minister Fischer.[23] As Fischer said, the massacres of Srebrenica in 1995 had convinced him that appeasement would only lead to further mass graves.[24]

Not all leading politicians engaged in the kind of "hypermoralization"[25] of the war as Foreign Minister Fischer and Defense Minister Scharping[26] did by using "dubious historical parallels" ("Never again Auschwitz"), creating the impression that they were trying to silence lingering doubts in their own minds.[27] In Chancellor Schroeder's rhetoric, the central historical reference point was not Auschwitz, but the rejection of a German *Sonderweg;* participation in NATO's fight was interpreted as an affirmation of the integration into the Western community, which he presented as part of Germany's *raison d'état*. This argument was much more palatable even to those conservatives who were unhappy with the rhetoric of the Auschwitz parallel. As the former Defense Minister Volker Ruehe and the chairman of the CDU (Christian Democratic Union) Wolfgang Schäuble warned, such a rhetoric could lead down the slippery slope toward the use of combat troops on the ground, toward unconditional surrender and total war.[28] At their party convention in April 1999, the CDU passed a resolution supportive of NATO's intervention, but with clear language that the party would not consent to any step that might trigger an uncontrollable military development in the Balkans.[29] The CSU (Christian Social Union), the Bavarian "sister party," was no less opposed to sending ground troops into combat, as the Bavarian prime minister Edmund Stoiber stated after visiting Moscow.

The de facto grand coalition in favor of limited military intervention reflected public opinion. Among the German public there was broad agreement, but in the course of the bombing campaign, support for NATO's military intervention gradually eroded.[30] In April 1999, 60 percent of the public considered it the right policy to bomb Yugoslavia; the number was even higher when people were asked whether it was right that the Bundeswehr was taking part in this intervention. In May 1999, support for the military intervention had declined to a bare majority of 52 percent. The percentage of those people who now thought it was wrong to attack Yugoslavia had risen from 35 percent to 44 percent. The decline of support was most pronounced among supporters of the Green Party. Whereas in April 1999, 57 percent of those people tending to the Greens were favorably disposed toward the Kosovo intervention, the number fell to 38 percent the following month.

Majority support for the intervention remained confined to supporters of the Social Democratic Party (SPD), the Christian Democratic Party (CDU/CSU), and the small Free Democratic Party (FDP). Supporters of the Socialist Party (PDS), which played a role only in the eastern parts of Germany, had been solidly opposed to the intervention from the beginning. But among the East German public, opposition to NATO's engagement in the Kosovo crisis extended well beyond the PDS and its supporters. Only 25 percent of the public in the eastern parts of Germany approved of NATO's Kosovo intervention, revealing a basic split in the attitudes toward NATO and its role among the eastern and western parts of Germany.[31]

In the western states of Germany, a majority believed that it was a task of NATO to intervene in countries where parts of the population were threatened or persecuted; only one-third of the public would have wanted to confine NATO's role to collective defense. In the eastern states, the prevailing attitude could hardly have been more different, reflecting a deeply rooted uneasiness with NATO and its missions. The majority in the east wanted to restrict NATO's functions to collective defense. In the eastern part of Germany, where hundreds of smaller rallies against the Kosovo war were taking place, the perception of NATO was still influenced by the Communist past.[32]

Thus the initial broad consensus in favor of NATO's Kosovo intervention was confined to the former West Germany. Despite its general favorable disposition toward the intervention and German participation in it, the overwhelming majority shared the pessimistic view that bombing alone would not be effective in forcing the Yugoslav government to fulfill NATO's demands. But this growing pessimism never translated into readiness to support the use of combat troops on the ground. A solid two-thirds majority was unwavering in its opposition to sending in ground troops even in the case that Serbia would not give in to NATO's demands. This opposition cut across party lines.

In the course of the bombing campaign, further cracks in the fragile consensus within the political class appeared. With NATO incapable of stopping the killing and expulsion of Kosovo Albanians, the main official justification of the intervention—stopping a "humanitarian tragedy"—was breaking apart; NATO's resolve, to intensify the bombing campaign against more and more targets in Serbia, led to concerns about the morally troubling turn the campaign was taking, leading to calls for stopping the air campaign and starting fresh negotiations.[33] Within the Social Democratic Party, which at a special party convention in mid-April had supported the policy of Chancellor Schroeder, critics received prominent support when the former party chairman Oskar Lafontaine made his public comeback on May 1, 1999. In a speech heavily critical of NATO's Kosovo strategy, he called upon European governments to make clear to the United States that sidestepping the United Nations and not including Russia were grave mistakes.[34]

The most vexing debates were taking place within the Green Party, where not all former nuclear pacifists had turned into humanitarian interventionists. The Greens were caught in a most severe dilemma, since in the Kosovo conflict the two basic goals of a Green foreign policy remained irreconcilable: on the one hand, the rejection of the use of force; on the other hand, the strong human rights commitment. With a highly emotional speech at a special party convention on Kosovo in mid-May 1999, Foreign

Minister Joschka Fischer persuaded the party delegates to reject a resolution demanding the unilateral halt of NATO's attacks—after he had categorically refused to take up this proposal if the party adopted it.[35] But the party delegates made clear that they would neither tolerate sending German troops into combat on the ground nor consent to a NATO ground war without German participation.[36]

With NATO forces targeting more and more the Serbian infrastructure and causing a growing number of casualties among the civilian population and apparently heading toward either failure or the decision to send in ground troops, support for the war within the SPD and the Green Party was eroding. Second thoughts were growing even among those who had initially supported military intervention.[37] Given the domestic situation in Germany, no government could have dared to participate in a ground war, since this would have raised enormous political and constitutional problems. Chancellor Schroeder's rather blunt rejection of deploying ground troops[38] mirrored the dominant sentiment within the German public and within the political class.

Bringing German Diplomacy Back In: The Dual Strategy

German military participation in what officially was never called a war mainly consisted of 14 Tornado aircraft equipped to suppress Serbian air defense. Militarily, this contribution was certainly not unimportant, since, within NATO, even the United States had insufficient suppression of enemy air defense (SEAD) capability, and German aircraft could make a unique contribution. In addition to 46 reconnaissance missions, German aircraft flew 394 sorties, firing 244 high-speed antiradiation missiles.[39] Hardly more could have been expected, since the rest of the German Tornado aircraft were armed with old-fashioned bombs, not well suited for the kind of air campaign planned against Serbian forces. With all in all a minor military part, Germany had little influence on the decisions about how to wage the war. The important decisions about the targets chosen were made by the United States, Britain, and France.[40]

But in political terms, the participation of German forces paid off, since the steadfast solidarity with the allies gave German foreign policy-makers the credentials to make a comeback with innovative ideas. Using the presidency of the European Council, the German government rallied support for an integrative, Marshall Plan-style, long-term vision for Balkan stability. Moreover, it pursued a "dual strategy" for ending the war: on the one hand, unwavering support for allied military pressure on Milosevic, thus avoiding any impression that Germany could be the weak spot in the Western coalition; on the other hand, new diplomatic efforts to end the war by involving

Russia and the United Nations and by injecting some flexibility into the Western negotiating position in order to induce Milosevic to make concessions.[41]

The German peace plan—the Fischer Plan, as it became known—was worked out after the initial hopes that Milosevic would give in to NATO's demands rather quickly proved to be false and the logic of military escalation seemed to develop its own dynamic. Domestically, it served to shore up eroding support for NATO's military campaign and contain criticism. The peace plan was based on the assumption that further air attacks combined with a Chapter VII Security Council resolution laying out the conditions for peace in Kosovo (essentially the withdrawal of all Serbian military, paramilitary, and police forces; acceptance of an international peace force with a Chapter VII mandate; and a transitory administration of Kosovo authorized by the United Nations) would bring Milosevic to the negotiating table. The highly controversial element in this plan was the offer to suspend the air strikes once Belgrade began to withdraw its forces and continued doing so—a proposal that Washington quickly rejected.[42]

With the Fischer Plan, German foreign policy was pursuing a delicate balancing act: staking out some independence of the United States while at the same time avoiding any impression that Germany would walk down a *Sonderweg*. In the end, German foreign policy-makers could luckily claim success: Belgrade accepted what became the Petersberg Peace Plan[43]— shortly before NATO and Germany had to face the most difficult decision: whether to invade Kosovo.

Conclusion: Lessons from the Kosovo Crisis

In the Kosovo crisis, as before in the Bosnian conflict, the willingness of the European allies to follow American leadership was foremost necessitated by their weakness.[44] With regard to Kosovo, Germany rather early realized that American commitment would be necessary—with the result that later it had little input into the American way of crisis management. The Kosovo conflict has left uneasiness about the dominating role of the United States and the way American-style coercive diplomacy had shut off other options, in the end leaving no other choice than military escalation.[45] Especially among Social Democrats and Greens, the "sin" of having to consent to military action without a United Nations mandate remains a vexing memory.

The lesson the "Red-Green" German government has drawn from the political and military weakness that the Kosovo crisis made plain is that the European Union must increase its capability to act autonomously in the process of preventing and managing crises in Europe so that Europe gains "real equity" (*wirkliche Gleichberechtigung*) with the United States.[46] In the aftermath of the Kosovo war and fed by the general perception—rightly or wrongly—that U.S. foreign policy has been drifting toward unilateralism, it has become almost a dogma among German policymakers that only a stronger Europe will get a hearing in Washington. Thus the Kosovo crisis gave new impetus to the old vision of a common European security policy; it acted as a "catalyst"[47] for the development of a European Security and Defense Policy, which, from the German perspective, lies in the political logic of the European unification process. In the German view, ESDP is seen as the basis for a new Atlanticism, for a real partnership based upon greater European strength.[48] Skeptics still have good reasons to doubt whether Europe will get its act together. But, as it has been rightly pointed out,[49] this time Europe cannot afford a failure, since so much political capital has been invested in this project and Europe's credibility is at stake.

Notes

*I wish to thank Thomas Frisch, Reinhard Wolf, and the editors for their helpful comments.

1. Adrian Hyde-Price, "Berlin Republic Takes to Arms," *The World Today*, June 1999, p. 13.
2. On German political-military culture, see Thomas U. Berger, *Cultures of Antimilitarism: National Security in Germany and Japan* (Baltimore: The Johns Hopkins University Press, 1998); on German political culture and foreign policy, see John S. Duffield, "Political Culture and State Behavior: Why Germany Confounds Neorealism," *International Organization* 53 (autumn 1999): pp. 765–803; on the evolution of Germany's attitude toward the use of force and the Kosovo conflict, see Hanns W. Maull, "Germany and the Use of Force: Still a 'Civilian Power'?" *Survival* 42 (summer 2000): pp. 56–80.
3. See Joachim Krause, "Deutschland und die Kosovo-Krise," in *Der Kosovo-Konflikt. Ursachen, Verlauf, Perspektiven,* ed. Jens Reuter and Conrad Clewing (Klagenfurt: Wieser Verlag, forthcoming).
4. See Berthold Meyer and Peter Schlotter, *Die Kosovo-Kriege 1998/99. Die internationalen Interventionen und ihre Folgen* (Frankfurt am Main: Frankfurt Peace Research Institute, 2000), p. 13.
5. The most detailed account of the evolution of German policy in the Kosovo crisis, based upon access to confidential files of the German foreign ministry and interviews with senior officials, can be found in Gunter Hofmann, "Wie Deutschland in den Krieg geriet," *Die Zeit,* May 12, 1999, p. 17.
6. Barton Gellman, "The Path to Crisis: How the United States and Its Allies Went to War," *Washington Post,* April 18, 1999, p. A1.
7. On the party positions, see Michael Damman and Jörg Nadolt, "Jugoslawienpolitik: Von der Ausnahme zur Regel?" in *Lehrgeld: Vier Monate rot-grüne Außenpolitik,* ed. Hanns W. Maull (Trier: Universität Trier, 1999), pp. 41–56.

8. See "Kosovo zwingt SPD zur Kurskorrektur," *Süddeutsche Zeitung,* June 15, 1998, p. 6.
9. Udo Bergdoll, "Nichts ohne den neuen Kanzler," *Süddeutsche Zeitung,* October 9, 1998.
10. The following account is based upon "Schröder für Härte im Kosovo-Konflikt," *Süddeutsche Zeitung,* October 10, 1998, p. 6; "Kabinett billigt NATO-Einsatz im Kosovo," *Frankfurter Allgemeine Zeitung,* October 13, 1998; Udo Bergdoll, "Poker mit 'deutscher Lücke'," *Süddeutsche Zeitung,* October 15, 1998, p. 10; "Lästiges Joch," *Der Spiegel,* October 19, 1998, p. 198.
11. As quoted in Hofmann, "Wie Deutschland in den Krieg geriet."
12. Later Holbrooke maintained that German and French concerns about military strikes without authorization by the United Nations Security Council had been delaying the success of his negotiating mission. See Stefan Cornelius, "Washington befürchtet den 'Saddam-Effekt,'" *Süddeutsche Zeitung,* October 30, 1998, p. 8.
13. "Der etwas andere Krieg," *Der Spiegel,* January 3, 2000.
14. As quoted in "Aus freier Überzeugung," *Der Spiegel,* April 19, 1999, p. 22.
15. See his speech in the debate of the Bundestag on October 16, 1998, reprinted in *Das Parlament,* October 30, 1998, p. 18.
16. See the speech of Chancellor Gerhard Schroeder at the Münchner Konferenz für Sicherheitspolitik, February 6, 1999, in Presse- und Informationsamt der Bundesregierung, *Bulletin,* February 22, 1999.
17. As quoted in "Aus freier Überzeugung," p. 22.
18. See "Deutsche Soldaten für Kosovo-Einsatz bereit," *Süddeutsche Zeitung,* October 17, 1998, p. 1. The debate in the Bundestag is reprinted in *Das Parlament,* October 30, 1998, pp. 17–21.
19. See Ulrich Fastenrath, "Es wird ein Präzedenzfall geschaffen," *Frankfurter Allgemeine Zeitung,* October 16, 1998, p. 5. For a detailed analysis of the decision of the Bundesverfassungsgericht, see Doris Koenig, "Putting an End to an Endless Constitutional Debate? The Decision of the Federal Constitutional Court on the 'Out of Area' Deployment of German Armed Forces," in *German Yearbook of International Law,* vol. 38, 1995 (Berlin: Dunker and Humbolt, 1996), pp. 103–128.
20. See Hofmann, "Wie Deutschland in den Krieg geriet."
21. See Thomas Blanke, "Das Dilemma zwischen Menschenrecht und Völkerrecht," *Frankfurter Rundschau,* March 29, 1999, p. 8.
22. See "Es ist eine barbarische Form des Faschismus," *Die Tageszeitung,* April 15, 1999, p. 3.
23. See his speech in Deutscher Bundestag, *Stenographischer Bericht* 32. Sitzung, April 15, 1999, pp. 2638–41.
24. See the interview "Milošević wird der Verlierer sein," *Der Spiegel,* April 19, 1999, p. 34.
25. The notion of hypermoralization (*Übermoralisierung*) is used by Gunter Hofmann, "Deutschland am Ende des Krieges," *Die Zeit,* June 10, 1999, p. S3.

26. In Scharping's view, what Milosevic was doing was fascist at core. Rudolf Scharping, "Der Stein auf unserer Seele," *Frankfurter Allgemeine Zeitung,* May 3, 1999, p. 55.
27. As Jürgen Habermas, one of Germany's most prominent intellectuals, succinctly pointed out in his own guarded defense of the intervention; see his "Bestialität und Humanität," *Die Zeit,* April 29, 1999, pp. 1, 6, 7.
28. See the speech of Wolfgang Schäuble in Deutscher Bundestag, *Stenographischer Bericht* 32. Sitzung, April 15, 1999, pp. 2623–27, and the interview with Volker Ruehe, "Überanpassung der Bundesregierung," *Süddeutsche Zeitung,* April 28, 1999, p. 7.
29. See "Frieden und Freiheit für den Kosovo," *Das Parlament,* April 30, 1999, p. S16.
30. See "Breite Zustimmung für die Luftangriffe," *Süddeutsche Zeitung,* April 17, 1999, p. 13; "Immer mehr Deutsche fürchten einen Krieg," *Frankfurter Rundschau,* April 8, 1999, p. 4; "Die Union hat die SPD wieder überholt," *Süddeutsche Zeitung,* May 22, 1999.
31. See Renate Köcher, "Das Kosovo spaltet Deutschland in Ost und West," *Frankfurter Allgemeine Zeitung,* June 16, 1999, p. 5.
32. See Heinz Boschek, "Honeckers langer Schatten," *Rheinischer Merkur,* May 21, 1999, p. 6.
33. See, for example, the op-ed pieces of the former leader of the Christian Democratic Party in the Bundestag, Alfred Dregger, "Den Krieg beenden," *Frankfurter Allgemeine Zeitung,* April 6, 1999, p. S16, and the Social Democratic minister of justice in Berlin, Ehrhart Körting, "Nothilfe: ja—Krieg zur Durchsetzung von Politik: nein," *Frankfurter Rundschau,* May 25, 1999, p. 7.
34. See "Man darf die UN nicht übergehen," *Frankfurter Rundschau,* May 3, 1999, p. 7.
35. See the excerpts of this speech in *Süddeutsche Zeitung,* May 14, 1999, p. 13.
36. See Bündnis 90/Die Grünen, "Frieden und Menschenrechte vereinbaren! Für einen Frieden im Kosovo, der seinen Namen zu Recht trägt!" Beschluß der 2. Außerordentlichen Bundesdelegiertenkonferenz, Bielefeld, May 13, 1999.
37. See Christiane Schlötzer and Christoph Schwennicke, "Der Rückhalt für den Krieg bröckelt," *Süddeutsche Zeitung,* June 2, 1999, p. 6.
38. See Roger Cohen, "Schroeder's Blunt 'No' to Ground Troops in Kosovo Reflects Depth of German Sensitivities," *New York Times,* May 20, 1999, p. A14.
39. See Anthony H. Cordesman, *The Lessons and Non-Lessons of the Air and Missile Campaign in Kosovo* (Washington, D.C.: Center for Strategic and International Studies, September 29, 1999), pp. 34, 189.
40. See Dana Priest, "Serbs Targets: NATO's Conflicting Views," *International Herald Tribune,* September 21, 1999.
41. For an interpretation and evaluation of this approach, see Frank Herterich, "Kriegswege, Friedensziele," *Frankfurter Rundschau,* May 12, 1999, p. 10; Ernst-Otto Czempiel, "Bekommt die NATO neue Kleider?" *Die Tageszeitung,* April 20, 1999, p. 10.

42. For the text of the peace plan, see *Frankfurter Allgemeine Zeitung,* April 15, 1999, p. 2; in addition, see "Fischer will G–8 Treffen in Bonn," *Frankfurter Allgemeine Zeitung,* April 14, 1999, p. 2; "Bonn: Friedenstruppen müssen von der NATO geführt sein," *Frankfurter Allgemeine Zeitung,* April 15, 1999, p. 2.
43. Chancellor Schroeder saw this as proof that Germany's dual-track policy was right, claiming that under the German presidency Europe demonstrated its capacity to lead politically. See "Ergebnisse des Europäischen Rates am 3./4. Juni 1999 in Köln und Stand der Friedensbemühungen im Kosovo-Konflikt, Erklärung der Bundesregierung," Presse- und Informationsamt der Bundesregierung, *Bulletin,* June 10, 1999, p. 381.
44. See August Pradetto, "Moral, Interessen und Machtkalkül in der Außenpolitik. Schlussfolgerungen ein Jahr nach dem Kosovo-Krieg," *Frankfurter Rundschau,* March 24, 2000, p. 14.
45. See the early critical remarks of the former Defense Minister Volker Ruehe, "Was die Kosovo-Krise lehrt," *Frankfurter Rundschau,* April 9, 1999, p. 6.
46. Rudolf Scharping, "Europäische Sicherheitspolitik und die Nordatlantische Allianz," speech on July 5, 1999, in Berlin; in addition, see the speech by Joschka Fischer, May 10, 1999, in Presse- und Informationsamt der Bundesregierung, *Bulletin,* May 26, 1999, p. 335.
47. Rudolf Scharping, "Die Kosovo-Krise wirkt wie ein Katalysator," *Frankfurter Allgemeine Zeitung,* March 24, 2000, p. 12.
48. See Karsten D. Voigt, coordinator for German-American cooperation, foreign ministry, "The Discussion of a European Security and Defence Policy: Labor Pains of a New Atlanticism," speech on March 8, 2000, in Washington, D.C.
49. See Christoph Bertram, "Partnerschaft und Divergenz. Die amerikanische Außenpolitik und die Zukunft der transatlantischen Beziehungen," in *Weltmacht ohne Gegner: Amerikanische Außenpolitik zu Beginn des 21. Jahrhunderts,* ed. Peter Rudolf and Jürgen Wilzewski (Baden-Baden: Nomos, 2000), pp. 395–400.

CHAPTER NINE

A Force for Good in the World? Britain's Role in the Kosovo Crisis

Louise Richardson

Britain was not only an enthusiastic supporter of the NATO action in Kosovo, but its prime minister, Tony Blair, soon assumed the role of the leading hawk in the West. Far from being a case of the United States imposing its will on its European ally, it was the British leadership that repeatedly maneuvered to strengthen U.S. resolve. More specifically, throughout the military campaign Britain argued relentlessly that the allies had to consider the option of sending in ground troops to evict the Serbs from Kosovo and to enable the return of the ethnic Albanians. The new Labour government, with its leaner, meaner army, its focus on force projection, and its oft-stated determination to reassert the ethical dimension in foreign policy, could be expected to support an effort to avert a humanitarian catastrophe in Kosovo. It is more difficult to understand why Britain would actually try to lead this effort, albeit rhetorically, not militarily.

Experiences in Bosnia, the Gulf, and elsewhere had persuaded the United States that Europeans would always have to be dragged along reluctantly. But this image never quite fit Britain. In light of the postwar history of British foreign policy it should not have come as a surprise that Britain would try to take a lead in Kosovo. The claims that it was Margaret Thatcher who stiffened the spine of President George Bush at their meeting in Denver after the Iraqi invasion of Kuwait are probably exaggerated.[1] But it is clear that in the Falklands War in 1982 the British took the lead and insisted on perceiving in the Argentine invasion of the Malvinas a test of the moral fiber of the West. It was the United States that had to be dragged rather reluctantly along. Earlier, in the Suez crisis in 1956, Britain tried to take the lead in standing up to what it perceived to be a case of aggression by Nasser, though in this instance it was brought swiftly to heel by President Eisenhower and a weakening pound.

The British Hawk

Britain was in no position to take a military lead in Kosovo, but the British prime minister led the charge on the issue of ground troops. Even before the fighting, the British argued that it would be necessary to plan a military invasion of Kosovo. Indeed, Britain already had such a plan.[2] British officials were convinced that the Americans consistently undermined the position of the West, both during the negotiations at Rambouillet, by failing to make credible threats to use force, and subsequently throughout the bombing campaign, by failing to prepare a ground invasion.

During the Rambouillet conference the British found that American efforts with the ethnic Albanians hindered the peace efforts. One official put it this way: "The American effort was to get to the end with the Serbs as the baddies."[3] Meanwhile the Serbs never quite realized how serious the threat from the West was. Another British official commented: "The Serbs were still laboring under misapprehension. They thought five cruise missiles would come floating down the road, and that was it. Even when I spoke to the Yugoslav minister in London to reiterate the threat, he still had not taken it on board. He said 'Two cruise missiles will not make us bow.'"[4] Prime Minister Blair clearly believed this too. Clare Short, the development secretary, describes Blair as saying: "Milosevic thinks he can get away with it, he is playing a game. He thinks we are unwilling to act. If he thought there was real steel in the threat he wouldn't get away with it."[5] This was essentially the same position the prime minister took throughout the crisis. Blair blamed the American reluctance to countenance the use of ground troops, not Milosevic's capacity for self-delusion, for the fact that the Serbs underestimated the determination of the West.

The clumsy handling of the Rambouillet conference by the Americans subsequently led many of the allies to feel that they had been manipulated by the United States, that they were not "forced allies" but rather "manipulated allies."[6] This interpretation appears to have received support from an unlikely source, Secretary of State Madeleine Albright, who said publicly of the conference: "Signing Rambouillet was crucial in getting the Europeans two things. Getting them to agree to the use of force and getting the Albanians on the side of this kind of an agreement."[7] The argument is that the United States never intended to reach agreement there but rather simply intended to attain international legitimacy for a military strike against Milosevic. American actions at Rambouillet are not inconsistent with this interpretation. No leader of the Serbs could possibly accept the terms presented to them, which were significantly harsher than those imposed after the bombing campaign. The insistence on NATO authority in Kosovo as well as the promise of a settlement based upon the wishes of the inhabitants in three years were both anathema to the Serbs, and they were both relinquished in the peace accords reached after the bombing campaign.[8] In particular, the eleventh-hour addition of a military clause insisting upon NATO access to all of Yugoslavia and the lack of public disclosure of this clause have generated suspicion that the agreement was designed to be rejected.[9]

This interpretation, while plausible, implies more clarity of thought and precision of execution than was evident in the conduct of American diplomacy at the time. It appears more likely that the American delegation, having convinced themselves, as they repeatedly said, that force was the only language understood by Milosevic, were convinced that Rambouillet would not work and fully expected to have to use force against him. Their conduct of the negotiations at Rambouillet then became a self-fulfilling prophecy, but it was not a case of self-conscious manipulation of their allies.

It also soon became apparent that the American officials vastly underestimated the amount of force needed to induce Milosevic to capitulate. Both Serbs and Americans were in agreement in expecting that the Serbian refusal to sign the Rambouillet accords would lead to a brief bombing campaign. The Serbs believed that the Alliance would not have the cohesion to be able to agree on more than that. The Americans believed that a brief, three-day campaign was all it would take to ensure Yugoslav compliance. Both were proven tragically wrong. The British believed that by failing to demonstrate resolve by ruling out a ground invasion, the Americans enabled the Serbs to withstand the bombing campaign.

The pattern persisted after Rambouillet. On the very day that Richard Holbrooke flew to Belgrade for the final meeting with the Yugoslav leader, Secretary Albright and Defense Secretary William Cohen were promising the American electorate that it would escalate no further. British officials described the comments as "not helpful." Former National Security Adviser Brent Scowcroft, elaborated: "It was a terrible military statement. If you tell Milosevic we're not going to put ground forces in, that makes him even more determined to ride out a bombing campaign."[10]

On March 24, President Clinton asserted in a televised address to the nation: "I do not intend to put our troops in Kosovo to fight a war." The British were joined by many American columnists in arguing that this was a mistake. Once the commitment was taken to fight Milosevic, Clinton's critics claimed, there was no acceptable alternative to NATO victory, and since ground troops might be required to achieve this goal, it was unwise to rule them out. They argued that knowing he would not have to face ground troops would help Milosevic withstand the air war. National Security Adviser Samuel Berger, who had written the key sentence in Clinton's speech, later explained why he did so: "[T]he American people would not have supported the war without European participation, and we never could have gotten all 19 allies on board at the outset if they thought we had any plan to use ground forces."[11] Two months later, on May 18, with the outcome of the bombing campaign still very much in doubt, President Clinton changed his tune, while characteristically denying that he was doing so. He said: "I don't think that we or our allies should take any options off the table, and that has been my position from the beginning."[12] This line was used repeatedly by Prime Minister Blair and his foreign secretary, Robin Cook, to refute allegations in the press and in the Commons of a rift in the Anglo-American alliance.

Berger was right in pointing to the hesitation of others in the Alliance on the use of ground troops. The biggest concern was that Germany might veto their use. Chancellor Gerhard Schroeder made little effort to hide his annoyance at British suggestions on the use of ground troops. He told a press conference at NATO headquarters: "I will not participate in this specifically British debate on war theory."[13] He argued that since the Bundestag was unanimous in its opposition, change in NATO strategy was "impossible." He pointed out: "The strategy of an alliance can only be changed if all the parties agree, so I trust that NATO's strategy is not going to change."[14] Schroeder went on to blame Britain for rifts in NATO unity. For the chancellor, who led a Red-Green coalition, it was a significant achievement to make these two parties agree to any military action at all. Schroeder was much more supportive of the operation in private than he could afford to be in public, and officials later confided that he was prepared to take on the challenge of rallying his government in support of ground troops if necessary, albeit with a limited German involvement.[15] The Italians shared the German position and the Greeks were even less enthusiastic. French officials privately expressed their mystification at Britain's permitting itself to be isolated by pushing for such a manifestly unpopular option.[16]

The British position, however, was not completely consistent. In March the defense secretary, George Robertson, had told British troops stationed in Macedonia that they would not have to "fight their way" into Kosovo.[17] He was criticized for this little-noticed statement, but he claimed that he had made it to maintain troop morale. He argued, moreover, that he was only stating the obvious, that it would have required an enormous effort to launch an opposed invasion, a fact that Milosevic was quite capable of figuring out for himself.[18] Nevertheless, from the summer of 1998, the British government publicly adhered firmly to the view that the resolution of the conflict in Kosovo would require the threat of force and the willingness to use force, even ground troops.[19]

In the House of Commons the day after Schroeder's press conference, the prime minister insisted that there were no rifts in the Alliance and that he agreed with Chancellor Schroeder that the current strategy was working. Paddy Ashdown, the leader of the Liberal Democrats, was free to say what the prime minister believed but could not say publicly: "By ruling out, as NATO did, the use of ground troops at the beginning, we left ourselves with only one means to prosecute the war and that was bombing. If bombing does not succeed, then we will leave ourselves only one means to prosecute peace and that is compromise."[20]

Speaking in Chicago on the eve of the NATO Summit, Blair assumed the mantle of leading hawk. He called for a "doctrine of international community" that would qualify the long-standing principle of noninterference. He argued that threats to international peace and security require intervention if they meet five conditions:

1 Is the international community certain it is in the right?
2 Have all diplomatic solutions been tried and exhausted?
3 Would military action be prudent and practical?
4 Could the military powers endure a long campaign to the finish?
5 Are national interests involved?

Blair also called for reforms in NATO and U.N. decision-making and for a Marshall Plan for the Balkans. On Kosovo, he insisted, in true Churchillian fashion, that "success is the only exit strategy I am prepared to consider."[21] This was quite a radical speech, greeted with derision at home and alarm abroad. As it turned out, the speech was overshadowed by the NATO Summit and the war itself, but it provides an indication of just how far ahead of the debate the British prime minister was to be found.

Deeply concerned that the NATO fiftieth-anniversary summit would be marred by disunity, President Clinton encouraged NATO secretary-general Javier Solana to remove the topic of ground troops from the table by offering to make arrangements to consider it elsewhere. At a dinner meeting on the eve of the summit, Blair tried to convince Clinton of the need to start contingency planning for a ground invasion. Clinton's goal was to maintain Alliance unity, which required preventing discussion of the divisive issue of ground troops. He persuaded Blair to stop talking publicly about an invasion because of the domestic problems it caused for European allies and because it undermined the Russians' willingness to help out diplomatically. In return Clinton agreed to allow NATO to update existing contingency plans.[22] Rumors of a rift in the Alliance were temporarily muted.

By mid-May the newspapers were again carrying constant accounts of differences between the United States and Britain. Both governments denied that there was any disagreement between them while at the same time publicly being quoted as saying quite different things. The U.S. defense secretary, William Cohen, insisted at a visit to a Louisiana air base that an air war was all that was needed to prevail over Serb forces. The same day the British foreign secretary, Robin Cook, in a series of radio and television interviews in the United States, refused to endorse the view that an air campaign alone could achieve NATO's objectives.[23] While agreeing on the ultimate objective—*Serbs out, NATO in, Refugees back*—there was a definite difference of emphasis. For the United States the emphasis was on the need to hold the Alliance together. For the British the emphasis was on not losing, and on being prepared to use ground troops to ensure that NATO did not lose. Both sides insisted publicly that any disagreements were completely overblown. Privately, however, Blair complained of "a deep sense of frustration" with Clinton's unwillingness to commit ground forces, and British officials expressed "a growing sense of frustration with the Clinton administration's intransigence."[24]

President Clinton's elliptical statement on May 24 that all options remained on the table enabled the Alliance to paper over the disagreements, at least until the period right before the Yugoslav surrender, when the allies finally were persuaded that a ground invasion should be prepared. On May 27 the defense ministers of the United States, Britain, France, Germany, and Italy met secretly in Bonn.[25] They were told by General Clark that a ground invasion would require 150,000 troops. George Robertson was familiar with the plans and argued the imperative of making immediate preparations in order to be able to act before the onset of winter. He argued that it would have to start by September 15. One of the participants described American defense secretary William Cohen as turning to Robertson and asking: "Well, how many troops are you prepared to commit?"

Robertson calmly replied, "Fifty thousand."

The participant describes a sharp intake of breath around the room, followed by a long silence. Then Cohen followed up: "For how long?"

"For as long as it takes," Robertson replied.[26]

The willingness of the British government to commit essentially its entire army to the operation showed that its position was more than political grandstanding. On May 31, four days after the secret meeting and three days before Milosevic conceded defeat, President Clinton gave General Clark permission to prepare for a ground invasion. Many officials believe that it was knowledge of this decision, leaked to him by the Russians, that was the crucial factor in forcing Milosevic to come to terms. More likely it was one of several factors, not least the costs of the intensification of the bombing campaign, the diplomatic pressure from Russia, and the terms offered by Viktor Chernomyrdin and Martti Ahtisaari that, while far from ideal, were considerably better than those available to him at Rambouillet.

The strength of the British commitment to the Kosovo campaign had been tested as the air war dragged on longer than anticipated. Initially the government committed just under 20,000 troops to KFOR, while 7,000 more British troops were stationed in Albania and Macedonia. Then Britain indicated its willingness to commit 50,000 to a 150,000-strong invasion force, which would have been the largest troop commitment since the Second World War.[27] Given the other standing commitments of the British army, a Kosovo force of this magnitude would have required essentially every available soldier and would have put an extraordinary strain on the military. Letters calling up 30,000 reservists had already been prepared for mailing.[28] There can be little doubt that the Labour government was deeply committed to the cause.

Explanations for the British Position

There are a number of possible explanations for British enthusiasm compared with American hesitation, German equivocation, and the downright skepticism of the Italians and Greeks. Prime Minister Blair described his own position: "The bottom line for me was we can't lose this. [...] I had a view, which was that we started it, and we had to see it through and finish it and win it."[29] There are broadly three types of explanations—strategic, domestic, and moral—for Britain's and particularly Blair's assumption of the leadership role in the NATO campaign. Strategic explanations are: the credibility of NATO, the "special relationship" as the cornerstone of postwar British foreign policy, and Britain's need to stake a claim to the leadership of European defense. Domestic considerations included the Labour government's interest in demonstrating that it was strong on defense, the need to showcase the new strategic concept set out in the Strategic Defence Review, and the intent to show that the prime minister was as skilled in foreign policy as he was domestically. The motivation could also have been moral; it could simply have been that participation in the war against Milosevic was the right thing to do. A final and pragmatic explanation is that somebody had to take the lead and Britain was the only government in a position to do so.

Strategic Explanations

NATO credibility. Tony Blair clearly believed the credibility of NATO to be at stake in Kosovo and that this fact alone required British participation in the effort against Milosevic. "I always used to go back to question, if we didn't act, then what? Then he ethnic cleanses [sic] Kosovo, and the whole region really is then totally destabilized. Europe and NATO are shown to be powerless, and a terrible act of barbarity has taken place with nothing happening from the international community. [...] I think the consequences would have been really immense, on the credibility of NATO, and on world stability."[30] Blair was concerned that if NATO were to fail to act, or to fail to see the campaign through to a victorious conclusion, despots the world over would soon challenge NATO authority. "Then the next time, say, if Saddam gets out of his box or somebody like that, and we say that we are going to take action, people would say, well, prove it."[31] This was a powerful argument that Blair constantly made to President Clinton, insisting that the bottom line was that NATO could not lose. Declaring NATO credibility to be at stake of course was one way of ensuring that NATO credibility was on the line.

Another possible approach, favored by some in Washington, was to downplay the entire incident as involving a little-known, faraway place. Having once committed NATO air power to extract a capitulation from the Yugoslav leader, however, this option became more difficult to sustain. The mass exodus of refugees also made it more difficult to declare victory and go home, as some might have been inclined to do. The importance of maintaining the credibility of NATO is an adequate explanation for British involvement in the air campaign but is not sufficient to explain the British assumption of a leadership role. While British security was undoubtedly based on the continuance of NATO, this equally true of other allies, yet they did not emulate the hawkish stance of the British government.

The special relationship. This term is no longer heard in Whitehall, having been banned from the lexicon of New Labour. Britain's role in the Kosovo crisis nevertheless demonstrated once again, and quite unequivocally, that the "special relationship" between the United States and Britain is alive and well. This term, attributed to Winston Churchill, initially referred to the extraordinary Allied cooperation during the Second World War. The Blair government made clear from the outset that it wished to retain close links with the United States, to retain the special relationship (in fact if not in name). For Blair, neither his efforts to end Britain's isolation from Europe nor his efforts to revamp European defense were in any way antithetical to good relations between the United States and the United Kingdom: "Stronger with one means stronger with the other. [...] We are the bridge between the U.S. and Europe. Let us use it."[32]

The special relationship has survived the advent to power of the successor generation with no memory of World War II and the dilution of the European focus of the American elite. It has survived, first, simply because the two countries with similar liberal traditions have tended to see the world in a similar way. Second, it has survived because of the transnational ties that emerged at subgovernmental levels due to involvement in the same international institutions and the sharing of military technology. Above all, it endures because it has served the interests of successive executives in both capitals. For the United States the special relationship has served to legitimize American action overseas by casting on these actions a veneer of multilateralism. The special relationship has allowed successive British governments to exercise more influence on the global scene than an objective assessment of Britain's capabilities might warrant, or, to use the boxing analogy favored by the Blair administration, to punch above their weight. Both of these interests were in evidence in the Kosovo crisis, as they had been in the Gulf War before it.

In the Gulf War of 1990, the British contributed less than 6 percent of allied troops against Saddam Hussein. But it served the interests of both the United States and Britain for Britain to play a leadership role publicly. As in the Gulf War, the British military commitment in Kosovo was not large compared with the American commitment, but it was, crucially, larger than that of other European allies. Britain contributed about 8 percent of NATO forces, compared with about 80 percent from the United States. Britain snagged the key public relations roles with NATO spokesman Jamie Shea, a nightly television fixture, quietly bolstered by the importation of media handlers from Downing Street and Washington. Later, the British commander of KFOR, General Sir Michael Jackson, became the military voice from the ground. The more elusive American general, Wesley Clark, was kept away from the cameras as he waged his virtual war from SHAPE headquarters in Belgium.[33] As in the Gulf War, the British were able to translate a relatively modest military contribution into an enormous political asset because it served the desire of Britain to punch above its weight and of the United States for multilateral legitimacy.

Throughout the Kosovo crisis the British displayed the same skills they had used in earlier crises to ensure that they got their way in Washington.[34] When the direct link to the White House was not proving successful, indirect links were tried. For example, Tony Blair put pressure on Hillary Clinton during a charitable trip to London, and Robin Cook lobbied key members of Congress, met with the editorial boards of powerful newspapers, and appealed directly to the U.S. public in a wide-ranging series of media interviews.

Even more important, the British identified those within the U.S. administration, particularly the military, who agreed with them, and helped them to make their case. A NATO military planning cell, meeting in London, had drawn up in June 1998 a secret plan, called Bravo Minus, for an opposed ground invasion of Kosovo involving more than 170,000 troops, including 50,000 British soldiers. After the campaign started, NATO's supreme commander, General Wesley Clark, launched secret planning for a ground invasion, relying heavily on the earlier British plans. Throughout, Clark argued to the skeptical national security adviser and defense secretary that the air campaign might not work and that contingency plans for a ground invasion were necessary. While American officials were optimistic that the air war would be over quickly, the British preferred to plan on the basis of a worst-case scenario.[35] Realizing that Clark was on their side, Downing Street took the remarkable step of permitting Clark to receive details of private telephone conversations between Prime Minister Blair and President Clinton. This was in an effort to ensure that he understood their positions perfectly and that he did not receive a doctored account from internal American sources.[36] This success in intervening in the internal debates within an allied government is a hallmark of the alliance politics practiced by Britain in its relations with the United States.

Far from being a forced alliance, the experience of Britain in the Kosovo conflict indicated that it entered the Alliance willingly and pragmatically. It served the long-standing British interest in having, in Churchill's words, "a place at the top table," or in Blair's rendition, "to punch above our weight." The experience of the war and the severe strain it placed and could have placed on the British armed forces indicate that even this cannot indefinitely be done on the cheap, as it has in the past. British participation in the Kosovo campaign is consistent with the special relationship, which required that Britain participate more fully and more enthusiastically than the other NATO allies. The core of the special relationship is the British claim, usually implicit, that they are the one ally who can always be counted on in the crunch. The special relationship, however, certainly did not require that Britain be more enthusiastic than the United States. Nor did it require that Britain try to force the hand of the United States as Blair repeatedly tried to do. Britain employed the mores of the special relationship not simply to support its ally but to induce the United States to share the British view of the importance of defeating Milosevic.

Taking the lead in Europe. Another possible explanation for the position Britain took in the Kosovo conflict is that the U.K. government seized the opportunity to stake its claim to the leadership of a key aspect of European integration, defense. Prime Minister Blair, himself a Europhile, opted for this position, the argument goes, having experienced some hesitation on the prospect of Britain joining the single European currency and in the wake of interminable acrimonious disputes over red meat and red tape. There is something to this argument. In May 1998, a Foreign Office diplomat,

Robert Cooper, prepared a confidential memorandum on maximizing the potential of the United Kingdom's future in Europe. A key recommendation of the influential report was that Britain exploit its military assets to develop a European capacity to act independently in the field of defense.[37] The plan, first announced at the EU summit in October 1998, was soon embraced by the French at Saint-Malo and then endorsed by EU leaders in Cologne and Helsinki. The plan had the added advantage of being popular with the British electorate, who, according to public opinion polls, are more in favor of cooperation in defense and foreign policy than in economic affairs.[38]

It is plausible that the British government took the position it did in Kosovo to assert its claim to leadership in the one area of European integration still in need of a leader and the one area in which Britain was best poised to lead. But this argument cannot explain why Britain went so far out in front of the others on Kosovo. Indeed it could be argued that Britain hurt its claim to leadership by insisting on an unpopular position and sticking to it in spite of all the domestic difficulties encountered by her European allies. If Britain's point was to lead Europe, then Britain would surely have been advocating the European position instead of advocating a British position that was not shared either in the EU capitals or in Washington.

Indeed the causal arrow appears to go in the opposite direction. The Kosovo crisis had a major impact on Britain's support for a European Security and Defense Identity. The Labour government was appalled to discover the scale of European dependence on the U.S. military. After the crisis, the Blair government became an ardent advocate for a more effective and independent European defense capability. After the air war, in summer 1999, Foreign Secretary Robin Cook observed that Britain must press her European allies to "professionalize and restructure" their armies to respond quickly to the next humanitarian crisis. In effect, other European governments were urged to conduct a strategic defense review along the lines of the British one, with an emphasis on more mobile forces and rapid reaction. Mr. Cook argued: "We have two million men and women under arms, yet we struggle to get 2.5 percent of them to provide a peacekeeping force in Kosovo. [...] Across the nations of Europe we spend 60 percent of the budget of the Pentagon, yet it is not at all clear we produce 60 percent of their output."[39] It would appear, therefore, that rather than using the Kosovo crisis to stake a claim to leadership of European defense, the experience galvanized the British to revive this claim and assert it vigorously.

Domestic Political Explanations

Countering Labour's perceived weakness on defense. The arguments that British participation in the Kosovo campaign and the assumption of a leadership position in that campaign can best be explained by domestic political imperatives are generally less persuasive. The first argument is that the government opted to take a strong line on Kosovo in order to eradicate an electoral liability, namely the view that Labour was weak on defense. In 1997 the party won its first general election since 1979. The Blair government came into office with an enormous electoral majority and with a determination to find a "third way" in domestic and international affairs. Defense had not been an issue in the 1997 election. Ever since the days of Labour support for nuclear disarmament the party was seen as vulnerable on defense. The Conservative Party had exploited this weakness in the 1982 and 1987 elections and, to a lesser extent, in 1992. For the first time since 1979, the Tories were actually seen as vulnerable on defense in 1997. Cuts in defense spending had led to low morale and underrecruitment in the armed forces, along with military overstretch and cost overruns. The Labour Party, no doubt conscious of its strong negatives on the defense question, decided not to try to take advantage of Conservative vulnerability on the issue, so defense was largely ignored in the 1997 campaign.

Undermining the view that Labour was soft on defense was undoubtedly an added bonus of involvement in Kosovo. This fact was probably not lost at the time in Labour Party headquarters, but there is no evidence that this factor influenced the government. The Labour Party had an enormous popular mandate, which suggested that the public either shared its views on defense or was relatively uninterested in them. In either case, embarking on a high-risk foreign venture was more likely to endanger that support than taking a safer, more moderate stance.

Showcasing the Strategic Defence Review. Much the same can be said of the related argument that the government's action was driven by a desire to showcase the strategic defense initiative. In the *Strategic Defence Review*, published in July 1998, the Labour government sought to move away from their predecessors' "crisis-management style" of foreign policy and to provide the basis for a coherent, long-term defense program that would be appropriate to the post–Cold War world. By 1997 the defense budget as a percentage of GDP was the lowest in the century, while the armed forces were smaller than at any point since the 1930s. Although the review was not as radical as promised, it went some distance toward adapting the British forces to their post–Cold War tasks, with an increase in power projection capabilities and improvements in strategic mobility. The fundamentals of British defense planning remained unchanged, with Europe and NATO remaining central elements, but new security risks were highlighted, such as ethnic and population pressures, terrorism, and drugs. Finally, considerable emphasis was placed on support services because of the belief that forces might be used on a more regular basis and maintained in theater for a long time.

Even after the review there remained a gap between Britain's international aspirations and its defense resources. Nevertheless the review was designed to permit the United Kingdom to respond expeditiously to precisely the type of crisis that occurred in Kosovo. The campaign confirmed the underlying assumptions of the review, but it also demonstrated its inadequacies by making even greater claims on military resources than the review anticipated. While the *Strategic Defence Review* enabled the government to participate more effectively in Operation Allied Force, it cannot reasonably be credited with influencing the decision to become involved.

Domestic politics. A stronger domestic explanation is that Tony Blair, a consummately political prime minister, was driven by a desire to ensure his popularity. This explanation for the government's participation in Operation Allied Force and for the prime minister's effort to lead this campaign was most frequently articulated in the opinion pages of the *Daily Telegraph*.[40] The argument is that Blair's role as the enthusiastic but constrained cobelligerent served his domestic political ambitions. If the war went well, he could claim vindication. If things went badly, it would permit him to argue that if only his advice had been followed and ground troops sent in sooner, then the war would have been won—a no-lose strategy for the prime minister.

Unlike several of his Alliance counterparts, Blair was in the happy position of not having to balance domestic considerations against Alliance commitments at the time of the Kosovo campaign. The British commitment of forces to Kosovo was popular both with public opinion and with the other political parties. Traditionally in Britain it has been the Labour Party that has opposed the use of force. The party's support for the Gulf War in 1991 had prompted a small internal rebellion, but if there was opposition to the Kosovo air war within the Labour Party, it remained quiet. The war was left in the hands of the triumvirate of Blair, Cook, and Robertson. Blair imposed an unprecedented degree of discipline on the parliamentary party that ensured that any internal opposition would be suppressed.

The Conservative Party did not want to give credit to the government but could not be seen as opposing the country's troops, so it gave sullen support to the government. The Liberal Democratic leader Paddy Ashdown even accused the Tories of wanting the NATO policy to fail so the Tory party could take political credit.[41] The prime minister skillfully exploited their discomfort. When the opposition leaped on the bombing of the Chinese embassy as an excuse to criticize NATO strategy, the prime minister and foreign secretary, sounding more Tory than the Tories, worried aloud about the impact on the men in the field of hearing criticism from home. The Conservatives were outraged by this questioning of their patriotism but were outmaneuvered.[42] Half the respondents to a poll in the *Sunday Telegraph* branded the Conservative criticism of the government "unpatriotic."[43] There can be little doubt that the position taken by each party served its political purposes. The Tory position enabled the opposition, if the war went badly, to claim that the prime minister was a reckless adventurer who committed British lives before thinking things through.

Public opinion polls are not consistent with the view that the Labour government policy on Kosovo was driven by domestic political considerations. The government and the prime minister's handling of the crisis received high praise throughout, but Blair's eagerness to explore the option of deploying ground troops was not shared by the British public. In March 62 percent of those polled disagreed with the statement that Britain should send ground troops into the conflict. Only 26 percent agreed. In April the figures were 43 and 47 percent respectively. Other polls pointed in the same direction. In a poll conducted just a few days after the bombing began, public support was two to one in favor.[44] By the end of April the support had risen from 58 percent to 72 percent. By mid-May it was 67 percent.[45] Polls also indicate that the British public was far from keen on expending British lives on Kosovo. When asked how many British lives would be worth losing to protect the ethnic Albanians in Kosovo, in March 56 percent, in April 57 percent, and in May 45 percent said none. Others indicated very low numbers or "don't know."[46] Thus it seems that Prime Minister Blair was leading rather than following his public, just as he was ahead of his allies, in his support of NATO's Kosovo campaign. Blair's role in the conflict was popular with the British public, but neither his participation in that campaign nor his effort to lead it can reasonably be attributed to domestic political considerations.

Moral Explanations

The right thing to do: the third way in foreign policy. The architects of the victory of New Labour in the 1997 British general election argued that the election heralded the advent of a third way in British politics. Shortly after taking office, the new foreign secretary, Robin Cook, articulated in a speech what the third way would mean for British foreign policy, setting out four goals. The first two, security and prosperity, would have been shared by any of his predecessors. The next two, the environment and the ethical dimension, were more novel and revealed the link with Labour's left-wing past. Mr. Cook described the fourth goal as "to secure the respect of other nations for Britain's contribution to keeping the peace of the world and promoting democracy around the world." He went on to say that the mission statement "supplies an ethical content to foreign policy and recognizes that the national interest cannot be defined only by narrow *realpolitik*."[47]

Mr. Cook concluded his speech with the exhortation to make Britain once again "a force for good in the world." This was a phrase that appeared time and again in the speeches of Prime Minister Blair and his foreign secretary. It was used both to articulate a goal of British foreign policy and as a description of American foreign policy. In November 1997 the prime minister said of the United States: "Leaving all sentiment aside, they are a force for good in the world. They can always be relied on when the chips are down. The same should always be true of Britain."[48] Over a year later he used the same words: "I also believe America at its best is a powerful force for good in the world; one of a few countries willing and able to stand up for what it believes."[49] The ethical dimension to the new government's foreign policy therefore was both an end in itself and a link to the United States.

Given the early and emphatic imposition of an ethical dimension on British foreign policy, it was fairly clear how the Labour government would be inclined to respond when faced with a humanitarian crisis. This inclination can only have been more acutely felt in light of the painful realization that this ethical dimension had not been much in evidence in the earlier Bosnian crisis. The crisis in Kosovo presented an opportunity to demonstrate that Britain was in fact a force for good in the world. The trauma of the Second World War has been a guiding analogy for all postwar British prime ministers, for whom *never again* meant *"Never again* should we appease dictators." The analogy was invoked by Eden against Nasser, by Thatcher against Galtieri, by Major against Saddam Hussein. But for a new generation of leaders, World War II and *never again* have meant something different. The analogy is no longer Munich and 1939 but rather the discovery of death camps and the apparatus of genocide. So when this group says *never again,* they mean: *"Never again* will we permit genocide to happen on our doorstep."

Blair clearly saw himself as operating in the long tradition of liberal intervention and enjoyed the comparisons made with Gladstone's outrage at the Bulgarian atrocities of the 1870s. He saw himself as motivated by moral outrage but not the type of outrage that had motivated Margaret Thatcher in the Falklands War. Then the prime minister linked the war with calls for national renewal, calls to make Britain great again. The "son of Thatcher" made no such calls. Instead he spoke constantly of the horrors inflicted on the ethnic Albanians and made a number of visits to refugee camps to see the evidence of these horrors firsthand. In his speech on March 26 asking for public support, he argued: "We are doing what is right, for Britain, for

Europe, for a world that must know that barbarity cannot be allowed to defeat justice."[50]

The one explanation that can account both for British participation in the campaign and for Britain taking on the role of chief hawk is the moral argument, that Blair was motivated by the belief that it was, as he put it, simply the right thing to do. It is obviously true that it is easier to do the right thing when one's power is secure. With a comfortable majority in the House of Commons and a commanding lead over the Conservatives in opinion polls, Blair enjoyed greater security of tenure than any of his allied partners. Moreover, unlike President Clinton, he enjoyed complete control over his legislature. Nevertheless, there is nothing to suggest that domestic considerations dictated his positions. As his biographer John Rentoul said: "He's an extremely cautious politician, but he hasn't acted like it. It must be deepseated, genuine moral conviction. He didn't need to do this."[51] War leaders invariably invoke moral arguments to cloak realpolitik designs. Britain fought two world wars to maintain the balance of power in Europe but sought to legitimize the commitment and mobilize support by invoking the plight of the "gallant little Belgians" and later the Poles. This time in his statement asking the public's support the prime minister spoke in terms of standing up for justice and defending the innocent against their evil oppressors.[52]

Undoubtedly, there were national interests at stake in Kosovo, first and foremost the credibility of NATO, but also stability in the Balkans. Demonstrating commitment to both the special relationship with the United States and the European ideal were also clear-cut national interests. All of these interests could have been served, as could the government's domestic interests, by being a loyal participant in Operation Allied Force. But Britain did more. Britain self-consciously assumed the role of leading hawk, and in so doing put some of these interests at risk. Had the Alliance refused to commit ground troops and had Milosevic refused to buckle, a compromise would have been necessary. By raising the stakes with moralizing rhetoric, Blair arguably put some of these interests in jeopardy. Such a compromise, which was at least conceivable, would have been deeply damaging both to British national interests and to Blair's domestic interests, all the more so because of the uncompromising position taken by the prime minister. It appears then that the leadership position Britain assumed in the Kosovo crisis can be understood only in the context of the prime minister's conviction that it was simply "the right thing to do."

Conclusion

When asked why Britain assumed the position of leadership in the campaign against Milosevic, one senior British cabinet minister replied with an explanation not yet mentioned. Displaying the pragmatism that has long marked the conduct of British foreign policy, he said simply: "Well, somebody had to and nobody else could. The American administration was preoccupied with the Lewinsky affair. The Germans couldn't, they were doing more than ever before. The French always have this difficult role. So there was nobody else."[53] This too is a plausible explanation, but it cannot quite account for the passion and energy of the prime minister in driving his counterparts to consider an option that would have been enormously difficult for them domestically.

There is very rarely a monocausal explanation for a complicated political decision. Instead politicians, like others, make decisions for a variety of reasons, some more self-interested than others. Having made a decision, they can usually find many other reasons to support it. To argue as I have done that the assumption of the role of leading hawk can be understood only if one accepts that Blair was driven by moral conviction is not to suggest that moral conviction is enough to explain his actions. Absent the many key strategic interests involved, moral outrage alone would not have induced the government to incur the costs Britain was prepared to incur in Kosovo, as any Rwandan can attest. The prime minister himself understood that the strategic and moral considerations were mutually reinforcing: "There were big strategic interests that would have justified intervention in their own right. But I felt that this was the closest thing to racial genocide that I've seen in Europe since the Second World War. I didn't feel that we could simply stand aside from that if we had the means, which we did, to intervene and stop it."[54] Britain's participation in Operation Allied Force was entirely in keeping with the principle and practice of British foreign policy since the Second World War. The British assumption of the role of the leading hawk of the Alliance can be understood only as a combination of the determination that allied force would remain a strong and credible force and that it would indeed serve, at least on occasion, as a force for good in the world.

Notes

1. See accounts in Margaret Thatcher, *The Downing Street Years* (New York: HarperCollins, 1993), pp. 816–22; George Bush quoted in Michael R. Gordon and Bernard E. Trainor, *The General's War: The Inside Story of the Conflict in the Gulf* (Boston: Little, Brown and Company, 1995), p. 49.
2. "Kosovo: The Untold Story," *Observer,* July 18, 1999, p. 13.
3. Ibid.
4. Ibid.
5. Ibid.

6. Alex MacLeod suggested this term at a panel discussion of several of the papers contained in this volume at the International Studies Association conference in Los Angeles, March 2000.
7. Quoted in Elaine Sciolino and Ethan Bronner, "Crisis in the Balkans: The Road to War," *New York Times*, April 18, 1999.
8. For a comparison of the Rambouillet agreement and the peace accords, see Barry R. Posen, "The War for Kosovo: Serbia's Political-Military Strategy," *International Security* 24 (spring 2000): pp. 79–81. For other accounts of the Rambouillet conference and its relationship to the military campaign, see Marc Weller, "The Rambouillet Conference on Kosovo," *International Affairs* 75 (April 1999): pp. 211–52; and Michael MccGwire, "Why did we bomb Belgrade?" *International Affairs* 76 (January 2000): pp. 1–24.
9. For an example of this line of argument, see Robert Fisk, "The Trojan Horse that 'Started' a 79-Day War," *The Independent,* November 26, 1999, p. 20. The clause in question is appendix (b), paragraph 8. For the full text of the Rambouillet agreement, see http://www.state.gov/www/regions/eur/ksvo_rambouillet_text.html.
10. "Kosovo: The Untold Story," *Observer,* July 18, 1999, p. 13.
11. Quoted in R. W. Apple, "A Domestic Sort with Global Worries," *New York Times,* August 25, 1999, p. 1.
12. Ibid.
13. Quoted in the *Daily Telegraph,* May 20, 1999, p. 18.
14. Ibid.
15. Interview with author, June 2000; the involvement would have been limited to the provision of field hospitals.
16. *Daily Telegraph,* May 19, 1999, p. 15.
17. Michael Evans, "Britain's troops train for peace role," *The Times* (London), March 3, 1999. *Daily Telegraph,* March 3, 1999, p. 14.
18. Interview with author, senior Ministry of Defense official, April 2000.
19. *Frontline* interview with Ivo Daalder, available at: http://www.pbs.org/wgbh/pages/frontline/shows/kosovo/interviews/daalder.html.
20. Quoted in *The Scotsman,* May 20, 1999, p. 13.
21. For accounts of this speech to the Economic Club of Chicago, see the *Scotsman*, the *Financial Times,* and the *Independent,* April 23, 1999.
22. Dana Priest, "A Decisive Battle That Never Was," *Washington Post,* September 19, 1999. For an account of this meeting, see also *Frontline* interview with Ivo Daalder, loc. cit.
23. John Morrison, "British-U.S. Rift Rumors Grow," *Toronto Star,* May 18, 1999.
24. Jonathan Carr-Brown and Stephen Grey, "Blair Frustrated Over Clinton's War Strategy," *Sunday Times,* May 16, 1999.
25. Steven Lee Myers, "Crisis in the Balkans: Strategy," *New York Times,* May 29, 1999. There were considerable recriminations about the leaking of the details of the conference, from which the smaller NATO allies were not happy to have been excluded. Robertson was blamed but forcibly denied that he was responsible for the leak.
26. Author interview with participant, April 2000.

27. All 50,000 might not come from the army; probably only about 30,000 would. The Royal Navy, whose strength had fallen from 63,000 in 1990 to 44,000 in 1999, and the RAF, whose numbers fell from 89,000 to 55,000, would also provide a significant number. For details, see Nicholas Watt, "British Army Faces Squeeze," *Guardian*, May 31, 1999, p. 5.
28. Steven Erlanger, "NATO Was Closer to Ground War in Kosovo Than Is Widely Realized," *New York Times*, November 7, 1999.
29. WGBH *Frontline*, "War in Europe Part Two: The Real War," February 29, 2000.
30. Text of *Frontline* interview at: http://www.pbs.org/wgbh/pages/frontline/shows/kosovo/interviews/blair.html.
31. Ibid.
32. Speech by the Prime Minister, Mr. Tony Blair, at the Lord Mayor's Banquet, Guildhall, London, November 10, 1997.
33. See Michael Ignatieff, "The Virtual Commander," *New Yorker*, August 2, 1999.
34. See Richard Neustadt, *Alliance Politics* (New York: Columbia University Press, 1970); and Louise Richardson, *When Allies Differ: Anglo-American Relations in the Suez and Falklands Crises* (New York: St. Martin's Press, 1996).
35. "Kosovo, the Untold Story," *Observer*, July 18, 1999.
36. "Kosovo, the Untold Story," loc. cit.; Dana Priest, "A Decisive Battle that Never Was," *Washington Post*, September 19, 1999.
37. Martin Walker, "NATO Today and Tomorrow," *Europe*, April 1999, p. 33.
38. Reginald Dale, "The Search for a Common Foreign Policy," *Europe*, July-August 1999, p. 29.
39. Quoted in the *Observer*, July 25, 1999. See also transcript of speech by Robin Cook welcoming the new presidency of the General Affairs Council, Brussels, July 19, 1999, at http://www.fco.gov.uk/news/speechtext.asp?2655.
40. See, for example, Boris Johnson, "Who Do You Think You are Kidding, Mr. Tony?" *Daily Telegraph*, May 19, 1999, p. 22.
41. *Guardian*, March 28, 1999, p. 2.
42. See Philip Webster, "Tories Accused of Unpatriotic Attacks on Allies," *The Times* (London) May 12, 1999.
43. Andrew Gilligan and David Bamber, "Tory Kosovo Criticism 'Unpatriotic' say public," *Sunday Telegraph*, May 16, 1999.
44. *Observer* poll, *Observer*, March 28, 1999.
45. Andrew Gilligan and David Bamber, "Tory Kosovo Criticism 'Unpatriotic' say public," loc. cit.
46. For detailed public opinion polls, see Market and Opinion Research International (MORI), *"Mail on Sunday*—Kosovo Poll," at http://www.mori.com/polls/1999/1999poll.htm.
47. Speech by the Foreign Secretary, Mr. Robin Cook, at the launch of the FCO mission statement, Locarno Suite, Foreign and Commonwealth Office (FCO), London, May 12, 1997.
48. Speech by the Prime Minister, Mr. Tony Blair, at the Lord Mayor's Banquet, Guildhall, London, November 10, 1997.

49. Speech by the Prime Minister, Mr. Tony Blair, at a luncheon to mark the 150th anniversary of the Associated Press, London, December 15, 1998.
50. Text in the *Guardian,* March 27, 1999, p. 4.
51. *USA Today,* May 20, 1999, p. 6A.
52. Text in the *Guardian,* March 27, 1999, p. 4.
53. Interview with author, April 2000.
54. Blair Interview for *Frontline,* loc. cit.

CHAPTER TEN

Italy and the Management of International Crises

Maurizio Cremasco

In any country, domestic politics influence the shape and conduct of foreign policy. In Italy, however, this influence is somewhat unique. In fact, the high fragmentation of the political system,[1] the transformism of the political class,[2] the number of parties in the coalitions, which were and still are the typical form of Italian government, and their ideological and policy differences, tend to make the system quite unstable and lead to considerable polemics. This, in turn, forces the premier to try to maintain the cohesion of the coalition through difficult balancing acts. Frequently, this leads to the external projection of a seemingly erratic policy. However, when it comes to the core pillars of Italian foreign and security policy—NATO and the European Union—the underlying course of Italian actions tends to remain fundamentally steady.

During the Cold War, Italy's foreign and security policy was almost a foregone conclusion. Membership in NATO, which had to be defended both in the Italian parliament and in some European capitals, provided the international legitimacy Italy needed and longed for. It also provided the basis for a special relationship with the United States, which continues today. The NATO choice was considered fundamental not only to clearly take sides in the East-West confrontation, but also to fulfill Italy's security and defense needs at an acceptable cost. A strong relationship with Washington was seen as a way to enhance Italy's position within the Euro-Atlantic community and to compensate for the instability of the domestic political system and the presence of the strongest communist party in the West, the Partito Comunista Italiano (PCI).

Once in the Atlantic Alliance, Italy was a faithful ally, and even though acceptance of NATO military requirements was often more formal than concrete, Italy played its part in all major NATO initiatives, notably the deployment of Euromissiles in 1979.[3] Nevertheless, governments maneuvered carefully to avoid adopting policies that could have seemed too openly pro-American, which would have made them vulnerable to attacks from the left, which was always prone to use anti-Americanism for propagandistic or electoral purposes.[4]

The image of *immobilisme* that often characterized Italian foreign policy during the Cold War was largely the result of the governments' fear that active diplomacy would lead to domestic political instability and that initiatives taken outside the Atlantic or the European framework might lead Italy to lose some of its international credibility. A notable change occurred in the early 1980s and continued through the 1990s. At that time, participation in all peacekeeping operations conducted within and outside the United Nations framework became a salient feature of Italy's international presence and the use of armed forces became a central element of its foreign policy. This was not an easy transition, however, and domestic factors, as well as the relationship with the United States, continued to play a significant role in the decision-making process before and during the conduct of operations.

The disintegration of the Soviet Union, the end of the Cold War, and the collapse of the Communist regimes in Eastern Europe brought about a revolution in the Italian political system. It freed the Italian Communist Party from that "exclusion" factor that had conditioned Italian political life since 1948—"frozen" was the word preferred by many political commentators and analysts. The new European security landscape also led to the rediscovery of the concept of national interest and it opened new options to foreign and security policy that Italy was willing to explore. Such exploration, however, has been somewhat constrained by the endemic instability of the Italian political system.

The effects of the sweeping international changes were domestically reinforced by Operation *Mani Pulite* (Clean Hands), an inquiry into corruption started in 1992, which wiped out the old political class and the parties that had governed Italy since 1949.[5] The Italian political scene was also profoundly changed by the transformation of the parties of the left and the right[6] and by the birth of two new political formations: the conservative Forza Italia! and the secessionist Lega Nord. The political system lost some of its predictability, because the post-Communists (and even the post-Fascists) could now be considered legitimate government participants. In the long run, perhaps, the partition of the center-left and center-right currents of the dissolved Christian Democratic Party might lead to a more coherent and less ambiguous political environment.

Nonetheless, the basic characteristics of the political system remain the same: proliferation of parties, preeminence of domestic over international issues, influence of internal political struggles on foreign and security decisions, recurrent political crises, unstable coalition governments, and political posturing of the Catholic Church. The tendency of Italian diplomacy to act together with its allies in NATO and the EU continued, but with the nuances, incongruities, and apparently autonomous stances imposed by the complexity and fragility of the domestic political situation.

It is against this background that I propose to analyze Italy's response to the post–Cold War crises that directly affected Italian security interests, including the Balkan crises and the war in Kosovo. Specific attention is given to an assessment of the impact of three factors on the decision-making process: international linkages, notably participation in NATO and the EU; the domestic political situation, including the reaction of public opinion; and the impact of the relationship with the United States.

Italy's Responses to the Yugoslav Collapse and the Crisis over Bosnia

As Italy confronted the Balkan crises of 1991–95, it remained largely in sync with its European partners. This does not mean that Italy did not have its own preferences about the policies the EC should follow, but its reaction to crises in the Balkans was clearly based upon the premise that a common European response should be privileged. Italy, like its European partners, was ill prepared to cope with the crisis, even if it developed somewhat predictably over several years and Yugoslavia was crucial for Italian security. It can be argued that Italy did not seriously address the Yugoslav situation before the Croatian and Slovenian declarations of independence on June 25, 1991. In fact, while the crisis was progressing toward its violent climax, Italy had to concentrate its attention on three events directly and indirectly affecting European security: the dissolution of the Warsaw Pact, leading to the uncertain evolution of its members toward democracy; the process of German reunification; and the Gulf crisis. Subsequently, the Gulf War, the collapse of the Soviet Union, and the failure of the Somali intervention coincided with the Yugoslav conflict's extension to Bosnia-Herzegovina.

Initially, like many other European countries, Italy favored a unified Yugoslavia, as it was felt that the breakdown of the federation would establish a dangerous precedent. This attitude was soon swept aside by events, and after Yugoslavia collapsed from within, the difficult problem arose of defending a country from itself. Then Italy took part in the EC's unsuccessful attempt at finding a diplomatic solution to the conflict, which by April 1992 had spilled into Bosnia-Herzegovina.

In fact, Italy, because of its geographic position, was able and willing to play a fundamental role in supporting the crisis management efforts of international organizations. It organized, coordinated, and directed OTRANTO, an aeronaval operation approved by the WEU with the aim of monitoring respect of the U.N. embargo against Serbia and Montenegro. When a NATO naval force was deployed in the Adriatic, command, control, and communications (C3) functions were assured from a NATO headquarters in Italy. The same was true when NATO and the WEU, in response to a U.N. Security Council resolution calling for a naval blockade, decided to conduct stop-and-search naval operations, with NATO assuming the operational control of the mission.[7] In addition, Italy provided the air bases and logistic support for NATO air forces throughout the crisis.

This progressive transformation of the Italian territory into a platform from which to intervene in the former Yugoslavia posed a series of problems. The Italian government wanted to be sure that NATO military operations were legitimized by appropriate UNSC resolutions. Furthermore, Italy requested to be fully informed of NATO military plans requiring the use of Italian bases. It showed its concern and expressed its disappointment that Italian support was not always adequately acknowledged politically. Italy, in fact, was excluded from the consultation that led to the establishment of the "safe areas" in Bosnia, even though their protection could be achieved only through the utilization of Italian facilities.[8] On this occasion, the Italian defense minister went so far as to voice a veiled threat: Italy could change its policy if similar events were to happen again in the future.[9]

Moreover, the high visibility of Italian involvement and the proximity to the conflict also posed new security risks, which in turn reverberated onto the domestic political arena and public opinion. For example, terrorism was a possibility, especially after the Serbian ultranationalist Vojislav Seselj openly threatened a missile attack against Italian territory if NATO aircraft intervened against the Serbs.[10] Other domestic security concerns were raised in southern regions, as the flow of refugees represented an increasing economic and organizational burden. Italy also participated in Operation Danube, agreed upon by the WEU countries to help customs authorities in Bulgaria, Hungary, and Romania to monitor and enforce the U.N. embargo on traffic toward Serbia via the Danube River.[11]

Finally, although the United Nations excluded the participation of military units from bordering countries in the force deployed in the former Yugoslavia (UNPROFOR), the Italian defense ministers in office in 1992 and 1993 repeatedly underlined Italy's willingness to contribute to the U.N. force.

While it remained within the mainstream of EC policy, Italy did not forgo autonomous initiatives, based on the optimistic view that there is always space for a political solution, and on a somewhat fanciful tendency to assign itself the role of peace broker. The Rome-Belgrade diplomatic channel was kept open and Foreign Affairs Minister Emilio Colombo visited Belgrade at the end of January 1993, a move strongly criticized by the media and political forces, even those belonging to the coalition government. The Ciampi government, which took office in April 1993, reiterated its preference for diplomatic rather than military tools and, in May, rejected the American proposals to suspend the embargo on the sale of weapons to the Bosnian Muslims and attack the Serbian artillery that was pounding Sarajevo. In the same month, the newly appointed foreign minister, Beniamino Andreatta, spoke in parliament of the need to continue to trust President Milosevic to find a solution to the conflict.

Obviously, Italians were worried about a conflict raging so close to home, and the government intended to be a player in the crisis management. Italy's insistence on providing a military contribution that nobody wanted (not even the Italian military, concerned about the range of peacekeeping tasks already undertaken, which had imposed a heavy burden on available capabilities and resources) should be set and understood in this perspective. Nonetheless, Italy was capable of conducting a high-profile foreign and security policy, even if it was confronted domestically with deep and recurrent institutional, political, and economic crises. This fact underscores the peculiar characteristics of the Italian political system, and the capacity of a succession of unstable governments to maintain a basically steady policy course. It also helps to better understand Italy's political and military response to the Kosovo crisis.

Actually, although Italy was not militarily involved in the Bosnian crisis except for the participation of Italian warships in NATO/WEU naval operations in the Adriatic, its logistic and technical support to NATO air forces was fundamental for the fulfillment of their mission. True, the fact that the NATO role was fully legitimized by UNSC resolutions allowed the Italian government a broader range of action, but the government had to cope with serious internal challenges during the short NATO bombings that preceded the peace negotiations in Dayton.

The Kosovo Crisis

Five elements formed the reference setting of Italy's response to the Kosovo crisis. First, the context was marked by the variegated composition of the center-left government of Massimo D'Alema, which included the DS (Democrats of the Left),[12] the PPI (Italian Popular Party),[13] the UDR (Union of Democrats for the Republic), DINI/RI (DINI/Italian Renewal Party), the Republican Party, the Italian Democratic Socialists, the Greens, and the Party of Italian Communists.[14] Each of these coalition members had its own approach to the problems of crisis management, Italian participation in peace support operations, and the use of force in international relations. Compounding this delicate position, D'Alema had to take into consideration the left wing of his own party, still attracted by old Communist political posturing. Not only Fausto Bertinotti's Communist Refoundation Party, but also Armando Cossutta's Party of the Italian Communists, as well as the Greens, were against a military intervention—particularly if conducted by NATO. Even the U.N. force they advocated was supposed not to engage in coercive operations, but to act as a typical Blue Helmet contingent with a specific humanitarian mandate. Throughout the conflict, these dissenting voices of the left were ubiquitous in the Italian media.

Second, a vocal pacifist front persists in Italy. During the Kosovo crisis, besides traditional components such as the supporters of the leftist parties and some sectors of D'Alema's own party, pacifist voices included high school students, the Church and all Catholic movements and associations, and the left wing of the former Christian Democratic Party, including even the president, Oscar Luigi Scalfaro.[15]

Third, public opinion was somewhat divided in its feeling that Italy should share Europe's responsibility in dealing with the crisis and, therefore, support the allies' initiatives. Among the public, there was deep concern for what was seen as an ill-timed military action. In fact, a poll conducted two days after the start of the NATO air campaign against Serbia reported that only 25 percent considered the NATO attack justified, and 50 percent felt that the attack was not justified "because there was still time to negotiate." Nonetheless, 75 percent agreed that Italy should collaborate at some level with its NATO partners. Only one respondent in seven expressed the opinion that Italy should dissociate itself from the NATO operation altogether.[16]

This underscored the fact that even though almost 50 percent did not approve of NATO military intervention, an even larger percentage felt that Italy should honor its commitments. This ambivalent attitude—yes to an Italian role because it would have been a disgrace to do otherwise, no to the timing of the air attacks—was fueled by anti-NATO and anti-American biases that have survived the end of the Cold War and are still influential in judging the actions of the government. D'Alema recognized that one of the obstacles to a smoother management of the Kosovo crisis was the strength of anti-American feelings in large sectors of the parties and society. In his view, the Italian left did not have a history of rejecting any use of force. In the case of Kosovo, "the taboo was the United States."[17]

Fourth, the majority of the combat sorties against Serbian targets were taking off from Italian bases. This was the clearest demonstration of Italy's willingness to play a crucial role, but it was bound to complicate the domestic situation and compound the work and responsibility of the antiterrorist and police forces. This element was underlined by Fabio Mussi, the House's whip for the Democratic Left, who stated: "Italy is on the front line and has assumed a serious responsibility and would like our allies to understand it. The NATO actions, after all, are launched from our territory."[18] As in the case of Bosnia, Italy became NATO's aircraft carrier. This time, however, NATO's air attacks differed from those conducted in 1995 to force Milosevic to the negotiating table, because they soon became a total air campaign. In this context, serious debates over targeting mishaps and civilian losses jeopardized the stability of D'Alema's government. NATO sorties took off also from other European countries, but the fact that the bulk of U.S. air forces was based in Italy tended to sharpen the impression that Italy's support for the "American" war was greater than that of other NATO allies. Moreover, the lack of a clear U.N. mandate this time raised questions about the legality of NATO actions.[19]

Fifth, there was a palpable uneasiness in Italy about an air war with no political outcome, limited military results, collateral damages and civilian losses, and above all the prospect of a politically disruptive ground war. These feelings were present in other NATO countries, but in Rome they represented bigger obstacles to government action than in Bonn, London, Madrid, or Paris. Throughout the crisis there were parallels between the German and Italian domestic political situations, but Chancellor Schroeder never had to deal with the challenges posed by D'Alema's coalition, and the attitude of the German Greens was certainly different from that of the Italian Greens.

On March 26, the Italian parliament voted a motion on Italy's position toward the war. It was crafted in such a way as to avoid alienating the Communists, who could resign from the government, thus triggering a serious political crisis, and at the same time to avoid hampering D'Alema's ability to maneuver. The motion explicitly called for an end to the air attacks as soon as possible and for diplomatic initiatives to be pursued immediately, and insisted that Italian forces should not participate directly in offensive air operations against Serbia.

As the first former Communist to occupy the function of premier, Massimo D'Alema was in an awkward position. His old party had maintained close links with the Soviet Union during the Cold War and consistently supported its foreign policy. In 1991 the PCI refused to support Italy's participation in the war against Iraq. D'Alema was aware that the Kosovo war was a sort of test that he and his government had to pass to confirm Italy's credibility as a reliable ally capable of assuming difficult political and military responsibilities.[20] The test was passed with flying colors. The Italian government rightly felt that Euro-Atlantic unity, NATO credibility, and stability in the Balkan area were worth a painful and politically risky decision, even though the government's survival was at stake. Actually, even if the Italian government might not have had the option of closing the door to any participation in NATO's air campaign while remaining a part of the Alliance, it could have adopted, as did Greece, a more limited and less committed role.[21]

On March 25, during the EU summit meeting in Berlin, D'Alema gave an optimistic assessment of the effects of the initial NATO air strikes on Serbian ethnic cleansing in Kosovo and declared that "the time to hand matters over to politics and diplomacy is approaching."[22] Within hours, he was rebuffed by Clinton's national security adviser, Sandy Berger, who contested the military evaluation of the Italian premier, while London and Washington asked for clarification out of concern that D'Alema's statement could weaken NATO's cohesion and send a misleading message to Belgrade.[23]

Though D'Alema's words seemed to hint that a pause in the raids was possible and desirable, Italy firmly supported NATO's air war. In fact, Italy backed the NATO decision to escalate the air war and to target political and military facilities in Belgrade. On the domestic front, this steadfast position was helped by the U.N. Security Council's rejection of the Russian resolution calling for an end to the bombing. D'Alema's capacity to stay the course in spite of significant domestic challenges tells a great deal about his personal political ability and about the world of Italian politics. Although Italy's policy remained basically firm, it was weakened by a number of factors, raising concerns among NATO allies. Notably, the government needed to do some posturing to maintain the cohesion of the coalition. The vocal antiwar position of the Catholic Church also had an impact on political parties and public opinion. Finally, one must not neglect the economic and social repercussions of a war conducted just across the Adriatic, disrupting civilian air traffic, commercial fishing, and tourism.[24]

In early April, the Party of Italian Communists and the Greens asked the government to distance its policy from that of NATO and to demand a bombing pause over Easter, threatening otherwise to leave the coalition. In his careful reply, D'Alema stated that Italy was strongly committed to a peaceful solution. He recognized that the Vatican's explicit antiwar position had an impact on political parties and public opinion[25] and noted that NATO's whole *modus operandi* in case of crisis would have to be discussed again after the end of the conflict. Nonetheless, the premier reiterated Italy's firm support for the NATO air campaign and clearly said that he would not be the first premier to endorse the reduction of Italy's role in NATO.[26] And, as a further indication of Italy's firmness, D'Alema rejected President Milosevic's call for a cease-fire, stating: "I share the view of our allies that

Belgrade's initiative of a temporary truce appears to be insufficient for a peaceful solution to the conflict to be found."[27]

The coalition's diverse, if not contradictory, positions on the war and on the policy responses to it contributed to a "personalization" of Italian foreign policy, often projecting an image of uncertainty and inconsistency. Apart from the Greens and the Communists, who constantly criticized the decisions of the government to the point of threatening to leave the coalition, there were also dissenting voices in the left wing of D'Alema's party and differences between the premier and Minister of Foreign Affairs Lamberto Dini that went beyond nuances of language.[28]

Commenting on these peculiarities of the Italian political picture, D'Alema noted that the way Italy coped with the war demonstrated that its institutions were still inadequate. He further added that there was an unwritten pact: the government performed its institutional tasks, while political forces were free to take their initiatives, even if they appeared to go in the opposite direction of the government's policy. The government took them into consideration, but always within the framework of its primary responsibilities and commitments. Thus, D'Alema explicitly recognized that this division of roles made it possible for Italy to overcome its institutional weaknesses, but also that the government did not have adequate powers to effectively manage a war.[29]

The restless attitude of the Party of the Italian Communists resulted from its peculiar interpretation of the Kosovo crisis, characterized by a strong pro-Serbia and anti-NATO bias, and pressure from the Communist Refoundation Party, which continually proclaimed that "true Communists" could not be part of a government that supported a NATO war.[30] In early April, Armando Cossutta, the secretary of the PCI, conducted his own peace initiative, flying first to Moscow and then to Belgrade, where he had talks with President Milosevic. It was certainly odd to see the leader of a party that was a member of a government supporting the NATO air campaign against the Federal Republic of Yugoslavia talking with the leader of that country about peace in Kosovo, while an entire population was being deported there and a humanitarian disaster was unfolding in Albania, Macedonia, and Montenegro.

By mid-April, EU diplomacy moved with more determination, trying to enlist the United Nations in the peace process, while Germany as the holder of the EU rotating presidency offered its own plan, which was judged as constructive and "within NATO parameters" by the U.S. State Department.[31] More European countries started to talk about a bombing pause and more direct involvement of the U.N. Security Council and Russia, which had been and were at the core of the Italian position.[32] The German and French diplomatic activity underlined, somewhat ambiguously, the need for a specifically European policy to counter what was perceived as American unilateralism and domination of NATO. Italy's diplomacy also stressed these themes.

Moreover, the fact that more than three weeks had passed since the beginning of the war and there were still no appreciable results, and the growing recurrence of pilots' errors in their bombing runs with an increasing number of civilians being involved, put even more pressure on Italian and allied governments and strengthened the widespread antiwar sentiments of the Italian population. Actually, the errors of NATO pilots struck a raw nerve in the country, fomenting demonstrations around Italian air bases, in particular Aviano, the home base of the American air armada in Italy. Meanwhile, questions were raised about whether NATO's overall strategy and air tactics were suited to the goals of Operation Allied Force, and whether these goals were appropriate.[33]

By mid-April, and even more by mid-May on the eve of a parliamentary debate on the war,[34] the contrast between the government's outward appearance of resoluteness and its internal struggles and antiwar tendencies had become very obvious. A reported escalation in the combat role of Italian aircraft brought the government close to another crisis. Again the premier had to walk the extra mile to convince his fractious coalition allies that the role basically had not changed and was still within the framework of the concept of an "integrated and active defense" approved by parliamentarians in March.[35]

In addition, the growing prospect of NATO being forced to use ground troops to impose a solution on Belgrade was emerging as another element of division among the allies, and it was seen in Italy as the straw that could break the government's back.[36] This prospect was also complicating European-American relations in terms of war objectives and Kosovo's future settlement.

Then again, it was difficult for Italy to maintain a steady policy course when the American administration seemed bent on following the mood of its public opinion. The messages emanating from Washington sometimes led to some confusion, such as when the Senate majority leader, Trent Lott, declared that it was time to stop the bombing, or when President Clinton hinted at the possibility of a bombing pause if there was at least a sign that Milosevic would begin to withdraw Serbian forces from Kosovo.[37]

Another moment of tension between Italy and its allies—the United Kingdom and the United States in particular—occurred in early May, when the moderate but controversial Kosovo leader Ibrahim Rugova was flown to Rome on a government aircraft. At the outset of the war, Rugova had attracted criticism for appearing with Milosevic on television, in what seemed like a reversal of the Albanian leader's long-standing opposition to the Serbian regime. Milosevic's motives for letting Rugova leave the country were not clear. There was concern that he might campaign against the Kosovo Liberation Army (KLA) and NATO bombing, thus sowing the seeds of division among the allies. When Rugova declared that the NATO operation was fully justified, the tension evaporated and the U.S. administration endorsed the Italian initiative.[38]

When Russia's special envoy Viktor Chernomyrdin stopped in Rome on his way to Belgrade in May, this was an opportunity for Premier D'Alema to call for more imagination and creativity in the search for a political solution, and for more flexibility on the command and control of the international force.[39] On May 16, after Russia and the G7 had drafted an ambiguous peace plan for Kosovo, and the diplomatic process had gained momentum with Russian mediation, D'Alema offered his own recipe. There were reasons for a political initiative at that time, as popular support for the NATO air campaign was steadily decreasing.[40] Other sources of pressure on D'Alema included a strong appeal by the pope for an immediate end to all hostilities[41] and, last but not least, the malaise within the coalition caused by the election of Carlo Azeglio Ciampi as president.

D'Alema's proposal was close to the German plan: if Russia and China voted a Security Council resolution to impose on Milosevic the withdrawal of his forces and the return of the refugees, under the protection of an international force, then a pause in the bombings could be the prelude to a diplomatic breakthrough. If Milosevic refused, NATO would then decide for a land intervention. D'Alema later explained his conviction that Milosevic would have given up if confronted with the real possibility of NATO obtaining a U.N. mandate on the basis of the G8 conditions. His proposal was thus aimed at "facilitating" Milosevic's surrender by having Russians on board and by putting the United Nations back onto center stage. His message was addressed mainly to Russia and China: If you do not want NATO to assume improper responsibilities, let the United Nations function. Otherwise, if the logic of the opposing vetoes prevails, decisions will be taken in other forums.[42]

D'Alema was unable to rally Chancellor Schroeder to his plan during the German-Italian summit in Bari on May 18, and responses from other NATO allies were even less enthusiastic. The next day, Downing Street explicitly turned down Italy's proposal for a pause in the bombings. The last major break in the coalition came in late May with declarations by Foreign Affairs Minister Lamberto Dini. Discussing the hypothesis of a land war, Dini warned that it would destroy 20 years of political and diplomatic work and added that, in such a case, Italy would be forced to dissociate itself from NATO.[43] Commenting on this episode, a journalist noted that many foreign observers had trouble understanding where foreign policy ended and where electoral posturing started.[44]

When the hostilities ended in early June, Italian authorities did not hesitate to attribute themselves part of the merit for the success of the NATO campaign, adding that their country would be willing not only to contribute to the NATO peacekeeping force, but also to play a leading role in the postwar settlement. Moreover, distancing his policy from that of his European partners, D'Alema announced the Italian government's willingness to provide aid to Serbia while Milosevic was still in power.

Conclusion

On the whole, the picture emerging from Italy's conduct during the Kosovo crisis offers more bright than gray or black spots, but the latter were nonetheless present. Throughout the crisis, Italy was able to maintain a steady policy course: full participation in the allied decision-making process and endorsement of NATO strategy; operational and logistic support to the NATO air forces; military participation in the NATO air campaign. And this was done while coping with a situation of endemic political instability and the high economic and social costs of the war.

Italy performed a notable military role, conducted a strong humanitarian effort (*Missione Arcobaleno,* Rainbow Mission), and pressed its own points of view in several international forums. Domestic problems, but also a genuine interest in seeking a political solution, led to declarations and diplomatic initiatives interpreted by the allies as a departure from common NATO positions. This was the case not only with D'Alema's unfortunate declaration of March 25, but also with his May 16 peace proposal. Yet, the basic element of that proposal was part of the one eventually accepted by Milosevic, and other elements of Italy's proposals were taken in the allied political initiatives, a demonstration of their validity, thus raising the question of whether for Italy it was just always a matter of bad timing or lesser international weight and credibility.

During the Kosovo crisis, Italy was the only country in which domestic terrorism struck significantly. In the midst of the bombing campaign, Red Brigade terrorism resurfaced with the killing of Massimo D'Antona, a university professor and government consultant on labor policy. The text of the document by which the Red Brigades claimed responsibility for this murder made explicit reference to the rejection of the "corporatist and anti-proletariat" social pact, and to Italy's participation in the NATO "imperialist war."

When at war, most countries tend to set aside internal divisions, and fractious groups tend to bow to the national interest. During the air war over Kosovo, even fragile governing coalitions formed by parties with different historical backgrounds, political ideologies, and traditions (such as the

SPD-Greens coalition in Germany) put national interest ahead of domestic political struggle. In Italy, however, political divisions not only continued but tended to increase throughout the crisis, as parties tried to use foreign-policy posturing to gain domestic support in view of the next elections, which always loom not too far on the Italian political horizon.

Massimo D'Alema wanted Italy to have a significant role in postwar Kosovo and become one of the principal actors in the efforts toward stability in the region.[45] In spite of his valiant efforts, however, Italy was excluded from the most important positions in the new administration. Bernard Kouchner, a French cabinet minister, was appointed as U.N. governor for Kosovo, with James Covey, an American, as his deputy; and Germany's Bodo Hombach was appointed as coordinator for the Balkan Stability Pact. Moreover, Italy was excluded from Kosovo's four Sector Directorates.[46]

In early September 1999, addressing a conference of Italian ambassadors, Premier D'Alema, while underlining that the Italian role in the Balkan crisis had conferred authority and prestige on the country, noted: "One cannot do without the U.N., but the U.N. is not enough and it is not able to guarantee, at least with its present functioning mechanisms, the kind of crisis prevention and crisis management that would be needed in today's world."[47] D'Alema's words should not be taken as an endorsement of the new NATO role as performed in the Kosovo crisis. They did not imply that NATO was now legitimized to provide the legal framework for crisis management. They were, in fact, the simple acknowledgment that "without a reference to international legality and the U.N. system—which is depositary of this legality—it is very difficult to find the political and moral force to solve the conflicts and guarantee a framework of stability and peace."[48] Thus, for Italy, the challenge is to ensure that the centers of legitimacy and authority in security matters are made to coincide again. In sum, if the management of the Kosovo crisis forced Italy to redefine its relationship with NATO and the EU in security matters, it also led its leaders to turn their attention to the revision of the United Nations Organization as a major policy objective.

Notes

1. Fifty-three parties and political formations participated in the April 1996 general elections. At the time of the Kosovo crisis, there were 46 parties in the Senate and the Chamber of Deputies.
2. As of December 1998, 140 members of the Chamber of Deputies and 76 senators elected in 1996 had changed political affiliation.
3. See Maurizio Cremasco, "The Political Debate on the Deployment of Euromissiles: The Italian Case," *The International Spectator* (April-June 1984): pp. 115–21.

4. The PCI formally accepted Italy's foreign policy, including participation in NATO, only in 1977. Obviously, this did not preclude the PCI from opposing policies related to NATO or assumed to be in support of the United States; Maurizio Cremasco, "Italy: A New Role in the Mediterranean?" in *NATO's Southern Allies: Internal and External Challenges,* ed. John Chipman (London: Routledge, 1988).
5. See Stanton Barnett and Luca Mantovani, *Italian Guillotine: Operation Clean Hands and the Overthrow of Italy's First Republic* (Lanham, Md.: Rowman & Littlefield, 1998).
6. In 1990, the Communist Party became the Partito Democratico della Sinistra (PDS; Democratic Party of the Left), while the "post-Fascist" Movimento Sociale Italiano (MSI; Italian Social Movement) became the Alleanza Nazionale (AN; National Alliance). In 1998, the PDS changed its name to Democratici di Sinistra (DS; Democrats of the Left).
7. The operation changed its name first to Maritime Guard and then to Sharp Guard.
8. The countries involved were France, Russia, Spain, the United Kingdom, and the United States.
9. Ettore Greco, "L'Italia e la Crisi Balcanica," in *L'Italia nella politica internazionale, Edizione 1994* (Rome: Editore SIPI, 1994), p. 111.
10. Ibid., p. 112.
11. Ibid., p. 114.
12. The secretary of the DS had become premier of a government supported also by the Party of the Italian Communists in October 1998.
13. The Partito Popolare Italiano (PPI; Italian Popular Party) is one of the three political formations born from the dissolution of the Democrazia Cristiana (DC; Christian Democratic Party).
14. Partito dei Comunisti Italiani, a split of the far left Rifondazione Comunista (Communist Refoundation Party).
15. President Scalfaro declared that "when weapons are used, it is a sign that thought, rationality and dialogue have been suspended, and that only muscles are being flexed," Laura Collura, *International Herald Tribune/Italy Daily,* March 26, 1999, p. 2.
16. *International Herald Tribune/Italy Daily,* March 27–28, 1999, p. 1.
17. Massimo D'Alema, *Kosovo: gli italiani e la guerra. Intervista di Federico Rampini* (Milan: Mondadori, 1999), p. 105.
18. Gabriel Kahn, "Italy Expresses Ambivalence toward NATO Operation," *International Herald Tribune/Italy Daily,* March 27–28, 1999, p. 1.
19. This issue was raised by Foreign Minister Dini at an international relations forum held in August 1999. *International Herald Tribune,* August 24, 1999, p. 5.
20. Romano Prodi was still premier when NATO approved the "activation order," the first step toward the air campaign against the FRY. On the tests Massimo D'Alema felt he had to pass, see D'Alema, *Kosovo: gli italiani e la guerra,* p. 3.
21. See D'Alema, *Kosovo: gli italiani e la guerra,* p. 109.
22. Laura Collura, "Italy Calls for NATO Pullback in Kosovo," *International Herald Tribune/Italy Daily,* March 26, 1999, p. 1; Gabriel Kahn, "D'Alema

Raises Concern on NATO Unity," *International Herald Tribune/Italy Daily,* March 27–28, 1999, p. 3. Arguably, D'Alema wished to set the stage for the forthcoming parliamentary vote by portraying a government eager for a diplomatic solution.

23. Federico Rampini, "Lo Strappo Italiano," *La Repubblica,* March 26, 1999, p. 1.
24. The fact that zones in the Adriatic were used by NATO aircraft to drop ordnance and that fishermen were wounded when canisters of cluster bombs were caught in their nets had a vast echo in the Italian press and affected the public's threat perceptions.
25. Angelo Panebianco, "Church and State, War and NATO," *International Herald Tribune/Italy Daily,* April 6, 1999, p. 2. There is little doubt that the Vatican's stance indirectly reinforced left-wing pacifists and divided Catholic public opinion. The public, however, was shocked by the magnitude of the ethnic cleansing in Kosovo, shown daily on Italian television.
26. *La Stampa,* April 1, 1999, p. 5.
27. Joseph Fitchett, "Milosevic Calls a Cease-Fire but NATO Stands by Terms," *International Herald Tribune,* April 7, 1999, p. 1.
28. For example, speaking at a meeting of the EU foreign ministers in Luxembourg in early April, Foreign Minister Lamberto Dini declared that Italy did not want to see the bombings go on for much longer and that the West should not try to impose a solution to the crisis, while urging NATO countries to discuss an exit strategy.
29. D'Alema, *Kosovo: gli italiani e la guerra,* pp. 34–35.
30. *La Stampa,* April 1, 1999, p. 5.
31. Joseph Fitchett, "Germans Propose 24-Hour Cease-Fire for Serb Pullback," *International Herald Tribune,* April 15, 1999, p. 1.
32. John Vinocur, "German and French Plans on Kosovo Reflect Political Needs at Home," *International Herald Tribune,* April 16, 1999, p. 2.
33. Italy had strongly objected to the targeting of the Serbian television headquarters and expressed deep concern about the bombing of the Chinese embassy in Belgrade.
34. Stefano Folli, "Sulla NATO la maggioranza non c'è, ma la rottura ha costi troppo alti" [NATO does not have majority support, but the costs of breaking away would be too high], *Corriere della Sera,* May 18, 1999, p. 8.
35. Christopher Emsdem, "Italian Jets Increase Role in NATO Bombing Raids," *International Herald Tribune/Italy Daily,* April 15, 1999, p. 1.
36. On April 22, 170 Chamber and Senate members of the governing coalition parties signed a cautious but firm appeal to D'Alema: In the event of a land war, they would not support the government. Giovanna Casadio, "No all'attacco di terra: è rivolta in Parlamento," *La Repubblica,* April 23, 1999, p. 10.
37. See "Appeasement Talk," *International Herald Tribune,* May 6, 1999, p. 8.
38. Gabriel Kahn and Alessandra Arachi, "From Rome, Rugova Says NATO Needed in Kosovo," *International Herald Tribune/Italy Daily,* May 7, 1999, p. 1.
39. Massimo Caprara, "E per D'Alema 'serve fantasia,'" *Corriere della Sera,* May 1, 1999, p. 5.

40. In an April 24 survey, 43 percent approved the air raids, while 33 percent were opposed. As of May 8, the percentages reversed to 35 and 42. See *Corriere della Sera,* May 10, 1999, p. 9.
41. Luigi Accattoli, "Il Papa richiama i cristiani: più audacia nel chiedere la pace," *Corriere della Sera,* May 10, 1999, p. 9; "I vescovi incoraggiano il governo di Roma a bloccare l'offensiva," *Corriere della Sera,* May 18, 1999, p. 4.
42. Massimo D'Alema, op. cit., pp. 57–58.
43. The declarations provoked a series of negative political reactions. The former Italian president Francesco Cossiga declared that those words were "incredible" and asked for D'Alema's intervention. *Corriere della Sera,* May 28, 1999, p. 6.
44. Maurizio Molinari, "Dini non può escludere un intervento di terra," *La Stampa,* May 29, 1999, p. 5.
45. Gabriel Kahn, "With Peace at Hand Italy wants a Lead Role," *International Herald Tribune/Italy Daily,* June 5–6, 1999, p. 1.
46. Ennio Caretto, "E l'Italia finisce esclusa da tutte le cariche," *Corriere della Sera,* July 4, 1999, p. 8.
47. "Intervento del Presidente del Consiglio, On. Massimo D'Alema, alla II Conferenza degli Ambasciatori Italiani nel Mondo," Rome, September 1, 1999; http://www.esteri.it/archivi/eventi/2conferenza/d010999dal.htm.
48. Ibid.

CHAPTER ELEVEN

Canada and the Kosovo War: The Happy Follower

Kim Richard Nossal and Stéphane Roussel

Twice in the 1990s the government of Canada went to war as part of a United States–led coalition. In January 1991, Washington and its coalition partners used force against Iraq after that country had invaded Kuwait in August 1990 and incorporated it into Iraqi territory. In March 1999, the United States and its allies in the North Atlantic Treaty Organization went to war against the Federal Republic of Yugoslavia after the government of Slobodan Milosevic refused to sign an international agreement intended to eliminate human rights abuses in the Yugoslav province of Kosovo. In both conflicts, Canada contributed minimally to the use of force. In the war phase of the conflict against Iraq, the main Canadian contribution was in the air: operating an air base in Qatar and committing CF-18s to escort missions—at least until the final hours of fighting, when these aircraft were authorized to use their munitions against Iraqi positions. On the ground, the Canadians contributed a field hospital based in Saudi Arabia.[1] In the war over Kosovo, Canada's contribution to the fighting was limited to air attacks against Yugoslav targets using 18 CF-18 fighter-bombers.[2]

Was Canadian participation in these wars *determined* by the coalition leader? Was it in any sense *forced* or *coerced* by the United States? The answers to such questions must, in both cases, be carefully qualified. For, on the one hand, it is true that in both cases, the smaller allies and coalition partners of the United States found themselves dragged into war by the coercive diplomacy of Presidents George Bush and Bill Clinton. In the case of the Gulf conflict, all of the 36 members of the international coalition were affected by the Bush administration's quite unilateral decision in November 1990 to change the purpose of the 36-member anti-Iraq coalition. No longer was the purpose of the coalition to defend Saudi Arabia and impose sanctions on Iraq; from November onward, the purpose was to expel Iraq from Kuwait, by using force if necessary. Likewise, in the Kosovo conflict, all the NATO allies of the United States could not help but be affected by the American decision to press at Rambouillet for an international force to occupy the province widely seen by Serbs as the cradle of the Serb nation, and then to make rejection of what any rational Serb leader would have to regard as an outrageous demand a cause of war.

In short, for all smaller coalition partners of the United States, both these conflicts had all the attributes of a hegemonic operation, albeit cloaked in the garb of multilateralism.[3] In each case, the preferences of the Bush and Clinton administrations became, perforce, the preferences of the entire coalition. All important decisions were made in Washington, from the broadest policy directions of the coalition (for example, the decision to transform the Gulf coalition from a defensive to an offensive posture, the decision to threaten the Milosevic government with the use of force if it did not sign the Rambouillet accords) to the smallest operational details (for example, the decision as to when to begin the bombing campaign in the Gulf War, or the decision to keep Apache attack helicopters out of the fighting in Kosovo).

Moreover, in each case, the smaller coalition partners found themselves tied tightly to the preferences of the coalition leader, but without any serious capacity to influence those preferences. The preferences of the smaller partners for alternative courses of action were routinely given short shrift by decision-makers in Washington. Thus, all members of the coalitions were stuck with the preferences of the leader, whether they agreed with them or not. For while leaving the coalition always remained a theoretical possibility, in fact defection was never seriously considered, given the huge costs involved. Like neophyte roller coaster riders who discover on the very first descent that they have made a dreadful mistake, the small coalition partners had little choice but to go along with the coalition leadership and grimly hang on until the end.

On the other hand, we have to acknowledge that just because the coalition leader set the pace, determined policy, ruled options in and out, and made the crucial decisions—all often unilaterally—it does not necessarily mean that the smaller coalition partner was *forced* into war. For it is possible that a smaller partner of a coalition leader might be enthusiastic about the leader's preferences, and a willing participant in the military option embraced by the leader. It depends entirely on what the motivation of the coalition partner itself is. Thus, in the case of the Gulf War, it was clear that the Progressive Conservative government of Brian Mulroney might have been caught off-guard by the unilateral decision of the Bush administration to change the purpose of the coalition, but it nonetheless turned into an enthusiastic supporter of the coalition's new goals.[4]

Our purpose in this chapter is to inquire into the motivations of the Liberal government of Jean Chrétien for Canada's participation in the Kosovo conflict. Seeking to reveal motivations through public statements and government policy, we will show that far from being forced into this war, the Canadian government was enthusiastic about NATO's use of air strikes to force the Federal Republic of Yugoslavia to relinquish de facto control of Kosovo. Thus the government was equally enthusiastic about Operation Allied Force. Indeed, it could be argued that the Canadian government would not have been unhappy had NATO embraced a more robust ground troops option earlier in the conflict, even though Ottawa did not follow the path of the British prime minister, Tony Blair, who openly campaigned for the use of ground troops. However, the impact of the Chrétien government on allied policy direction was as minimal as that of other small states, and largely for the same reason. Canada, like all other small coalition partners, was unwilling to contribute more than a token to the actual fighting: 18 fighter-bombers and some 800 ground troops (a contingent so small that, in an eerie replay of another conflict 100 years earlier, they had to be attached to British forces deployed to the theater). In other words, even though the Canadian government's participation in the Kosovo conflict was in all important ways determined by policy decisions taken by the United States government, that participation nonetheless accorded with Canadian preferences. In the Kosovo conflict, Canada was indeed the happy follower: it was happy to be involved in a campaign that was being portrayed as a humanitarian mission; it was (in general) happy with the policy preferences of the United States as coalition leader; and it was particularly happy that it did not have to contribute anything more than token forces.

Possible Canadian Motivations: Overview

In the course of a debate in the House of Commons on April 12, 1999, Prime Minister Jean Chrétien outlined the basis of Canadian participation in these words: "It is these three elements—our values as Canadians, our national interest in a stable and secure Europe and our obligations as a founding member of NATO—that led Canada to take [up] arms with its NATO partners. It is because of our values, our national interest, and our obligations that we must see the job concluded."[5] In so doing, the prime minister based his justification for Canadian participation on three arguments that, while not necessarily incompatible, were nonetheless of very different orders. To establish the relevance and logic of these arguments, and at the same time to measure the government's rationale against the arguments being advanced by others, it is useful to resituate the various points of view expressed over the course of the conflict—not only the arguments in favor of Canadian participation, but also the criticisms—in the context of several key hypotheses formulated to explain coalition behavior.

We hypothesize that Canadian participation in the war against the Federal Republic of Yugoslavia could have been a function of one or more of the following factors: a concern to advance or maintain Canada's national security; alliance entrapment, in which the Canadian government was dragged into the war reluctantly as nothing more than a function of its membership in the Atlantic Alliance; the lessons of history; domestic politics; and humanitarian motivations. These factors are most often mentioned in the theoretical literature on foreign policy and the causes of war.[6] They reflect very different approaches to international relations, in particular the traditional distinction between defensive realism (considerations of national security, alliance entrapment, and lessons of history) and liberalism (domestic politics and humanitarian concerns). But variables such as the lessons of history or humanitarian concerns put more emphasis on ideas, values, and standards than on material or institutional factors, and inspire approaches such as neoclassical realism[7] or even constructivism.[8] To an assessment of each of these factors we now turn.

National Security

One of the most common hypotheses advanced by theories of alliances and coalitions is that states seek to join alliances in order to counter other states that might constitute a threat to their security.[9] To what extent were the policies of the government in Belgrade a threat, real or perceived, to Canadian security?

Every Canadian government since the Second World War has defined Canadian security interests in terms of European security; every European conflict was seen in Ottawa as imperiling Canada's military, diplomatic, political, and economic interests. It was this logic that led a succession of Canadian governments to embrace Atlanticism as a long-term cornerstone of foreign policy: in the late 1940s by attaching itself to the idea of an Atlantic Alliance, and then by stationing Canadian forces in Europe between 1950 and 1991.[10] In the post–Cold War period, the collapse of the former Yugoslavia was seen in Ottawa as a threat to the stability of Europe as a whole. It was for this reason that both the Progressive Conservative government of Brian Mulroney and the Liberal government of Jean Chrétien involved Canada in multilateral attempts to secure the peace in Croatia and Bosnia.[11]

A posteriori, it is possible to explain Canada's participation in NATO's operations against Yugoslavia by using the concept of "national interest." On the one hand, the Canadian government, like the majority of its allies, had every interest in ensuring the survival of the Atlantic Alliance. The operations against the Serbs would certainly show the need for maintaining an American military presence in Europe—and thus for preserving the NATO alliance. Thus, Canada's participation would have made it possible to reinforce the transatlantic link and to show the importance that Ottawa attached to this institution. Moreover, the embrace of crisis management in Europe as a central mission of the Alliance was in line with the ideal of NATO as a "cooperative security alliance" being articulated by Canadian leaders.[12] This evolution could only make NATO more valuable for Ottawa.

On the other hand, the involvement of Canadian forces would have served to shore up Canada's credibility as an Alliance partner and reverse the long-standing view among the allies that Canada was an "odd man out" in NATO.[13] Given this, it is not at all surprising that right from the outset of hostilities, the Department of National Defence was keen to stress the qualitative importance of Canada's contribution: although the 18 Canadian CF-18s constituted only 2 percent of the 912 NATO aircraft involved, the Canadian planes flew fully 10 percent of the missions and recorded a relatively high rate of "successful hits" compared with the European allies. Likewise, the performances of the Coyote reconnaissance vehicles attached to KFOR also produced a favorable impression among the other allies.[14]

The idea that Canada's security interests demanded Canadian involvement in the multinational use of force against the Federal Republic of Yugoslavia for its policies in Kosovo was expressed on occasion. We have noted the prime minister's comments above; reference to strategic calculations was also made by some commentators outside the government. For example, writing in *Le Devoir*, Marcel Belleau noted that intervention would guarantee "regional stability, by preventing an extension of the conflict to neighboring countries, notably Macedonia."[15] Likewise, some commentators noted that NATO's use of force in Kosovo was designed to preempt possible comparable ethnic cleansing in the one other Yugoslav republic, Montenegro, or, more ominously, in the Vojvodina region in Serbia, where there was a significant Hungarian ethnic minority.[16]

On the whole, however, the strategic argument was not prominently heard in the justifications of government officials, parliamentarians, or media commentators. No Canadian politician tried to replicate for Canadians the brief lesson in geopolitics given by President Bill Clinton to the American people on the night of March 24, when he tried to lay out in clear terms why American security interests were threatened by the possibility of spillover from Kosovo. Rather, in Canada the strategic argument was sometimes even explicitly denied: for example, Frederic Wagnière, writing in *La Presse,* welcomed Canadian participation, but rejected the idea that this represented an appropriate Canadian investment in European security;[17] for his part, Marcus Gee opposed Canadian participation on any grounds, including the strategic rationale.[18]

Sometimes the strategic rationale was presented half-heartedly, or even added as an afterthought. For example, speaking before the Standing Committee on Foreign Affairs and International Trade at the end of March, the defense minister, Art Eggleton, expressed it this way: "The objective of NATO's air campaign is to diminish the capacity of the Yugoslav forces to attack and inflict atrocities against the people of Kosovo, and to bring that government back to the negotiating table. Our military operations are intended to avert an even greater humanitarian catastrophe and prevent the prospect of wider regional insecurity and instability."[19]

For his part, Lloyd Axworthy, the foreign minister, tended not to focus on the strategic considerations alone, but to put them in the wider context of other motivations. To the Standing Committee on Foreign Affairs and International Trade, he claimed: "I think most Canadians are aware that Kosovo is important to them. [...] The events there have been happening in the heart of Europe, a continent where most Canadians find roots and where we have *vital interests in terms of our security and in the economic, cultural, and human fields.*"[20] A week later, he again mentioned the strategic rationale, but again in passing:

> It was and is the humanitarian imperative that has galvanized the alliance to act. To be sure, strategic considerations played a role. The risk of the conflict's spilling over into the Balkans, in particular into Albania and the Former Yugoslav Republic of Macedonia, was and is a concern. However, NATO's actions are guided primarily by concern for the human rights and welfare of Kosovo's people.[21]

In short, the connection between Canada's "national interests" in Europe and the intervention against Yugoslavia seemed more virtual than real.

Alliance "Entrapment"

Derived from the theory of alliances, alliance entrapment seeks to explain how a state, after having joined an alliance or a coalition, can be dragged by its allies into conflicts that it might not necessarily consider important to its interests but that it agrees to fight because of its fears of being abandoned or marginalized by its allies.[22] Junior partners in an alliance or an international coalition can also become "trapped" by coalition leaders when the nature of the coalition changes after the smaller state joins the alliance, as occurred in the Gulf conflict in 1990–91, when the coalition leader unilaterally changed the purpose of the multinational coalition ranged against Iraq.

At first blush, it might appear that this dynamic applied to the case of the Canadian participation in the Kosovo conflict in at least two ways. First, it can be argued that simply by being a member of NATO, the Canadian government had no other choice but to participate in the military operations against Yugoslavia, whether it wanted to or not. To paraphrase the formulation employed by Sir Wilfrid Laurier to describe an earlier period in Canadian history: when the Atlantic Alliance is at war, Canada is also at war.[23] Moreover, this participation was seen as necessary if the Canadian government wanted to preserve a degree of credibility with its European partners, which too often tended to see Canada as little more than part of the "American pillar" of the Atlantic Alliance. In the second place, the Canadian government had already tied itself to NATO policy. By sending six CF-18 fighter-bombers to Italy in October 1998, the Canadian government placed itself in a situation from which it would be virtually impossible to disengage if the Alliance eventually decided to resort to force.

This situation was clearly recognized, and admitted, by policymakers. When John McKay (Liberal: Scarborough East) asked whether it was possible, at least in theory, for a NATO member to have refused to participate in the conflict, Paul Meyer, director of international security affairs in the Department of Foreign Affairs, responded:

> It's my understanding, from a political perspective [...] Of course, it's always a choice of national governments as to whether to participate or not; no one is forced to participate in a NATO operation if they've taken a sovereign decision not to. You know that even among the NATO member states there is a variety of different types of participation or nonparticipation in the allied military efforts that are going on. *But I think there is a premise of overall political solidarity, which has continued to characterize the attitudes of member states. You're also right that at any time [...] when there are leaders gathering, there could be changes in the nature of participation by states.*[24]

Certainly the prime minister stressed Canada's "obligations" as a founding member of NATO. And in a similar fashion, commentators and editorialists alike agreed that maintaining solidarity with the Alliance was a given in the Canadian government's decision to participate in the air war against Yugoslavia.

A good illustration of Canada's commitment to Alliance solidarity was the issue of ground troops. The Chrétien government consciously agreed to give up part of its capacity to make decisions to the Alliance as a whole. It consistently refused to hold a debate on the possibility of using ground forces—on the grounds that it would not be appropriate to anticipate the decision of the Alliance as a whole. Thus, when the defense minister, Art Eggleton, let slip that Canada was looking at the possibility of using ground troops, he was quickly contradicted by a Pentagon spokesman,[25] and after this episode Chrétien made a point of stressing that the Canadian approach to the use of ground troops would be determined by NATO decisions. On the eve of the Washington fiftieth-anniversary summit, he said, "If everyone agrees, I will not be the only one not to agree."[26]

This drew considerable criticism from opposition spokesmen. One Reform MP complained: "It should be a Canadian decision. Why is [Chrétien] letting NATO tell us what to do?" The New Democratic Party accused the government of being a "lap dog of the United States."[27] Moreover, several editorials and commentators expressed a similar point of view.[28]

This line of criticism represented a less sophisticated version of the "alliance entrapment" thesis, one that stressed the degree to which the Canadian government was being dragged into war not by NATO, but by the United States. It also represented a faint echo of the vitriolic anti-American discourse that marked the Canadian debate during the Gulf War, when one of the principal criticisms of the Mulroney government was that it was in Washington's pocket.[29]

Interestingly, the same accusation could have been levied against the Chrétien government in 1999, given that it was engaged in an operation directed more by Washington than by Brussels (to say nothing of New York). However, this opinion was not widely expressed, either by the opposition in Parliament or by public opinion. None of the opposition parties in the House of Commons used this argument to oppose the government's Kosovo policy. Indeed, a number of newspapers explicitly rejected it: *La Presse* argued that "the decision to bomb Yugoslavia was not made to support the United States, but it was made because Canada could not remain indifferent to what was happening in Kosovo."[30]

One of the reasons that could explain the fact that the Chrétien government did not suffer the same epithets that had been leveled at the Mulroney government during the Gulf War is that since coming to power in 1993, the Liberals had been very careful not to get too close to Washington. There had been no "Shamrock Summit" between Chrétien and Clinton, nor any ostentatious manifestations of friendship or complicity.[31] Thus, people tended to believe the prime minister when he declared on April 20: "We are taking collective decisions. These are not the Americans' decisions. Of course, the United States has a weight that is proportional to its importance in the attacks, but all decisions are made in the form of a consensus."[32]

Indeed, the record supports the prime minister's view: there is no evidence that the Canadian government was pressured by either the Americans or the Europeans. In fact, one of the main worries of the government was how to dampen the ardor of the opposition parties, which wanted to move further and more quickly than the NATO allies. In short, there is a difference between being "entrapped" by alliance commitments and willingly agreeing to forgo unilateral decision-making in favor of a more collective approach. There is little evidence that the Chrétien government was in any sense trapped into a commitment that Ottawa did not want.

The Lessons of History

The lessons that policymakers and analysts draw from past experiences can also constitute an important element in decision-making. When confronting a new and unclear policy situation, policymakers tend to look at comparable cases in the past, and draw inspiration from these cases to orient their decision. This hypothesis is particularly applicable to grave national decisions, such as entering alliances or going to war.[33] During the Gulf War, the "lessons of history" were used by numerous coalition policymakers to embellish their policy positions. While the comparison between Saddam Hussein and Adolf Hitler that was popular in the United States was not widely used in the Canadian debate, there were nonetheless constant references to the past as the proper guide for Canadian policy.[34] Can we see a similar pattern in 1999?

Most of the "historical" references used by government ministers and other members of Parliament focused on the behavior of the Yugoslav government in the recent past. Mention was often made of Milosevic's apparent difficulty in keeping his commitments (notably during the war in Bosnia). As Axworthy said to the Standing Committee: "One needs to recognize that with Milosevic, if one does not have the capacity to make him keep his agreements, he will not meet his obligations. It has always been this way for ten years."[35] This argument, it might be noted, also made its appearance in newspaper editorials.[36]

The Canadian government also justified NATO's operations against the Serbs by invoking the necessity of not repeating the errors of the past. As Axworthy told members of the Standing Committee on Foreign Affairs and International Trade: "Given our horrible experience in Bosnia and Rwanda, we decided that it was incumbent on the international community, using NATO as the intermediary, to have an effective response [to attacks on civilians]."[37]

Finally, history was a source of inspiration to commentators who doubted the efficacy of NATO's strategy of limiting its military operations to air strikes. Using examples drawn from the Second World War, the

Vietnam War, and the Gulf War, some parliamentarians, together with a good number of analysts, raised questions about the approach adopted by the Atlantic Alliance.[38]

In effect, these critiques could serve either as justification for a ground operation or (more rarely) as a condemnation of using force. Curiously, however, virtually all commentators forgot to make reference to the case of Bosnia in 1995, when NATO air strikes contributed to bringing the Bosnian Serbs to the negotiating table, paving the way for the Dayton Accords.[39] On balance, however, the lessons of history did not seem to constitute a clear or visible motivation for the Canadian decision to participate in the attacks on Yugoslavia.

Domestic Politics and Public Opinion

It is also possible that the Canadian government's approach to the conflict in Kosovo was determined by domestic politics. There are several variables associated with the "domestic politics" approach: type of regime, bureaucratic politics, elite bargaining, public opinion, style of decision-making, electoral politics, etc. For the purpose of this chapter, we will concentrate primarily on the reactions of members of Parliament, commentators in the press, and public opinion. In our view, this element is particularly significant given the importance of domestic politics the last time that Canada had gone to war—during the Persian Gulf conflict of 1990-91.

While there was considerable opposition to Canadian participation from Canadians of Serbian origin—manifested most visibly in violent street demonstrations at the outset of the conflict—there was also considerable consensus that this was, in Gwynne Dyer's phrase, a "good war."[40] Certainly the principal daily Canadian newspapers—such as Toronto's *Globe and Mail* and *National Post*, or Montréal's *Le Devoir* and *La Presse*—argued that the "international community" should adopt an increasingly firm attitude toward Belgrade. Indeed, much of the criticism leveled at the Canadian government—and at NATO—in the media tended to focus on the strategies employed. Of the four main dailies, only *Le Devoir* pronounced the air strikes "illegal and illegitimate."[41]

There was also widespread consensus among the various parties in the House of Commons about the appropriateness of the Canadian response to the Kosovo crisis; the principle of Canada's participation in NATO operations inspired next to no opposition in Parliament. On the contrary, there was a quasi-consensus among the main opposition parties—Reform, the Bloc Québécois, and the Progressive Conservatives. The intransigence of the government in Belgrade, and the massive exodus of the Kosovar Albanians from Kosovo generated unanimity among Canadian parliamentarians on the issue of air strikes. When the air operations were formally announced on March 24, all the opposition parties gave their approval for the NATO initiative. It is true that the unanimity was not unqualified. Some MPs, such as David Price of the Progressive Conservatives and Daniel Turp of the Bloc Québécois, openly deplored the absence of a mandate from the Security Council of the United Nations.[42] And on March 31, 1999, the New Democratic Party changed its mind, calling for a cessation of the bombing and a return to negotiations. But on the general approach, the major parties were in agreement. If anything, the main opposition parties were out in front of the government in their enthusiasm for a forceful response to the Kosovo crisis, inclined to try to prod the Liberals on the issue of a ground operation.

If there was general agreement on Canada's Kosovo decisions, there was little agreement on the way in which those decisions had been made. Much of the parliamentary debate fixed on process, with the government, in effect, continually pestered to recall Parliament, which had recessed on March 25, the day after the bombing started, and hold a debate on an eventual ground war.[43]

Public opinion tended to mirror the attitudes of the political elite. Canadians appeared unwilling to oppose the decision to participate in NATO operations. One of the first polls, published on April 10 in the *National Post,* indicated that fully 79 percent of respondents approved of the NATO air strikes and that 57 percent were in favor of launching a ground operation against the Serbs in Kosovo. Two weeks later, a *Globe and Mail*/CTV/Angus Reid poll showed that 69 percent of Canadians approved of the bombing and that 59 percent wanted to send ground troops to Kosovo if that were the only way to stop the humanitarian crisis there. In Quebec, where there is generally more reticence than in English Canada when it comes to dispatching troops for service overseas, similar opinions were expressed. A poll published on April 26 in *Le Devoir* revealed that 73 percent of Quebecers approved of the bombing and that a slim majority, 52 percent, would approve of sending ground troops to expel Serb forces from Kosovo, at least "as a last resort."[44]

When one notes the widespread consensus in Canadian society on the appropriateness of the use of force in response to the Kosovo crisis, one might well conclude that the enthusiasm of the Chrétien government for participation in a multilateral use of force was in part determined by the permissive domestic political environment in Canada. And, if there were few overt demonstrations by Canadians in favor of an even more forceful and muscular response, there was open support for the use of force for humanitarian purposes.

Humanitarian Motivations

In recent years, notions such as values, standards, ideas, and culture have made a comeback in the analysis of international relations: constructivists, critical theorists, and, to a lesser extent, neoclassical realists all stress the importance of these notions. One of the hypotheses advanced by constructivists consists of linking definitions of interest and identity and the policies of international actors to the normative environment in which they operate.[45] Indeed, one of the significant components of the contemporary international environment—at least for Western states—would be all of the norms relating to humanitarian intervention, which were gradually introduced over the last 150 years and which were appreciably reinforced in the decade after the Gulf War of 1991.[46]

Canada could be one of the countries most sensitive to this normative environment. Canadian foreign policy is still strongly marked by the idealism of Lester B. Pearson.[47] It is deeply based on the respect for the Charter of the United Nations and the search for international stability. The participation in both missions and in an active pursuit of human rights policies constitutes elements of foreign and security policy that garner the most support among Canadians. It is thus not surprising that policies based on humanitarian grounds are given considerable support in Canada.

One of the reasons why the Canadian debate did not emphasize either strategic considerations, alliance entrapment, the lessons of history, or domestic politics was that the debate was so dominated by humanitarian concerns, and in particular by the "human security" discourse championed by Lloyd Axworthy, the minister of foreign affairs. Canadian officials and commentators were in broad agreement that the Serb forces in Kosovo were not threatening the "national" security interests of Canada as a state, but rather the "individual" security interests of hundreds of thousands of Kosovar Albanians.

The humanitarian plight of the Kosovar Albanians in early 1999 fitted perfectly with the "human security" perspective that Axworthy had been pushing since his appointment to the foreign affairs portfolio in 1996. In this view, the traditional focus of foreign and defense policy on "state security" was no longer appropriate. In the post–Cold War era, when intrastate conflicts killed far more people than interstate war, what was needed was a focus on "human security"—in other words, putting the security needs of the individual ahead of those of the state.[48] Axworthy's highly successful campaign for a global ban on antipersonnel landmines in 1997 reflected that view.[49]

The situation in Kosovo over the winter of 1998-99 proved to be a quintessential example of the need for a "human security" perspective. The persistent refusal of the government in Belgrade to provide security for the

Albanian majority and the accumulating evidence that the Milosevic government was about to launch a massive ethnic cleansing campaign in the spring combined to convince Axworthy of the need for, and the appropriateness of, robust and muscular action by the NATO alliance.

It is true that a number of observers pointed out that Axworthy's "human security" perspective was not fully worked out, particularly in cases like the Kosovo conflict in which a recourse to force prevailed over all other measures.[50] Moreover, even if all the logical consequences of the concept of human security are not yet clear, it seems evident that the notion of "human security" belongs in a different intellectual universe: it is a post-Westphalian, essentially nonstate conception of security that sits uneasily with the logic of a realist state-centric perspective.[51]

Regardless of the intellectual complications of the term itself,[52] there can be little doubt that Axworthy's "human security" discourse was widely embraced in the debate about Kosovo in Canada. Much of the official justification embraced by the Canadian government stressed that the primary purpose behind the use of force against the Federal Republic of Yugoslavia was to safeguard the human rights of Kosovar Albanians threatened by Serb security forces, both local militias and army and police units from Serbia proper. In his public statements, for example, the prime minister routinely referred to the importance of the humanitarian element and the deteriorating condition of Kosovar Albanians.

Not surprisingly, the humanitarian aspect was also uppermost in Axworthy's own justifications for Canada's participation. As he put it in April 1999:

> NATO's actions are guided primarily by concern for the human rights and welfare of Kosovo's people. NATO's recourse to air strikes was precipitated by evidence that the regime of repression by the Serb government was on the rise and accelerating. [...] NATO did not provoke this tragedy—it responded to it. And the decision to act was not motivated by a military threat to Alliance territory, but by an affront to Alliance values and a belief—perhaps more explicit in some capitals than in others—that human security matters. Alliance members could not turn away from the humanitarian crisis taking place on NATO's European doorstep. That is why Canadian pilots are part of the effort, why we are providing humanitarian relief and why we are offering sanctuary to 5,000 refugees.[53]

Indeed it can be argued that this humanitarianism was already deeply entrenched in Canadian political discourse by the time the Kosovo conflict broke out. One of the early warning signals that Canadian public opinion had shifted occurred in July 1995, at the time of the massacres that followed the fall of the Bosnian Muslim city of Srebrenica, an enclave long protected by Canadian Blue Helmets. A second signal was sent in November 1996, when a humanitarian crisis erupted in the Great Lakes region of Africa. Stung by public opinion still outraged by the Rwandan massacres of 1994, the Chrétien government tried to form an international coalition to bring aid to the Rwandan refugees. While the initiative collapsed when the refugees returned en masse to Rwanda at the end of November,[54] the lesson was clear: Canadians would no longer tolerate their government remaining indifferent in the face of humanitarian calamities. And the Liberal government, which had made "human security" such a cornerstone of its foreign policy, was naturally inclined to respond to such public pressure.

Overall, the arguments justifying Canadian participation on the basis of respect for human rights were the most frequently heard. The prime minister made frequent reference to this aspect. Nearly all of the public pronouncements of cabinet ministers were embellished with reference to such phrases as "the humanitarian catastrophe in Kosovo," "ethnic cleansing," "atrocities committed by Serb forces," and, most frequently of all, "protection of human rights."[55] On at least one occasion, Axworthy left no doubt in his view about which factor best explained Canadian participation: "Humanitarian considerations," he said on the day the bombing began, "are the principal motive for our action."[56] Opposition members of Parliament were no different. Daniel Turp of the Bloc Québécois expounded on numerous occasions his belief in the necessity of "preventing a genocide,"[57] and used this argument to press for setting in motion a ground operation in Kosovo. And, as noted above, comparable ideas were expressed by all of the parties represented in the House.

The lessons of the events in Bosnia and Rwanda indicate that Canada's participation in the Kosovo operation—and the tendency of the government to justify its participation using the discourse of humanitarianism—was no accident. It reflected the logical continuation of policy evolved in previous engagements. It also demonstrated the degree to which norms relating to humanitarian interventions have become anchored more and more deeply in both civil society and the political elite in Canada.

Conclusion

Our survey of the different possible factors that motivated the Canadian government to participate in the NATO attacks on Yugoslavia reveals little support for what might be thought of as the classical concerns of realism in international politics. The Canadian government did not contribute the few resources it did to this fight for national security reasons. Nor was it a victim of alliance entrapment. While Canadian policymakers were not oblivious to the broader geostrategic implications of allowing Kosovo to be cleansed by

Serb forces, and while Canadian policymakers were only too aware of the dynamics of Alliance politics, they were also seized by what they saw as the essential rightness of the use of force in these circumstances. Moreover, as we have shown, they were operating in a domestic political environment that was not only permissive but also generally supportive (with the notable exception of numerous Canadians of Serb origins, who remained unaffected by the humanitarian crisis caused by the mass expulsion of Kosovar Albanians and persisted in their staunch opposition to the campaign).

While this case might offer little support to realists, it does lend a certain credence to constructivist hypotheses. There was an almost complete absence of any mention of the concept of national interest in the government's justifying rhetoric; rather, Canada's participation was justified using the language of humanitarianism, reinforcing the constructivist hypothesis that the normative environment is an important determinant of foreign policy decisions. This is all the more plausible since the Canadian reaction to the events in Kosovo does not seem to be an isolated or aberrant policy. Rather, it seems to be the latest stage in the process of the integration of norms, a process started after the Second World War and dramatically accelerated by the events in Bosnia and in Rwanda. Thus, our conclusions reinforce—and indeed go well beyond—the observations of Peter Katzenstein, who noted that "Canadian identity on the question of security is defined in terms of international peacekeeping rather than the defense of national sovereignty." In this sense, "Canada [is] arguably the first postmodern state par excellence."[58]

We have characterized Canada as the "happy follower" in the Kosovo conflict. The above account suggests that the Canadian government was happy that the international community (or, more properly, NATO) was taking human security seriously. It was enthusiastic about the use of force, for it was widely believed that the use of force in Kosovo would finally bring an end to ethnic cleansing in the former Yugoslavia. Ottawa was also happy that the government in Washington was in command, for that ensured that the superordinate power of the United States would be committed to the campaign. But most of all, the Chrétien government was happy because Canada could participate in what was widely perceived to be a just cause without having to devote any serious Canadian blood or treasure to the enterprise. In short, if the Canadian government was a "forced ally," it was forced by the internal logic of its own well-established foreign and security policy, and not by the coalition leader or the hegemonic power.

Notes

1. For an examination of the middle-power contributions to the Gulf War, see Andrew F. Cooper and Kim Richard Nossal, "The Middle Powers in the Gulf

Coalition: Australia, Canada, and the Nordics Compared," in *Friends in Need: Burden Sharing in the Gulf War,* ed. Andrew Bennett, Joseph Lepgold, and Danny Unger (New York: St Martin's Press, 1997), pp. 269–95.
2. David Price, a Progressive Conservative member of Parliament, claimed that members of Canada's antiterrorist unit, Joint Task Force 2, were operating in Kosovo behind the lines with the Kosovo Liberation Army, along with comparable units from other NATO countries. This was flatly denied by Art Eggleton, the Canadian defense minister. *Globe and Mail* (Toronto), April 20, 1999, p. A1.
3. For a discussion of this dynamic, see the contributions in Michel Fortmann, S. Neil MacFarlane, and Stéphane Roussel, eds., *Tous pour un ou chacun pour soi: promesses et limites de la coopération régionale en matière de sécurité* (Sainte-Foy: Institut québécois des hautes Études internationales, 1996).
4. See, for example, Martin Rudner, "Canada, the Gulf Crisis and Collective Security," in *Canada Among Nations, 1990–91: After the Cold War,* ed. Fen Osler Hampson and Christopher J. Maule (Ottawa: Carleton University Press, 1991); Kim Richard Nossal, *Rain Dancing: Sanctions in Canadian and Australian Foreign Policy* (Toronto: University of Toronto Press, 1994), chap. 9.
5. *Le Devoir* (Montréal), April 13, 1999, p. A8 (our translation).
6. For an overview of the contemporary debate in foreign policy, see Margot Light, "Foreign Policy Analysis," in *Contemporary International Relations: A Guide to Theory,* ed. A. J. R. Groom and Margot Light (London: Pinter, 1994), pp. 93–108.
7. Gideon Rose, "Neoclassical Realism and Theories of Foreign Policy," *World Politics* 51 (October 1998): pp. 144–72.
8. Peter J. Katzenstein, ed., *The Culture of National Security: Norms and Identity in World Politics* (New York: Columbia University Press, 1996).
9. The classic formulation is to be found in Stephen M. Walt, "Alliance Formation and the Balance of World Power," *International Security* 9 (spring 1985): pp. 3–43; also Walt, *The Origins of Alliances* (Ithaca: Cornell University Press, 1987).
10. Kim Richard Nossal, "Un pays européen? L'histoire de l'atlanticisme au Canada," in *La politique étrangère canadienne dans un ordre international en mutation* (Sainte-Foy, Québec: Centre québécois de relations internationales, 1992), pp. 131–60; Nils Ørvik, "A defense doctrine for Canada," *Orbis* 27 (spring 1983): pp. 185–206; Stéphane Roussel, "Amère Amérique... L'OTAN et l'intérêt national du Canada," *Canadian Defence Review/Revue canadienne de défense* 22 (February 1993): pp. 35–42.
11. André P. Donneur and Stéphane Roussel, "Le Canada: Quand l'expertise et la crédibilité ne suffisent plus," in *Intérêt national et responsabilités internationales: Six états face au conflit en ex-Yougoslavie (1991–1995),* ed. Alex Macleod et Stéphane Roussel (Montréal: Guérin, 1996), pp. 143–60.
12. David G. Haglund, "The NATO of Its Dreams? Canada and the Cooperative-Security Alliance," *International Journal* 52 (summer 1997): pp. 464–82.
13. Joseph T. Jockel and Joel J. Sokolsky, *Canada and Collective Security: Odd Man Out* (New York: Praeger, 1986).

14. Interview, Department of National Defence, Ottawa, June 1999.
15. Marcel Belleau, "Le Canada devait-il participer aux bombardements en Yougoslavie?" *Le Devoir,* April 7, 1999, p. A7.
16. See, for example, Kim Richard Nossal, "Another march of folly? Hardly," *Globe and Mail,* April 15, 1999, p. A15.
17. Frederic Wagnière, "Les Canadiens en Europe," *La Presse* (Montréal), June 3, 1999, p. B2.
18. Marcus Gee, "NATO's unjust war," *Globe and Mail,* April 21, 1999, p. A10.
19. Canada, Parliament, House of Commons, Standing Committee on Foreign Affairs and International Trade, *Minutes of Proceedings and Evidence,* March 31, 1999; emphasis added. For the full text, see: http://www.parl.gc.ca/ InfoComDoc/36/1/FAIT/Meetings/ Evidence/ faitev111-e.htm.
20. Ibid.; emphasis added.
21. Lloyd Axworthy, "Kosovo and the human security agenda," Canada, Department of Foreign Affairs, *Statements and Speeches* 99/28, April 7, 1999, Woodrow Wilson School of Public and International Affairs, Princeton University. For the full text, see: http://198.103.104.118/minpub/Publication. asp?FileSpec=/Min_Pub_Docs/100194.htm.
22. This dynamic is best explicated in Glenn H. Snyder, "The Security Dilemma in World Politics," *World Politics* 36 (July 1984): pp. 471–77.
23. In 1910, Sir Wilfrid had said, "If England is at war, we are at war and liable to attack." C. P. Stacey, *Canada and the Age of Conflict,* vol. 1: *1867–1921* (Toronto: Macmillan, 1977), p. 135.
24. Standing Committee on Foreign Affairs and International Trade, *Minutes of Proceedings and Evidence,* April 22, 1999; also at http://www.parl.gc.ca/ InfoComDoc/36/1/FAIT/Meetings/ Evidence/faitev 118-e.htm; emphasis added.
25. Jeff Sallot, "The federal government wants NATO to consider sending ground troops into Kosovo to halt ethnic cleansing by Serb forces," *Globe and Mail,* April 8, 1999, p. A1.
26. *Globe and Mail,* April 21, 1999, p. A1.
27. *National Post,* April 22, 1999, p. A1; *Globe and Mail,* April 22, 1999, p. A8.
28. For example, *Le Devoir* editorialized that "le gouvernement Chrétien obéit aux ordres." *Le Devoir,* April 14, 1999, p. A8.
29. See Jocelyn Coulon, *La dernière croisade. La guerre du Golfe et le rôle caché du Canada* (Montréal: Méridien, 1992).
30. *La Presse,* May 3, 1999, p. B2 (our translation).
31. Roy Norton, "Posture and Policymaking in Canada–US Relations: The First Two Mulroney and Chrétien Years," *Canadian Foreign Policy* 5 (winter 1998): pp. 15–36.
32. Cited by Manon Cornellier, "Le Canada se ralliera à l'OTAN," *Le Devoir,* April 21, 1999, pp. A1, A8.
33. Dan Reiter, *Crucible of Beliefs: Learning, Alliances, and World Wars* (Ithaca: Cornell University Press, 1996); Reiter, "Learning, Realism, and Alliances: The Weight of the Shadow of the Past," *World Politics* 46 (July 1994): pp. 490–526.

34. Kim Richard Nossal, "Quantum Leaping: The Gulf Debate in Australia and Canada," in Michael McKinley, ed., *The Gulf War: Critical Perspectives* (Sydney: Allen and Unwin, 1994), pp. 58–63; Cooper and Nossal, "The Middle Powers in the Gulf Coalition."
35. Standing Committee on Foreign Affairs and International Trade, March 31, 1999, 1200hrs.
36. For example, *La Presse,* October 15, 1998; "A peacekeeper goes to war," *Globe and Mail,* April 14, 1999.
37. Standing Committee on Foreign Affairs and International Trade, March 31, 1999, 1145hrs.
38. See the comments of the following MPs on the Standing Committee on Foreign Affairs and International Trade: John O'Reilly (March 31, 1215hrs), Keith Martin (June 1, 1530hrs). Also Robert Pelley, "Participer à la guerre au Kosovo: soyons prudent," *Le Soleil,* May 3, 1999, p. B9.
39. However, according to Adam Roberts, NATO policymakers drew the wrong lessons from Operation Deliberate Force, undertaken in Bosnia in 1995, when they estimated that air strikes alone would be enough to convince the Serbian government to agree to the conditions of the Rambouillet agreement. Adam Roberts, "NATO's Humanitarian War Over Kosovo," *Survival* 41 (autumn 1999): pp. 102–23.
40. Gwynne Dyer, "At last, a good war," *Globe and Mail,* April 17, 1999, p. D1.
41. Guy Taillefer, "La guerre illégitime," *Le Devoir,* April 1, 1999, p. A6.
42. *Le Devoir,* March 25, 1999; "La fermeture des frontières du Kosovo fait des Kosovars des prisonniers chez eux," *Communiqué of the Bloc Québécois,* April 9, 1999. Price began by calling the NATO bombing a violation of international law, but was quickly reined in by his leader, Joe Clark, who issued a statement disavowing Price's view and supporting the NATO bombing. *National Post,* March 25, 1999, March 26, 1999.
43. Manon Cornellier, "L'opposition pourrait appuyer l'envoi de troupes au Kosovo," *Le Devoir,* April 13, 1999.
44. *National Post,* April 10, 1999; *Globe and Mail,* April 12, 1999.
45. Alexander Wendt, *Social Theory of International Politics* (Cambridge: Cambridge University Press, 1999); Ronald L. Jepperson, Alexander Wendt, and Peter J. Katzenstein, "Norms, Identity, and Culture in National Security," in *The Culture of National Security,* ed. Peter J. Katzenstein, pp. 33–75.
46. Martha Finnemore, "Constructing Norms of Humanitarian Intervention", in *Culture of National Security,* ed. Peter J. Katzenstein, pp. 153–85.
47. As Canada's foreign minister from 1948 to 1957, Pearson inspired the U.N. peacekeeping force deployed in the wake of the Suez crisis of 1956, which earned him the Nobel Peace Prize. He later became prime minister, from 1963 to 1968.
48. For a formal statement, see Department of Foreign Affairs, *Human Security: Safety for People in a Changing World* (Ottawa: Department of Foreign Affairs, April 1999).
49. For an excellent survey of the "Ottawa process" and Axworthy's role in it, see the various contributions to *Canadian Foreign Policy* 5 (spring 1998).

50. Christian Geiser, "Fin du conflit au Kosovo: Le danger de la 'sécurité humaine,'" *Le Devoir,* June 14, 1999, p. A7; for a critique, see Fen Osler Hampson and Dean F. Oliver, "Pulpit Diplomacy: A Critical Assessment of the Axworthy Doctrine," *International Journal* 53 (summer 1998): pp. 379–406.
51. See Stephen M. Walt, "The Renaissance of Security Studies," *International Studies Quarterly* 35 (June 1991): pp. 211–39.
52. For critiques of the concept of human security, see, in particular, Myriam Gervais and Stéphane Roussel, "De la sécurité de l'État à celle de l'individu: l'évolution du concept de sécurité au Canada (1990–1996)," *Études internationales* 29 (March 1998): pp. 25–52; Fen Hampson and Dean Oliver, "Pulpit Diplomacy."
53. Axworthy, *Statements and Speeches 99/28,* April 7, 1999.
54. Myriam Gervais, *Le concept de sécurité humaine et ses applications: Afrique des Grands Lacs et Bosnie* (Ottawa, Canadian Center For Foreign Policy Development, June 1998).
55. See, for example, Art Eggleton's interventions to the Standing Committee on Foreign Affairs and International Trade, March 31, 1999.
56. Lloyd Axworthy, *Statements and Speeches 99/23*, March 24, 1999.
57. See, for example, "La fermeture des frontières du Kosovo fait des Kosovars des prisonniers chez eux," loc. cit.; also Turp's interventions before the Standing Committee on Foreign Affairs and International Trade on March 31, 1999, 1145hrs.
58. Peter J. Katzenstein, "Conclusion: National Security in a Changing World," in Peter J. Katzenstein, *The Culture of National Security,* pp. 535 and 518 fn. 48.

CHAPTER TWELVE

The Atlantic Alliance and the Kosovo Crisis: The Impact of Expansion and the Behavior of New Allies

Milada Anna Vachudová[*]

Poland, Hungary, and the Czech Republic became members of the Atlantic Alliance just days before the launch of military operations against the Federal Republic of Yugoslavia (FRY) in March 1999. What impact did expansion have on the political cohesion and military performance of NATO during the Kosovo crisis? Did it cripple the Alliance, as some observers feared? This chapter first explores whether expansion strengthened or weakened NATO's ability to intervene militarily against the FRY. Second, it seeks to account for variation in the level of political commitment and domestic support for NATO among the three new members. NATO's war against the FRY on the heels of its expansion created an immediate test: Would new members meet their Alliance commitments? To what extent would they model their comportment toward the war on the expectations of NATO and the United States? Third and fourth, this chapter analyzes more closely the domestic political debates surrounding NATO's military intervention against the FRY in Hungary and the Czech Republic, respectively. Fifth, it explores how the behavior of Bulgaria, Romania, and Slovakia during the Kosovo crisis was shaped by the aspiration of these states to join NATO in the future.

The Impact of Enlargement

Did Expansion Make NATO Weaker?

One argument against NATO expansion was that new members from the former Soviet bloc would weaken the Alliance. In this view, new members would undermine political cohesion because more members would make it more difficult to reach a consensus, and because the political behavior of newly democratized states would likely be destabilizing. Moreover, these new entrants would be a security liability, bringing only backward and incompatible armed forces into the Alliance while exposing it to a host of new security threats. They might, for example, entangle the Alliance in disputes with neighboring states over borders and ethnic minorities.[1]

The *bilan* of the Kosovo crisis is mixed, but favorable to expansion. As regards political cohesion, two out of the three new members provided steady support for the Alliance. The Polish government championed NATO's attack on the FRY and supported its American architects more actively than any veteran NATO member besides the United Kingdom, while the Hungarian government took considerable risks in providing political and material support for air strikes against its immediate neighbor. In contrast, while the Czech government met its procedural obligations to the Alliance, the two largest political parties broadcast a great number of statements that made it clear that they did not, in fact, approve of NATO's actions in the Balkans.

Instead of being a security liability, the new members were an asset to the Alliance despite the inadequacy of their armed forces. Expansion improved NATO's ability to conduct a bombing campaign against the FRY and to deploy peacekeeping troops in the Balkans because, absent expansion, the Czech Republic and Hungary would likely have lent far less support. While the Czech Republic's disposition may have been irrelevant, Hungary's provision of military bases, transportation routes, and other forms of logistical support was strategically significant. Hungary's commitment to the Alliance compelled the government to support, with some restrictions, NATO's strategy to pacify the FRY despite the precarious position of some 300,000 ethnic Hungarians living under the rule of Yugoslav president Slobodan Milosevic in the Vojvodina region.

Alongside Hungary, NATO strategists needed to cooperate closely with several southeastern European states bordering the FRY and aspiring to NATO membership. In an effort to bolster their credentials as future allies, the Bulgarian and Romanian governments provided political and logistical support, including air and land corridors for NATO's military operations, in the face of strong domestic opposition and threats of retaliation from the FRY. Both governments could expect their countries to suffer substantially from lost trade, lost foreign investment, and environmental damage as a result of the Kosovo crisis, sinking NATO's reputation even further with their electorates. Coping with the Bosnian wars and complying with the embargo against the FRY had taught Bulgarian and Romanian leaders to expect little Western compensation for the economic costs of being frontline states, no matter how cooperative.² Without the potential reward of NATO membership, these governments had few incentives to assume the domestic costs of cooperating with the Alliance and appearing as instruments of American power.³

Geography lent Hungary, Bulgaria, and Romania strategic importance in the Kosovo crisis. If one allows for future expansions of NATO and predicts that NATO's future engagements will be on the peripheries of Europe, then expansion will continue to strengthen the Alliance. New members will adjust their behavior to meet Alliance commitments, while prospective members will provide valuable assistance in an attempt to signal their fitness for future membership. Indeed, serious prospective members may turn out to be more reliable than a number of existing ones.

Did NATO Expansion Make Europe Less Stable?

Another argument against NATO expansion was that it would undermine European stability by drawing new dividing lines on the Continent and by making Russia more belligerent toward the West. Here I do not seek to fully evaluate Russia's reaction to NATO expansion or the effect of expansion on Russia's conduct during the Kosovo crisis. There is, however, evidence that NATO expansion (in tandem with that of the EU) has improved relations between new NATO members and neighboring states left outside of the Alliance, because the prospect of membership has helped Western-oriented reformers get elected and elected governments pursue reform.⁴ This dynamic played a role in the ouster of destabilizing nationalist leaders such as Vladimir Meciar in Slovakia, Ion Iliescu in Romania, and Franjo Tudjman in Croatia. The replacement of nationalist political parties by pro-European parties intent on meeting the requirements of NATO membership improved the treatment of ethnic minorities and restarted economic growth in the region.

Meanwhile, for Hungary, the Czech Republic, and Poland, accession to NATO allowed for closer cooperation with their eastern and southern neighbors. They had previously avoided close ties in order to avoid being associated by the West with their less reformed eastern neighbors. Once in NATO, the new members became sincere advocates of their neighbors' entry into the EU and NATO, perhaps chiefly to improve the lot of coethnic groups living across the border. Whatever their motivation, this translated into a policy of supporting democratic reformers and restraining demands for autonomy on the part of coethnic groups, which in turn increased political stability and cooperation in the region. NATO membership for some postcommunist states—but not others—posed no significant border problems. This is in contrast to a future enlargement of the EU, which will create new dividing lines by way of tighter visa regulations separating members from nonmembers.

The Domestic Politics of Joining NATO

There are several criteria to evaluate the political performance and military utility of NATO's newest members during the Kosovo crisis. The most interesting may be to assess the political commitment of the government to the Alliance against the domestic political costs for the government of lending such support. Geographic proximity to the conflict is critical, because it is likely to raise both the costs of assistance for the government and the utility of that assistance to the Alliance. Other criteria include the level of domestic support for NATO membership, the quality of the military, and the respect afforded the military by the public.

Poland, for its part, firmly supported NATO's air strikes against Yugoslavia and offered substantial military assistance; indeed, the Poles, along with the British, seemed the only ones willing to put their soldiers in harm's way for Pristina. Polish political parties were united behind NATO membership, some 80 percent of citizens approved of Poland's accession, and the United States was held in the highest esteem. The Polish army is the largest, best equipped, and publicly the most respected in eastern Europe, making its potential military contribution to a NATO operation the most valuable (though severe interoperability problems could persist for as long as a decade). But the Polish government's enthusiasm for NATO's war in Kosovo was perhaps aided by the fact that Poland was geographically far removed from the conflict; it thus had politically and economically little to lose from the war, on the one hand, and logistically little to offer, on the other.

In contrast, Hungary, a neighbor of the FRY, was gravely concerned by the approximately 300,000 ethnic Hungarians who lived in the Serb-controlled province of Vojvodina. A valuable host to NATO troops and aircraft, it was nevertheless trying to restrain its participation in NATO's military operations, for fear of retaliation by Belgrade against the Vojvodina Hungarians. Its proximity to the conflict generated significant economic losses, high numbers of refugees, and palpable security concerns. Hungary therefore faced the greatest test of its commitment to the Alliance. As it turned out, all of the main Hungarian political parties actively supported the military operations, albeit with restrictions on NATO's use of Hungarian territory; the government was subsequently successful in making the Alliance respect some of these restrictions. During the air strikes, domestic support for NATO, generally around 60 percent, did not decrease significantly. The Hungarian army, however, did not have much to offer besides regional expertise: it is the smallest and least well equipped of the three, and it earns a low level of respect from the Hungarian public.

The Czech Republic was, like Poland, geographically removed from the conflict and had no concerns about coethnics in the Balkans, but its government, political parties, and public gave substantially less support to the Alliance than those of Poland or of Hungary. For its part, the Czech military also had little to offer, though it is in slightly better shape and earns slightly more respect than that of Hungary. Support for NATO membership was as low as 45 percent during the air strikes. Technically, the government fulfilled all of its obligations to the Alliance, such as granting the use of Czech territory in a timely manner. But the lukewarm commitment of the Czech political class to NATO was underscored by the Czech government's peace initiative, drafted with NATO's traditional miscreant, Greece. The "Czech-Greek initiative" earned Prague the considerable displeasure of the American government.

While the Czech Republic incurred virtually no costs or risks from the air strikes, Czech political leaders denounced NATO's military intervention in the FRY. For this they were heavily criticized by Western journalists and government officials as unreliable allies. Czech politicians did tend to question NATO's values and intentions, rather than thoughtfully criticizing NATO's bombing strategy. Whatever the merits of their arguments, however, this revealed an interesting tension between political parties participating in a vigorous democratic debate about Alliance membership and governments ensuring that the state upheld its Alliance commitments.

Complacency and Reform of the Left

For NATO's eastern members and candidates, membership offers clear benefits. First, membership places the state in the security alliance of the Western democracies; along with EU membership, it confirms that the political and cultural goal of "returning" to Europe after decades in the Soviet bloc has been fulfilled. Second, it presents itself as a far more effective way to guarantee state security than the alternatives of neutrality or alliance with Russia. Third, it proves to be considerably less expensive than paying for a state's own defense, and provides momentum and assistance for the essential task of modernizing the military. Finally, NATO membership furthers other goals, such as attracting foreign investment and improving a state's credentials for joining the EU.

Why do the elites and publics of Hungary and Poland value NATO membership more highly than those of the Czech Republic? Two factors help explain this: the attitude of the political class toward state security, and the reform of the former Communist Party. First, a consensus exists among mainstream Hungarian and Polish political parties as to the importance of NATO as a provider of security. For both states, long borders to the east and to the south underscore the need for a sound national security strategy; this is punctuated for Poland by its history of invasion and partition, and for Hungary by the Yugoslav wars. For the Czechs, however, the lack of obvious security threats makes NATO membership less crucial. Moreover, the Czechs always seemed assured of inclusion in the first wave of expansion, no matter how little their successive governments did to shore up public support or to meet the military requirements of membership. Thus, Czech approaches to NATO have been marked by a high degree of complacency.

Second, the evolution of the political debate on NATO depended largely on whether the former Communist Party reformed itself after 1989. For decades, the populations of Warsaw Pact states were indoctrinated with propaganda that equated NATO with the enemy; in Poland and Czechoslovakia, this was reinforced by strong anti-German sentiments. After 1989, mainstream left-wing public opinion tended to equate NATO membership with membership in the Warsaw Pact: it did not seem advisable to trade the tutelage of Moscow for that of Washington or Brussels or Bonn. Moreover, there were valid concerns about the costs of meeting NATO military standards and of antagonizing Russia. Since populations were very poorly informed about NATO, what politicians told them played a decisive role, and those who most needed to be convinced were voters of the left.

In Poland and Hungary, the communists reformed themselves in the early 1990s and supported NATO membership upon their subsequent return to power as social democrats. They gradually persuaded a substantial portion of their core voters on the "conservative" left to take a pro-Western stand on NATO as well as on other issues. As a result, a strong political consensus in favor of NATO membership developed in 1990-91 and held fast until membership was attained in 1999. All moderate political parties of the left and the right supported NATO membership as a matter of basic state interest.

In the Czech Republic, by contrast, the Communist Party did not reform itself and remained vehemently anti-NATO, while the newly established Social Democratic Party did not exert itself to create a pro-NATO consensus within its own ranks or among its electorate.[5] Instead, Social Democratic politicians remained lukewarm on accession in an attempt to win Communist votes. More generally, they followed public opinion instead of shaping it. This was compounded by the bizarre anti-NATO (and pro-Milosevic) stance of the country's most powerful right-wing politician, former Prime Minister Vaclav Klaus. As a result, political consensus on the value of Alliance membership was elusive, and approaches to NATO were highly contentious.

NATO and Domestic Politics in Hungary

The two pillars of Hungarian foreign policy since 1989 have been integration into NATO and the EU, on the one hand, and the improvement of the situation of ethnic Hungarian minorities abroad, on the other. By linking NATO membership with the imperative of regulating relations with neighboring states, NATO required Hungary to subordinate its support for Hungarian minorities abroad to its goal of joining NATO. During NATO's military operations against Yugoslavia, Hungary carved out a distinct position and lent qualified support in order to balance conflicting interests in safeguarding ethnic Hungarians under the rule of Belgrade and proving its merits as a new member. Despite the problems this caused NATO's military planners, Hungary's position was generally respected in the Alliance.

The political consensus in support of NATO membership amongst Hungarian political parties was impressive, especially since Hungary's precarious position with respect to the wars in Yugoslavia could have created substantial disagreements. Political parties generally kept questions of NATO membership and national security separate from the arena of political competition.[6] In the November 1997 referendum, 85 percent of the voters supported Hungary's accession (though participation stood at only 50 percent). In a poll conducted in January 1999, 65 percent of the population supported while 20 percent opposed NATO membership.[7]

Despite a broad political consensus on the desirability of NATO membership, how best to secure this membership became a significant issue in Hungarian domestic politics after 1989. Hungary's first democratic government, led by Jozsef Antall of the Hungarian Democratic Forum (MDF), worked through European institutions to internationalize the problems faced by ethnic Hungarian minorities in Slovakia, Romania, and Serbia and to codify minority rights.[8] In several statements, however, it implied support for peaceful border changes.[9] Instead of signing basic treaties with Slovakia and Romania, it worked to isolate internationally the Slovak and Romanian governments due to their incorrect treatment of Magyar minorities. In consequence, Hungary's foreign policy became viewed as nationalistic and potentially destabilizing for the region. In 1994, some Western observers contemplated a first expansion of NATO without Hungary.

The Socialists and the Free Democrats came to power in 1994, charging that the previous government's preoccupation with the interests of ethnic Hungarians abroad had sacrificed those of Hungary itself with respect to NATO and EU accession. The government of Gyula Horn signed basic treaties with the Slovak and Romanian governments, despite their hostile stance toward the collective rights of their ethnic Hungarian citizens. The pressure of NATO and the EU were decisive in compelling the Slovak and

Romanian governments to sign treaties with such ambitious provisions, and in compelling the Hungarian government to resign itself to their likely non-implementation.

The 1998 elections were won by the right, now dominated by the Federation of Young Democrats (Fidesz), who formed a coalition with the MDF and the Independent Smallholders (FKGP). During the campaign, Fidesz blamed the Socialist-Free Democrat government for being too subservient in meeting the requirements of NATO and particularly EU membership. The return of the right to government (albeit in a more pragmatic form) and several statements by Prime Minister Viktor Orban again stirred concern about Hungary's treatment of its neighbors. However, the election of democratic reformers in Romania and Slovakia, who invited ethnic Hungarian parties to join the government, ushered in a period of good relations with Hungary.

Hungary and the Kosovo Crisis

The tension between acceding to NATO membership and defending the interests of ethnic Hungarian minorities abroad came to the fore with NATO's intervention in the Bosnian wars.[10] These wars have affected Hungarian security profoundly because of their geographic proximity and because of the 350,000 ethnic Hungarians living in Vojvodina, a region of northern Serbia bordering Hungary and Romania. From 1991, Hungary faced an influx of refugees and ever-worse reports of the mistreatment of ethnic Hungarians living in the Serb-controlled Vojvodina region. Vojvodina's autonomous status had been revoked by Belgrade in 1989 along with that of Kosovo, but Hungarians comprised only 15–16 percent of Vojvodina's population in 1999.[11]

The Kosovo crisis and NATO military operations against Yugoslavia launched in March 1999 created much greater tension between NATO and the protection of Magyars in Vojvodina than had NATO's intervention in the Bosnian wars. Hungary worked to limit its participation in NATO's military attacks for fear of retaliation by Serbia against ethnic Hungarians living in Vojvodina. However, because of geography and of NATO bases in Hungary, it was in fact expected to contribute much more than the Czech Republic or Poland.[12]

By the time of the Washington summit in April 1999, Hungary had carved out a fairly clear position with respect to the conflict: it would support but not participate in the air strikes against the Yugoslav regime, and no NATO ground invasion could be launched from Hungarian territory.[13] Parliament had voted overwhelmingly on October 14, 1998, to allow the unrestricted use of Hungarian airspace by NATO aircraft; this was extended to the use of military airfields on March 24, 1999. Only the extreme rightwing Hungarian Justice and Life Party (MIEP) voted against the measures. However, it was understood that NATO combat aircraft would not take off directly from Hungary to carry out their bombing missions against Yugoslavia.

The Orban government also declared that no Hungarian soldier would set foot on Yugoslav soil, even as part of a peacekeeping mission; Hungary would contribute only technical and medical units outside Yugoslavia. Several hundred ethnic Hungarians were conscripts in the Yugoslav army, and Orban stated in July 1998 that "Hungarian soldiers can under no circumstances face [other] Hungarian soldiers."[14] Despite the potential for large numbers of refugees and significant economic costs, public support for the air strikes in April 1999 was high at 60 percent (with 31 percent against). Moreover, the six parliamentary parties achieved impressive political consensus on Hungary's stance during the air strikes (save for the dissent of the MIEP, which called the Kosovo crisis an opportunity to redraw Hungary's southern border).

Some Vojvodina leaders warned that cooperation with NATO could lead to brutal retribution against ethnic Hungarians and charged that the Orban government was proving its loyalty to NATO in a way that jeopardized the Vojvodina Hungarians.[15] According to Jozsef Kasza, chairman of the Alliance of Vojvodina Hungarians (SVM), Budapest made a serious mistake in allowing the use of its airports. Kasza also described Orban's statement that "human and historical justice is on NATO's and our side" as irresponsible.[16] The Hungarian press reported in March that anti-Hungarian sentiment was growing amongst Serbs in Vojvodina, in part because "Belgrade television and military officials repeatedly stressed that NATO has conducted its assaults in Vojvodina (including on Novi Sad) from the direction of Hungary."[17]

After ongoing NATO missile attacks in Vojvodina, Foreign Minister Martonyi wrote to Kasza that NATO combat aircraft were not taking off from Hungary and that even the NATO aircraft securing Hungarian airspace operated from Italian bases.[18] He indicated that Hungary would put pressure on NATO to limit as much as possible military strikes in Vojvodina, and would draw attention to the threatened situation of the Vojvodina Hungarians at every possible occasion. Meanwhile, Martonyi reaffirmed Hungary's support for the military strategy of the Alliance, and ceded several times to the logistical requests of NATO military planners.

In the political aftermath of NATO's air strikes, Hungarian leaders and commentators urged a diplomatic solution to the Kosovo crisis that would guarantee security for all ethnic groups, including the Hungarians in Vojvodina."[19] The Orban government tried to parlay its support for the Alliance into guarantees for the autonomy of the Vojvodina province.

It pushed the West Europeans and especially the United States to include a separate chapter on autonomy for the Vojvodina region in the Stability Pact for South Eastern Europe, but was unsuccessful.

While Hungarian diplomacy earned the respect of the Alliance, the crisis revealed the weakness of the Hungarian military.[20] It is considered by many to be in the worst shape of the three new members, with government policy being the least supportive of defense spending and conscription. Subsequent to Hungary's difficulties in providing a very small force for KFOR, Orban ordered a thorough review of the military, which may lead to political support for essential reform.

NATO and Domestic Politics in the Czech Republic

For much of the 1990s the Czech Republic perceived itself, and was generally perceived by others, as the most pro-Western state in eastern Europe and perhaps the most deserving of NATO membership. In reality, the Czech Republic's accession to NATO posed substantial problems of both domestic political consensus and public support.[21] But however provincial and chaotic the Czech debate on NATO became, the Czech Republic, since the divorce with Slovakia, has encountered few security risks. It borders neither the former Soviet Union nor the former Yugoslavia, there are no substantial coethnic populations in neighboring states, and there are no minorities within the state who seek greater autonomy.[22] A Czech government has therefore been unlikely to create problems of international security. Of course, the Czech Republic's entry into NATO in March 1999 made this less true: the Czech Republic stood to become an undependable and internally fragmented ally.

Of the five parties in Parliament in 1999, all supported Czech membership in NATO except the Communists.[23] However, the two largest parties, the Social Democrats (CSSD) and the Civic Alliance Party (ODS), have proved unwilling to treat NATO membership as a matter of basic state interest and provide the Alliance with strong support. The right-wing ODS-led coalition government of Prime Minister Vaclav Klaus, in power from 1992 to 1997, conducted a resolutely pro-NATO foreign policy. However, the diverse domestic requirements of accession, including building public understanding and support for membership, were neglected. Klaus, who always privately disapproved of NATO membership, condemned NATO's air strikes against Yugoslavia in March 1999.

The new Social Democratic Party (CSSD), created after 1989, never took a strong stand in favor of NATO; instead of convincing its "conservative" left-wing electorate of NATO's advantages, it preferred a vague, shifting approach to membership. This amounted to supporting NATO membership as a matter of foreign policy but sporadically catering to anti-NATO voters on the domestic political scene. The rifts within the party between a pro-Western and a provincial wing came to the fore when the Social Democratic minority government, in power since June 1998, had to cope with the Kosovo crisis in the spring of 1999. In contrast to Hungary and Poland, the Czech government offered only the most tenuous support for the air strikes against Yugoslavia, though it did assent to their taking place. Public support for NATO membership and for the air strikes was significantly lower than in Poland or in Hungary. With no clear political leadership from the dominant political party of the left or, remarkably, of the right, this was not surprising. Only President Vaclav Havel and the two small centrist parties, the Christian Democrats and the Freedom Union, have consistently and articulately supported the Alliance.

More generally, the Czech political establishment failed to identify membership in NATO as a matter of state interest: legislation required for accession became embroiled in various domestic political fights and was not accorded the political weight that it deserved. This was a symptom of a broader disregard for reformulating the security concept of the state, stemming in part from the absence of perceived threats. Czech commentators and President Havel also pointed to the long-standing approach of Czechs to history, which assumes that the nation will bump along through history rather than set national goals and pursue them with determination.

The Czech Republic and the Kosovo Crisis

The onset of NATO bombing in Yugoslavia was met with a barrage of conflicting political statements on the Czech political scene. President Havel spoke out in support of NATO's operations; the CSSD government and the ODS opposition did not. The lack of political consensus was vividly displayed. The failure of the government to take a clear stand was symptomatic to many observers of the inability of Czech politicians to formulate Czech interests and obligations with respect to NATO.[24] Despite recent accession, there was no consensus as to the interests of the Czech state with respect to the Yugoslav conflict, and to its responsibilities toward its new allies. The war did not have any repercussions for the Czech Republic, such as economic loss, regional instability, or the risk of an influx of refugees, which might explain such a hostile political reaction. Meanwhile, the media and governments of other NATO states remarked upon the disunity in Czech domestic politics, as well as the lack of solidarity displayed by the government of a new ally.

The Zeman government initially issued a statement in late March disapproving of the air strikes against Yugoslavia. It claimed that NATO had decided on the attacks some days before the Czech Republic had joined NATO, and therefore the Czech government had not been consulted. Five days later, the government was forced to admit that it had lied: it had in fact approved the strikes in the NATO Council, but had covered up its assent for fear of losing public support.

The crisis revealed deep divisions within the Social Democratic Party itself and belied all previous claims that the party unambiguously supported Czech membership in NATO. The gap between the party's declared pro-European identity and its actual domestic political behavior became ever more evident. To start things off in late March, Prime Minister Zeman characterized the air strikes as the work of primitive troglodytes, and questioned the legitimacy of NATO siding with the Kosovar Liberation Army. Some weeks later, Vice Prime Minister Egon Lansky declared that Milosevic's ethnic cleansing of Kosovo was morally justified because of the NATO bombing.[25] Meanwhile, a few CSSD deputies, heralding traditionally strong ties between Serbs and Czechs, set off to Belgrade to express their support for Milosevic.

The Zeman government did respect its NATO obligations and support the Alliance in deeds, if not in words. On April 2, 12 CSSD ministers voted to allow NATO to use Czech airspace, while 4 abstained. On April 21, the Parliament approved by a wide margin the use of Czech airfields, roads, and rail facilities for the transit of NATO military forces (with the Communists and a handful of Social Democrats in dissent). Foreign Minister Jan Kavan consistently presented a pro-NATO foreign policy on behalf of the government. But though it pledged its participation in a future NATO-led peacekeeping mission in Kosovo, at the close of the Washington summit the government vocally excluded the participation of Czech troops in a ground invasion of Yugoslavia. It was considered unfortunate by many, including President Havel, that such strident statements were made when NATO had not even presented plans for a ground invasion.

The largest opposition party, the ODS, condemned the strikes, and its leader Vaclav Klaus, proclaimed that it was NATO's bombing that caused Milosevic's ethnic cleansing campaign in Kosovo.[26] Those on the Czech political scene who supported the strikes he characterized as warmongers. Klaus has a long history of anti-Western foreign policy activities and views, including an unusually amicable stand toward the Yugoslav regime. For example, he paid a friendly visit to Milosevic in 1996 and observed that it was best not to take a black-and-white view of the conflict in Bosnia.[27] Klaus's condemnation of NATO, however, seemed unlikely to bring political benefit, since the right-wing Czech electorate is pro-NATO. Indeed, many of Klaus's voters were dismayed and confused by his statements.

President Havel responded forcefully to the domestic debate, declaring that "Czech politicians, who publicly condemn NATO's military intervention, are responsible for the creation and the support of isolationist and, from the long term perspective, very dangerous moods in society."[28] The mainstream Czech media criticized both the CSSD and the ODS, observing that the Czech Republic was proving to be an unreliable ally, that Czech affirmations at accession of "shared responsibility for the values espoused by NATO members" were ringing rather hollow. For its part, the Czech public could only be unconvinced by inconsistent and usually brief political pronouncements on the Yugoslav crisis: few politicians attempted to explain to the Czech public the purpose of NATO's air strikes. Support for the strikes stood at 34 percent, with 48 percent against, in April 1999, while support for the Czech Republic's accession to NATO had declined somewhat to 49 percent in early March 1999.[29]

Slovakia, Romania, and Bulgaria: Aspiring Allies

For NATO's still aspiring members—Romania, Bulgaria, and Slovakia—NATO's intervention in Yugoslavia provided an opportunity to demonstrate solidarity with the Alliance in hopes of bringing them closer to membership. This was particularly attractive as, in all three states, democratic governments worked to undo the damage to reform and reputation wrought by years of rule by unreconstructed nationalists.[30] The Slovak government, closest to NATO membership and furthest from the conflict, was most keen. The reform-oriented governing coalition was nearly unanimous in its support but for some members of the post-Communist party, who abstained from cabinet and parliamentary votes endorsing military operations.

The Romanian and Bulgarian governments had to balance the desire to support NATO with the need to manage a strong domestic opposition to the strikes, stemming from the security and economic concerns of the population and from the vigorous anti-NATO campaigns of nationalist political parties in opposition. The Bulgarian government worked hard to impress the Alliance by adopting Bulgaria's new military doctrine in advance of the Washington summit. But the government's pro-NATO stance was made more difficult by a stray NATO missile that damaged a house in the Sofia suburbs in late April. Still, both the Romanian and the Bulgarian government announced their support for NATO, and by early May the Romanian and Bulgarian parliaments had approved the use of their airspace by NATO military aircraft.

NATO's strikes against Yugoslavia brought out the most anti-Western side of the unreconstructed Communists-turned-nationalists in Romania, Slovakia, and Bulgaria. In government until the mid-1990s, they sought to use the Kosovo crisis to undermine their more liberal successors.[31]

In Bulgaria the post-Communist Bulgarian Socialist Party (BSP) had never supported NATO membership. In Romania and Slovakia the nationalist parties, led by Ion Iliescu's PSDR and Vladimir Meciar's HZDS, were nominally pro-NATO while in power, and their party programs continued to support membership out of power. In opposition, however, many of their members turned against NATO and attempted to gain as much political capital as possible from NATO's military strikes against Yugoslavia. The daily newspapers controlled by the BSP, the PSDR, and the HZDS ran strident opinion pieces siding with the Serbs and against NATO and their respective governments.[32] Extremist parties in Poland, Hungary, and the Czech Republic also opposed NATO and denounced the strikes; however, they were politically much more marginal than the once-ruling nationalist parties in Romania, Bulgaria, and Slovakia.

NATO's Engagement in Kosovo as a Precedent for Ethnic Conflict Regulation

NATO's engagement on behalf of the Kosovar Albanians in 1999 linked the protection and promotion of minority rights with the activities of the Alliance.[33] The support of NATO for extensive territorial autonomy (and perhaps eventually independence) for the Kosovar Albanians was perceived by nationalist parties in Slovakia, Romania, and Bulgaria as inimical to their states' interests. All three states harbor a single, politically cohesive ethnic minority whose aspirations for greater autonomy are threatening to some part of the majority nation.[34] Nationalist parties suggested that in the future, if NATO should be displeased with their government, it will support the secessionist projects of ethnic minorities and use the government's opposition to such projects as a pretext for bombing and invasion.[35] This rhetoric was embraced by Meciar's HZDS in Slovakia and Iliescu's PSDR in Romania, as well as by vocal extreme right-wing parties in both states.[36] In Bulgaria, the BSP adamantly denounced the attacks but was more restrained when suggesting that Bulgaria's ethnic Turkish minority had an irredentist agenda.[37]

In addition, nationalists in Bulgaria and Romania lamented that NATO attacked the Serbs, a fellow Slavic and Orthodox nation. They routinely accused the government of concealing NATO's use of the country's territory and airspace for its military operations.[38] They pointed to Russia's condemnation and to the grave consequences of arousing Russia's displeasure by supporting the strikes. Not surprisingly, concerns about Russia held the most sway in Bulgaria, while charges that NATO would use the treatment of ethnic minorities as a future pretext to violate national sovereignty received the most column inches in Romania.

Bulgarian and Romanian nationalists also accused the government of servility to Western masters and of acting counter to the nation's interest. They charged that their states had been asked to host large numbers of NATO troops, without any firm security guarantees or promises of early NATO membership.[39] Moderate Romanian and Bulgarian politicians suggested that since their states suffered the most insecurity and the greatest economic losses from the Kosovo crisis, NATO owed them early membership. Many voices in the Bulgarian debate called for NATO to admit Bulgaria because of both its substantial security needs and its impressive contributions to regional stability.[40]

Can governments of democratic reformers be discouraged and domestically discredited by exclusion from NATO? After the July 1997 Madrid summit, Romania's newly elected democrats believed that they lost momentum in their reform program because of high expectations followed by severe disappointment over NATO's decision not to admit Romania in the first wave. Bulgaria's reform government was more realistic and thus less dismayed by the decision. After the Washington summit of April 1999, the governments of Slovakia, Bulgaria, and especially Romania all regretted that a firm date had not been set for their accession to NATO, in recognition of recent democratic and economic reforms but also of their politically taxing cooperation with the Alliance during the Kosovo crisis.[41]

Conclusion

The differences between domestic approaches to NATO membership in East European states cannot be explained solely with reference to the strategic environment. While a sense of insecurity—based on past security failures and on proximity to contemporary areas of conflict—played an important role, so did the evolution of domestic politics after the fall of communism. The quality of the domestic debate on NATO shaped how publics and elites viewed the costs and benefits of NATO membership, and how elites used the question of NATO membership in domestic competitions for power. Domestic political factors, particularly the reform of the post-Communist left, helped account for different levels of political commitment to the Alliance in Hungary, the Czech Republic, and Poland.

The evolution of domestic political thinking on NATO demonstrates that the incentives of NATO membership and the signals sent by NATO governments can shore up pro-Western security strategies and strengthen the hand of liberal democratic elites in post-Communist states. If NATO's only concern in admitting post-Communist states was to create reliable new allies, it would have to strike a difficult balance between holding the applicants to extensive requirements while also being careful not to discourage or discredit Western-oriented reformers working in a difficult political environment. This balance is even more difficult to achieve, however, given that NATO's agenda on expansion is influenced by many factors unconnected with the character of domestic politics in the candidate states.

Notes

*For comments on an earlier draft, my thanks to Anne Deighton, S. Neil MacFarlane, Tim Snyder, and Kieran Williams, and to participants in a seminar at the Center for Science and International Affairs (CISAC) at Stanford University.
1. The classic is John J. Mearsheimer, "Back to the Future: Instability in Europe After the Cold War," *International Security* 15 (summer 1990): pp. 5–56. See also Andrew Hurrell, "Explaining the resurgence of regionalism in world politics," *Review of International Studies* 21 (October 1995): pp. 331–58; and Edward D. Mansfield and Jack Snyder, "Democratization and the Danger of War," *International Security* 20 (summer 1995): pp. 5–38.
2. Without a place at the EU table, they could not bargain for compensation for taking part in the sanctions. See Edward D. Mansfield, "Alliances, Preferential Trading Arrangements and Sanctions," *Journal of International Affairs* 48 (summer 1994): pp. 119–39.
3. On conditionality as a tool to bolster European security, see Stephen Van Evera, "Primed for Peace: Europe After the Cold War," *International Security* 15 (winter 1990–91): pp. 5–57; and Van Evera, "Managing the Eastern Crisis," *Security Studies* (spring 1992): pp. 361–81.
4. See Milada Anna Vachudová, *Revolution, Democracy and Integration: East Central and South Eastern Europe since 1989* (Oxford: Oxford University Press, forthcoming).
5. In a November 1997 poll, 36 per cent of Czech respondents said they would vote for NATO membership if a referendum was held; 22 percent were against and 21 percent were undecided. In Bulgaria, 37 percent were for, 14 percent against, and 22 percent undecided. In Hungary, 47 percent for, 22 percent against, 15 percent undecided; in Poland, 61 percent for, 4 percent against, 18 percent undecided; in Romania, 67 percent for, 9 percent against, and 11 percent undecided. The numbers for Slovakia—31 percent for, 27 percent against, and 24 percent undecided—were affected by the spoiled referendum of the previous spring. Support for NATO increased over the course of 1998 in all of the states. *Central and Eastern Eurobarometer* 8 (March 1998).
6. All five major political parties—the Hungarian Socialist Party (MSZP), the Alliance of Free Democrats (SZDSZ), the Federation of Young Democrats (Fidesz), the Hungarian Democratic Forum (MDF), and the Independent Smallholders (FKGP)—support NATO membership. In parliament, only the small, extreme right-wing Hungarian Justice and Life Party (MIEP) opposes

membership (as does the tiny, extreme left-wing Workers Party outside of parliament).
 6. See Lajos Pietsch, *Hungary and NATO* (Budapest: The Hungarian Atlantic Council, 1998). My analysis of Hungary benefited from conversations with Rudolf Joo, Laszlo Poti, Geza Jeszenszky, and Laszlo Valki.
 7. This represents a substantial increase: in September 1996, 48 percent were for, 27 percent against, and 25 percent undecided on NATO membership. In a *Eurobarometer* survey conducted for the European Commission in November 1995, the respective figures were 32 percent for, 22 percent against, and 46 percent undecided. "Two-Thirds Support for NATO Membership," Budapest *Nepszabadsag,* March 8, 1999, p. 1, FBIS-EEU–1999-0309; and Zsofia Szilagyi, "Poll Shows 48 percent of Hungarians in Favor of NATO Membership," *OMRI Daily Digest,* October 2, 1996.
 8. Istvan Szonyi, "Hungarian State Strategies and International Institutions After the Cold War," *TKI Working Papers on European Integration and Regime Formation,* no. 20, Thorkil Kristensen Institute (TKI), Esbjerg, 1997.
 9. Hungary's foreign minister from 1990 to 1994 refutes that border changes were an issue; see Geza Jeszenszky, "Hungary's Bilateral Treaties and the Issue of Minorities," *Ethnos-Nation* 1–2 (1996): pp. 123–28.
 10. As NATO prepared for air strikes against Bosnian Serb positions in February 1994, Premier Peter Boross (MDF) asked the Alliance's reconnaissance planes to leave Hungary's airspace during eventual air strikes in Bosnia. This measure was aimed at reassuring Belgrade, for fear that Hungarian involvement in military action could endanger the Magyar minority in Vojvodina.
 11. By 1993, about 50,000 Hungarians had fled the region to escape harassment, economic privation, and conscription into the army of the rump Yugoslavia.
 12. In 1995 NATO requested that Hungary provide an air base on its territory for American forces in IFOR. This gained strong support from the parliamentary parties in anticipation of Hungary's becoming the first former Warsaw Pact country to host NATO troops and thus earning its future membership. Important bases were established at Kaposvar and Taszar.
 13. Foreign Minister Martonyi declared that this could be ruled out "categorically." Janos Martonyi, interview, Budapest *Duna TV,* April 18, 1999, FBIS-EEU–1999-0418.
 14. Matyas Szabo, "Hungary Will Not Send Troops to Kosovo," *RFE/RL Newsline,* July 30, 1998.
 15. Slovakia also has a small minority in Vojvodina. Some members loyal to Belgrade accused the Slovak government of "betrayal" for granting permission to NATO aircraft to use Slovak airspace. These accusations were dismissed by the foreign ministry, which observed that the Slovak communities "did not raise their voices when the Serbian army fought against Croats and Slovenes." Prague *CTK,* March 31, 1999.
 16. "The SWM Criticizes Budapest—According to Kasza, Orban's Statement Was Irresponsible," Budapest *Nepszabadsag,* April 7, 1999, p. 3, FBIS-EEU-1999-0407.
 17. In the Budapest daily *Nepszava,* as reported by Budapest *MTI,* March 29, 1999, FBIS-EEU-1999-0329.

18. "Martonyi's Answer to Kasza—No Combat Aircraft Take Off From Hungary," Budapest *Magyar Nemzet,* April 21, 1999, p. 3, FBIS-EEU-1999-0421.
19. In 1991, Antall had underscored that conflicts in Yugoslavia could not be settled without "due consideration for the legitimate aspirations" of Albanian, Hungarian, and other ethnic communities within the Yugoslav republics. József Antall, Address to the United Nations, October 1, 1991, published by the Hungarian Ministry of Foreign Affairs in *Current Policy* 34 (1991): p. 3.
20. The weakness of the Hungarian military should be reassuring to Hungary's neighbors: Hungary could not hope to ride to the military rescue of coethnics in neighboring states.
21. See Milada Anna Vachudová, "The Czech Republic: The Unexpected Force of Institutional Constraints," in *Democratic Consolidation in Eastern Europe,* ed. Alex Pravda and Jan Zielonka (Oxford University Press, forthcoming).
22. There is a grave problem with racism against the Roma minority and their mistreatment by state organs, but as the Roma have no external protector state, they are unlikely to cause international conflicts or problems (unless their mistreatment and exodus attracts international attention, as was the case in 1998).
23. From the left to the right of the political spectrum, they were the Social Democrats (CSSD), the Christian Democrats (KDU-CSL), the Freedom Union (US), and the Civic Democratic Party (ODS); the Czech Communist Party (KSCM) never reformed itself, and although marginalized since 1989, it sits in Parliament with 11 percent of the vote and remains vehemently anti-NATO. My analysis of the Czech Republic benefited from conversations with Petr Lunak, Jiri Sedivy, Karel Kovanda, Josef Zieleniec, Jiri Pehe, Pavel Seifter, Ivo Silhavy, and Jacques Rupnik.
24. Ivan Gabal in "Cesti politici se k utoku NATO nehlasi," *Lidove Noviny* (Prague), March 26, 1999, p. 1.
25. Martin Schmarcz, "Lansky: vina NATO," *Lidove Noviny,* April 6, 1999, p. 10.
26. Vaclav Klaus, interview by Ondrej Drabek, "Za odsun Albancu muze NATO," *Lidove Noviny,* April 8, 1999, p. 1.
27. Viliam Buchert, "Klaus selhava v zahranicni politice dlouho," *Mlada Fronta* (Prague), March 30, 1999, p. 12.
28. "Nazory na uder dale stepi politickou scenu," *Mlada Fronta,* March 27, 1999, p. 2.
29. "IVVM: Polovina obcanu souhlasila se vstupem do NATO," *Lidove Noviny,* April 10, 1999, p. 2.
30. Reformist governments were elected in Romania in 1996, Bulgaria in 1997, and Slovakia in 1998. Up to the July 1997 Madrid summit, the Meciar government still held some hope for early NATO membership. Once it was excluded, the Slovak government turned to Russia. Some officials suggested that neutrality might be more suitable for Slovakia than NATO membership, and that Russia could become the guarantor of that neutrality. See Martin Butora and Frantisek Sebej, eds., *Slovensko v sedej zone? Rozsirovanie NATO, zlyhania a perspektivy Slovenska* (Bratislava: Institute for Public Affairs, 1998).

31. On the attacks of Romania's nationalists on President Emil Constrantinescu, see Alina Mungiu-Pippidi, "The War That Never Was," *East European Constitutional Review* (summer 1999): pp. 41–46.
32. For example, Stefan Prodev, "NATO's Night," *Duma* (Sofia), March 26, 1999, p. 7, FBIS-EEU-1999-326.
33. See the contribution by S. Neil MacFarlane to this volume.
34. While Poland, the Czech Republic, and Hungary are relatively homogenous, in Slovakia, Bulgaria, and Romania one cohesive ethnic minority forms about 10 percent of the population. There are some 600,000 ethnic Hungarians in Slovakia (11 percent of the total population), 2 million ethnic Hungarians in Romania (8 percent), and 800,000 ethnic Turks in Bulgaria (10 percent).
35. At a NACC meeting in early 1999, the Russian delegation provocatively asked whether NATO would support the demands of Romania's ethnic Hungarians for an autonomous Transylvania. The PSDR in Romania has long accused the Hungarian minority of secessionism and linked it to NATO; Michael Shafir, "Romania Fears NATO Bases in Hungary," *OMRI Daily Digest,* July 24, 1996.
36. In the debate on NATO's request for unrestricted access to Romania's airspace on April 21, Ion Iliescu, head of the largest opposition party, the PSDR, warned that the Kosovo precedent might encourage the separatist and secessionist tendencies within Romania's ethnic Hungarian minority. Bucharest *Radio Romania Network,* April 21, 1999, FBIS-EEU-1999-0421.
37. One editorial in the BSP daily warned that Bulgarian leaders "should realize that where Kosovo is involved, the Serbs' interests and drama are analogous with our national drama, which could be set alight by [...] the Atlantic interest." Svetlana Mikhova, "There is Another Choice Providing We Have a Conscience," *Duma,* March 25, 1999, p. 5, FBIS-EEU-1999-0325.
38. The Bulgarian government condemned this as dangerous, for it implicated Bulgaria in the conflict and reportedly provoked an anti-Bulgarian campaign in Belgrade. This undermined Bulgaria's state interests and was likened by some to "treason." Neven Kopandanova, "Dangerous Liaisons," *Demokratsiya* (Sofia), March 31, 1999, p. 1, FBIS-EEU-1999-0331; "BSP's Liquidator Becomes Traitor," *Standart News* (Sofia), March 27, 1999, p. 1, FBIS-EEU-1999-0327.
39. Bogdan Chirieac, "NATO Officially Asks Romania to Grant Unlimited Access to Its Airspace," *Adevarul* (Bucharest), April 20, 1999, pp. 1, 15, FBIS-EEU-1999-0420; and Cristian Tudor Popescu, "The Imperial Logic," *Adevarul,* April 14, 1999, FBIS-EEU-1999-0414.
40. Indeed, Bulgaria has promoted stability in the Balkans since 1989 by respecting the independence of "coethnic" Macedonia and establishing generally friendly relations with its neighbors. Maria Koinova, "Bulgarian Foreign Policy toward the States of Southeastern Europe, 1989–98," M.Phil. thesis, Central European University, June 1998. Some argue that Bulgaria deserved NATO membership even more than the three new members; see Yuri Mikhalkov, "We Must Also Have a Clear Invitation From NATO," *Standart News,* March 11, 1999, p. 8, FBIS-EEU-1999-0311.

41. For the view that although NATO's first expansion created no major problems, other means besides a second expansion should be used to consolidate a new security order in Europe, see Kori Schake, "Europe After NATO Expansion: The Unfinished Security Agenda," Institute on Global Conflict and Cooperation working paper, March 1998.

CONCLUSION

Balancing Acts: NATO's Unity and the Lessons to Learn

Mark R. Brawley and Pierre Martin

The NATO intervention in Kosovo in the spring of 1999 exemplified the challenges of an old alliance that has to adjust to a new world, where enemies and threats are no longer quite as clearly defined. Of course, the NATO presence in Kosovo is far from over and the conflict it was meant to address is far from settled, so it is still too early to cast a definite judgment on the success or failure of Operation Allied Force. What can be said, however, is that the intervention itself showed that the Alliance was able to maintain an impressive degree of cohesion in a situation in which such cohesion was in no way guaranteed at the outset. We now review the reasons why the Alliance stuck together, and draw some conclusions about the cohesion of the Alliance in future similar actions.

Having now completed an overview of the theoretical issues surrounding Alliance politics, and also having examined the various national perspectives, we wish to pull the different pieces together into a single framework. To understand how NATO was able to hold together despite various strains in the Alliance, we must examine the interaction of domestic and international factors. The top leadership of NATO's members—including the White House—wanted to see NATO perform well in this crisis, and more importantly, the leaders of each member of NATO wanted their country to be seen as an active partner in the Alliance. What is of greater interest, perhaps, is why the various governments took such positions, for they were not all motivated by the same needs and desires, despite accepting to play a role in Operation Allied Force. In the end, of course, the Alliance did manage to stick together, and all members stayed more or less in tune. There was, however, sufficient variation in the way the various members reacted to the crisis to warrant explanation.

In formulating our summary account, we follow the general argument presented by Stephen Walt in his overview of the crisis in terms of the theory of alliances. In his contribution, Walt makes a pitch for accepting the utility of various approaches to understanding NATO's persistence, the evolution of its mission, and its first offensive military operations in Operation Allied Force. We shall first examine the strength of a rationale based on realist notions to understand the positions taken by NATO's non-American members. We examine the extent to which security needs alone might explain the participation of some NATO members in Operation Allied Force. Then, following another approach discussed by both Walt and David Haglund, we turn to the sort of evidence a constructivist might look for, as well as the evidence an expert on domestic sources of foreign policies might gather. Although these approaches are usually pitted against each other and often characterized as irreconcilable, we find some common ground between them.

By examining the relationships between domestic pressures and the positions governments took in balancing domestic and international demands, we can construct an argument that explains much of the observed variation in policy stances. This perspective, made by combining domestic pressures and the security needs associated with the allied intervention, provides a valuable counter to those who argue that shared identity might have encouraged these states to act together in this instance. Reflecting on the impact and interplay of domestic pressures and security needs, in the end, points to a different, simpler explanation.

The Security Needs of NATO's Members

From the systemic-level arguments, it is clear that most if not all of NATO's members are keen to keep the Alliance in place for the time being. Their reasons vary, of course, but security concerns should not be ignored, despite the end of the Cold War. The United States is in the best position to jettison NATO. It is the one state best positioned to defend itself without allies, and as several contributors have underscored, there is a pervasive tendency among some U.S. policymakers—and many opinion shapers—to portray membership in the Alliance as more of a burden than a benefit. Yet NATO still serves an important political role for its dominant member by providing multilateral cover for military actions that might otherwise suffer from a lack of legitimacy (both externally and domestically).

For the other major powers in NATO, American participation is a mixed blessing. Clearly, the governments and publics in Britain, Germany, and even France prefer having an American involvement or presence in the provision of European security, despite the fact that each of these countries can meet its own individual, direct security needs. They need allies in order to confront more distant threats, or to deal with situations on Europe's periphery. Despite spending plenty of money and generating certain special military forces (e.g., two of the three have their own nuclear forces), these three lack other important military capabilities, which limit their abilities—either singularly or even in combination—to project their power. They lack adequate lift and resupply capacity, electronic/satellite intelligence gathering, fully interoperative communications equipment, forward repair facilities, and other forms of logistical support needed to keep a large force in the field. By some estimates, the European members of NATO could deploy and maintain a force of up to 20,000 troops out-of-area—compared to the Americans' ability to field and supply a force greater than ten times that size.[1] Given the disparity in capabilities, even the strongest European states will continue to turn to the United States when they seek to undertake out-of-area military operations.

The three foremost European powers view NATO differently because they differ in their calculations of the costs and conditions of American involvement. Certainly, when it came to the Kosovo campaign, the British and the Americans saw things more "eye-to-eye," and therefore Britain perceived little cost to having the United States actively lead the Alliance. Tony Blair worked hard to elicit that leadership. France does not agree on policy as often or as readily, however. French policymakers usually are more skeptical about the benefits of American leadership than their neighbors across the Channel, thus France bristles under American leadership. Germany had disagreements on policy with the United States but also feels a greater need for guaranteed allies given its geographic position and recent history. Germany perceives a cost to American leadership but, unlike France, it is willing to pay that price.

Even among NATO's larger members, then, we can observe how security needs grow as we travel eastward. This evaluation is more accurate when assessing the situations of the smaller members of the Alliance. On the eastern edge, the newest members of NATO clearly desire membership because they continue to feel a real threat emanating from the East. This observation, which is consistent both with basic geopolitics and with a conventional realist analysis of regional security, is also supported at the level of public perceptions. In a multination survey conducted during the first week of the Kosovo episode for the *Economist,* 45 percent of respondents in the three newest members of NATO (Poland, the Czech Republic, and Hungary) saw a world war as likely in the coming ten years, while 45 percent saw this as unlikely. Among the western European members, however, these figures were respectively 35 and 61 percent. Although North Americans were even more pessimistic than the East Europeans (54 percent likely; 45 percent unlikely), it is probably the case that fewer perceive that a conflict would threaten their homeland.[2]

We should be clear that this threat of a possible large-scale conflict is generated by uncertainty about the future directions that might be taken by Russia and by the other successor states to the Soviet Union. Although, as Neil MacFarlane notes in his contribution, it is unlikely that the instability observed in areas of the former Soviet Union will spill over to the extent that it would pose a serious military challenge to the territorial integrity of most NATO members, this pervasive uncertainty provides ample reasons not to let down the guard. The perception of a threat of large-scale conflict could therefore recede in the future, but it is highly unlikely to disappear. More likely, uncertainty will linger. Logically, the need to attain a higher level of security would cause Poland, Hungary, and the Czech Republic to accept a higher price for NATO membership. This was clearly evident in the ways in which the Czech Republic and Hungary behaved in Operation Allied Force, as outlined in Milada Vachudová's contribution. In the Czech Republic, the public was not terribly supportive of NATO's actions, yet the government upheld its modest obligations. In Hungary, support was high—if not necessarily ironclad—but participation also entailed much greater risks, and the government did as much as it could to meet its obligations.

Among the other NATO members, Italy may be a special case. War in the Balkans has more direct spillovers into Italian affairs, in the form of refugees or smuggling, and it threatens to add significantly more dangerous elements, such as terrorism or a retaliatory missile strike. Italy's general security position may not be very different from France's or Belgium's (though it has a dangerously erratic neighbor to the south in Libya), but Italy's leaders have more direct and pressing concerns involving its neighbors across the Adriatic. From a geopolitical perspective, thus, it would make sense for Italians to welcome a vigorous American involvement in the Balkans, while still debating among themselves the degree of American leadership to accept. As Maurizio Cremasco's chapter explains, the importance of Italy's security needs in relation to the Kosovo crisis was compelling enough to allow a government of the left to ride out the crisis in spite of a sizable domestic opposition to NATO's actions.

For the other NATO members discussed in this volume, Canada and Spain, direct threats to their security have also been of declining importance in recent years. In *Shaping the Future of Canadian Defence: A Strategy for 2020* (the assessment of threats and priorities recently published by Canada's Department of National Defence), the authors note that "Canada faces no direct conventional military threat." Instead, the authors stress

Canada's need to maintain combat capabilities in order "to protect and promote its interests and values." To protect the country's physical well-being, NORAD is probably of more immediate importance than NATO; being under the protective umbrella of America's National Missile Defense may well be the best way to safeguard Canadian territory from the most serious direct threats in the future.

In sum, the evidence supporting a purely realist calculation—that the members had some strategic interests directly involved, or that they needed to follow the U.S. lead in this instance against their initial preferences—is mixed. It cannot be ignored, but it does not explain the behavior of several alliance members. Several NATO members had good reasons to follow along with American desires in Operation Allied Force, simply because they needed to maintain their strategic ties to the United States and others in the Alliance. Straightforward security concerns can account for the actions of a number of NATO members—especially the most recent additions, but also others in central or eastern Europe, perhaps even including Germany.

The evidence supporting this assessment will only be stronger once we examine the domestic pressures on these same governments, for many of them had to present the case for acting within NATO against the opposition of their publics. Yet the evidence presented so far also implies that a number of countries, perhaps even the majority of NATO members, need the Alliance for security purposes less and less. This has given cause for some authors to stress the growth of a community of states, sharing a set of norms and beliefs. These norms are constitutive: they shape a state's self-image and therefore help define its shared identity within this community. That at least is the argument presented by some authors.[3] To test its strength we need to examine the depth of support for Operation Allied Force among the allies that remain in NATO but do not face pressing military threats.

Domestic Calculations on Kosovo and Operation Allied Force

Just as there was some variation in the degree to which each member needs the Alliance to face systemic demands, we observe some degree of variation in support for Operation Allied Force at the domestic level. In several countries, there was widespread approval for putting pressure on Serbia to resolve the crisis over Kosovo, and to use force if necessary. In these countries governments led the charge and even put pressure on the United States to consider the deployment of ground troops on the Kosovar territory. Elsewhere, although there was a willingness to use threats, that support grew softer as the application of military force became a reality. There, governments managed to support NATO but they often had to tiptoe their way between the pressure to conform to Alliance norms and the reluctance of their publics to support the Alliance's actions. Even in the United States, which to a great extent dictated the shape of the diplomacy and the air campaign, any support that might have developed was constrained to a large extent by a persistent unwillingness to accept significant casualties in a war over Kosovo. It is therefore no surprise that among the allies, there would be states also unwilling to risk loss of life in this military intervention.

Among the Alliance's members, the British public was much more willing to use force to impose peace on Serbia. Not only did this reflect the broad acceptance of the principles that NATO declared itself to be pursuing, it also reflected some degree of acceptance by the British public of the risks involved in undertaking military operations.[4] Britain more than any other NATO member was willing to pursue a policy that risked trading off the lives of British soldiers and airmen for the principles at stake. This allowed the British government to not only stand firmly by the Americans' side, but to even move out ahead of it on some subjects, most significantly in urging the deployment of ground forces into the region as the first step to a ground invasion of Kosovo. It is no accident as well that we associate British faces with NATO—Jamie Shea, Robin Cook, and others—for British officials were backed not only by their convictions but also by their public.

Survey data support this perception of the British public, although they are not unambiguous. For example, a multicountry survey conducted by the *Economist* showed that support for the broad outlines of NATO actions in the early stages of the intervention was comparably high in Britain (68 percent in support and 23 percent opposed), the United States (68 and 27), Denmark (74 and 19), Norway (64 and 23), and Canada (64 and 33).[5] Other polls showed the limits of this support, however, as Louise Richardson notes in her assessment of British support. On April 2, 1999, when asked how many British lives they would be willing to lose to defend the ethnic Albanians in Kosovo, 57 percent said "none," while only 19 percent agreed to mention a number—and the numbers mentioned were very low.[6] Still, public satisfaction with the Labour government and particularly with Prime Minister Tony Blair himself remained high throughout the conflict, even if Blair was an outspoken proponent of participation in a large-scale land operation in Kosovo.[7] Whether Blair actually believed that such an operation had any likelihood of materializing in the face of staunch American opposition, however, is another question.

Canada was another country where the public supported military operations fairly strongly, but in Canada there was even less willingness to accept casualties than in Britain. Pursuit of principles was tempered by the potential costs, as in the United States. And unlike in the United States, Britain, or many other European members, the political debate on the subject was shallow. The government acted, and the parties in opposition questioned some aspects of Canada's participation, but the core decisions were largely unchallenged. The Canadian military was fairly secretive about its involvement in the early days, suggesting some fear that the Canadian public would not appreciate the job it was doing—and it was doing a good job, as David Haglund reminded us. Therefore there is evidence that Canada did more than simply stand by its allies, by urging action sooner than others and contributing meaningful forces to the operation quite quickly. Yet public support was somewhat soft. The question of whether Canadians would have continued to approve the intervention if things had turned sour for their country's men and women in uniform remains open. Perhaps the best explanation for Canada's support in the absence of a direct threat to its own security is that Canadian decision-makers, and perhaps also the public, wanted to assert a set of values that define a shared identity, as well as defend their country's stake in the Alliance. As Canada's defense minister, Art Eggleton, put it in the speech he made to open the conference on which this book is based, Canada "followed its instincts as well as its allies" in this instance.[8]

For Germany, there was support for the end goals NATO was aiming for, but there was less support for the means employed. Certainly in Germany there was no desire for a ground campaign to restore peace to Kosovo, even if that ground campaign promised to deliver peace more quickly. As Peter Rudolf notes, Germany's foreign policy goals have been consistently oriented around the principles at stake here; but Rudolf also noted that the German public constrained what the government could do in pursuit of these goals. In the early stages of the intervention, like the public in France and Italy (albeit to a lesser extent), the German public was more supportive of returning to the diplomatic table rather than pursue the use of force initiated by the United States.[9] Even if public opinion was a constraint on the German government, however, the public was willing to give its recently elected government a greater margin to maneuver, because it was a coalition of the left. In all likelihood, a Conservative-led government would have faced a much tougher barrage of criticism for similar actions. Acceptance of the goals is not the same as accepting sacrifices for those goals; Germans were willing to make sacrifices but they put a lower price tag on achieving peace in Kosovo than the British or Canadians.

The interesting parallel to the German case is Poland. The Polish public supported action against the Milosevic regime. Indeed, of the three new NATO members, the Polish public was the most supportive of NATO action.[10] Also, the government wanted to support the Alliance as it was led by the Americans into Operation Allied Force. As noted above, Poland needs the Alliance to ensure its future security. The Polish case, in this sense, may be "overdetermined." All the reasons we can identify with the theories under consideration here point to the same position taken by its government.

The French government and public questioned American leadership as much as any within NATO. The French government in particular sought to move policy discussions to other forums, in which American leadership would be limited, such as the United Nations. In Italy and Spain, the governments supported Operation Allied Force more strongly than indications of public support should have warranted. The Italian and Spanish publics were never as hawkish on these issues as their governments. This created situations quite different from those observed in Britain, Canada, Germany, or elsewhere. For example, as Maurizio Cremasco shows, Italy's prime minister D'Alema was able to manage the pressures of his public by trying—with little success—to mobilize allied support for renewed diplomatic efforts in the midst of the heaviest bombing in Serbia.

Since the French, Spanish, and Italian governments contributed forces to Operation Allied Force above what their publics would have demanded, each was undoubtedly interested in meeting requests coming from outside the country. What did these governments hope to gain—or to maintain—by participating in NATO's war? Here we go back to the systemic/security needs of the countries in question. But even then, the arguments are not all that compelling. Only Italy could be said to face local threats of such a nature that it would submit to the wishes of an ally that strongly countered its own views. We may find that these countries' governments participated because their real desire was to prove their solidarity with the rest of NATO—and with their European allies in particular.

As already mentioned, the publics in several countries were not supportive of the war. Most clearly this included Greece, but also the Czech Republic. Both countries remained members of the Alliance, but neither was called on to contribute forces. Both were asked to allow NATO forces to transit through their territory and airspace, to which they agreed. For both, the need to acquire security seems the paramount reason for their actions. These reluctant allies were wary of direct involvement, but not enough to relinquish their long-term commitment to the Alliance as a broader security guarantor. In the case of Greece, the government's tacit acceptance of NATO's actions can perhaps be interpreted as a clear sign of commitment to the Alliance, given the tensions involved in its own relationship with its northern neighbor. In the case of the Czech Republic, the leadership role played by President Vaclav Havel in resisting the temptation to follow his public in condemning the allied action can probably also be interpreted as a clear sign of long-term commitment to the Alliance as a security guarantor.

In summary then, the domestic support for Operation Allied Force varied from those member states where it ran deep and strong to those lacking any substantial support for hostilities. We have also already established that the NATO members to the east have, in general, greater security needs and therefore need to maintain good standing with other Alliance members. Combining these two types of information, we develop a simple framework in the next section.

A Framework for Understanding Support for Operation Allied Force

Plotting these issues together may help get a better picture of how each member acted, in comparison with the others. We simply combine the information provided above to develop a picture of groupings of states in terms of their relations with the United States in Operation Allied Force. Figure 1 presents the basic groupings of member states on two axes, while Figure 2 uses available data on domestic support and a summary ranking of security needs on the external dimension to illustrate the central point: NATO members did not need to be coerced into responding to the Kosovo crisis, because those who lacked domestic support had strong security rationales to join in the effort, while those who had little direct security incentives to participate were able to count on solid support for the normative principles underpinning the intervention.

To this general framework can be added further variables, which matter on a case-by-case basis (e.g., the institutional setup in Italy, which tends to create coalition governments whose behavior is often difficult to predict). Such refinements would not alter our main argument, however. As it is, our representation only captures the interplay of only the two most important variables we have isolated in this instance. If we were to turn to other

Figure 1: A typology of Allied reactions to the U.S.–led NATO intervention in Kosovo

	Less Domestic Support for Action	Some Domestic Support for Action	Greater Domestic Support for Action
Greater Fear of Future Threats	Reluctantly Faithful, or "Internal Compellence" (Czech Republic, Greece)	Faithful Follower (Hungary, Germany)	Eager Follower (Poland)
Less Fear of Future Threats	Forced Ally	Reluctant and/or "Frustrated" (France)	"Front-Runners," or "Happy Followers" (Britain, Canada)

Figure 2: Spatial distribution of NATO countries by security needs and public approval of operation Allied Force*

Higher Security Needs
Poland
Hungary
Czech Rep.
Germany; Turkey**
Greece**

| **Domestic Opposition** | *Italy* 50/50 | *U.S.* | **Domestic Support** |

Norway
France — *U.K.; Denmark*
Benelux**
Canada

Lower Security Needs

Note for Figure 2:
* In Figure 2, domestic support or opposition is measured by the balance of approval and disapproval for NATO's intervention as taken in a cross-national poll in the early part of the conflict (the *Economist*/Angus Reid Group, 1999). As an indication, the balance of approval and disapproval is −22 in the Czech Republic, 0 in Italy, +7 in Hungary, +21 in Germany, +41 in the United States, +45 in the United Kingdom, and +55 in Denmark. Security needs are a combination of geopolitical consideration and public perception of a threat of war, as reported in the same cross-national survey.
** Turkey, Greece, and the Benelux countries were not part of this survey, and their placement in the chart is an approximation.

opportunities to use NATO as an intervention force, we might find other factors entering our calculations.

The framework we develop to capture the mix of pressures governments were under can also then be adapted and employed to identify the degree of robustness NATO will exhibit in future non–Article 5 (or "out-of-area") operations. While security needs will not change all that rapidly (our list of countries confronting a higher degree of uncertainty in their defense posture today is unlikely to be different two years from now), the domestic support for future interventions is likely to be much more volatile. It is possible to make the case that some countries have established track records in support of humanitarian interventions and may be expected to behave consistently in the future. Britain and Canada have participated in almost every multilateral operation for establishing peace on the ground, or peacekeeping, in the last decade. These countries are more likely to be involved in future operations of this sort, especially if NATO takes the lead. Other countries have already exhibited quite different levels of support for recent operations, showing how factors such as location, past history, and cultural ties can influence support for NATO action. Finally, another source of potential variation in a model such as this one is the ability of member states to maintain political support for intervention in the face of mounting material and—particularly—human costs.

Any ability to make a prediction about future non–Article 5 operations rests on another question: How will the United States behave? Indeed, the best way to interpret the graph above is to note the distance of each country from the American position. Those most distant would have the greatest degree of difficulty maintaining their position in the Alliance once it undertakes offensive operations—but in the case of those with higher security needs, the governments must provide leadership and explain to their populations why their countries should support NATO action. Any states in the lower left-hand quadrant would be the most likely to opt out of the operation, if not of the Alliance itself.

On the other hand, any future situation on Europe's periphery in which military intervention might be demanded on humanitarian grounds may be handled in a very different manner, depending on the institutional changes currently being aired. Some experts have already noted that the uncertainties generated by the end of the Cold War have led Europeans to develop an overlapping array of alliances and security organizations. Moreover, the demands put on the existing ones by the breakup of Yugoslavia have shown several of these to be unworkable.[11]

To the extent that several NATO members chafed under American leadership in Operation Allied Force, they have now set about designing arrangements within and/or alongside NATO for potentially independent action. Of course, they will also need to create the necessary military forces to undertake an intervention without U.S. forces, which will not happen in the short term. Yet, as the *Economist* editorialized, "Shamed by their modest contribution to last year's war over Kosovo and by the time it took most of them to get their troops there to keep the subsequent peace, this is their best chance in a generation to buff up their military boots."[12] The members of NATO may well make some fundamental changes to the security architecture of Europe, and if they do, the lessons learned here may no longer be appropriate.

Projecting the Findings: The Basic Lessons Learned

To anticipate NATO's future performance, we must take note of the likelihood of further conflicts on Europe's periphery. In the face of such conflicts, however, the degree of domestic consensus *both within and across* NATO members matters greatly. While some theorists might expect this consensus to build over time, it should not be taken for granted. As future cases for NATO action emerge, the strength of the consensus behind military action is likely to vary. Moreover, the degree of "internal compellence" to participate (generated by external threats) will wax and wane as well. It is not that difficult to imagine a call for intervention that would cause the Alliance to fracture. Just as a systematic, consistent policy regarding future multilateral interventions is unlikely to be designed, so too will it be hard to evaluate NATO's future on anything but a case-by-case basis. Yet hopefully the framework established here is a first step toward recognizing the limits of NATO's new agenda. If there is any single lesson to be drawn, it is that Operation Allied Force exposed weaknesses as well as strengths. The most important work to complete before any future operation will be to identify the weak links in the Alliance so that they may be strengthened before being once again put to the test.

Finally, we should also note that NATO's experience in this episode is still evolving. The war may be over, but future evaluations of Operation Allied Force may vary with time, as NATO conducts a series of more drawn-out conflicts to "win the peace." As an editorial in the *Economist* concluded: "Having taken responsibility in Kosovo, NATO must make a success of it. Failure there would risk failure on a much wider front, certainly throughout the Balkans, probably even farther afield: the future of armed intervention for humanitarian ends, no matter where, would be set back years."[13]

Although the success of Operation Allied Force was far from total, it was a success nonetheless, notably in that the allies were able to act, on the whole, in concert. As it turned out, as David Haglund aptly pointed out, the Delian League is not the correct model to understand today's NATO. No one, it seems, needed to be "forced" into action in Kosovo. Now NATO and the other major players in European security face the more long-term— and much more difficult—challenge of bringing the pieces of the former Yugoslavia to make peace with each other and with the world. Whether the combination of strategic necessity and moral obligation that allowed the allies to hold together and to keep their publics on board in NATO's "first war" can be maintained in the long run will be the crucial test of its newly found vocation as the pillar of European security in this new century.

Notes

1. See Bruce Clark, "Survey: NATO," *Economist,* April 24, 1999, especially pp. 11–14.
2. *Economist*/Angus Reid Group poll, "NATO and the War in Kosovo/Yugoslavia: A Report on International Public Opinion" (press release), April 23, 1999.

3. Thomas Risse-Kappen, *Cooperation Among Democracies: The European Influence on U.S. Foreign Policy* (Princeton: Princeton University Press, 1995); Emanuel Adler and Michael Barnett, *Security Communities* (New York: Cambridge University Press, 1998). See the assessment of this literature provided by Kirsten Rafferty in her unpublished Ph.D. dissertation, McGill University.
4. We thank Anne Deighton for pointing this out during our conference at Harvard.
5. *Economist*/Angus Reid Group poll, "NATO and the War in Kosovo/Yugoslavia," Chart 1.
6. Market & Opinion Research International (MORI), *Mail on Sunday— Kosovo Poll* (April 2, 1999), available at http://www.mori.co.uk/polls/1999/ms990402.htm.
7. MORI, *Times-MORI Satisfaction Ratings* (monthly polls), available at http://www.mori.co.uk/polls/trends/satisfac.htm.
8. The Honourable Art Eggleton, "Canadian Lessons from the Kosovo Crisis," speaking notes for the Honourable Art Eggleton, Minister of National Defence, Harvard University, Cambridge, MA, September 30, 1999. The full text of the speech is available at http://www.dnd.ca/eng/archive/speeches/30SepHarvard_s_e.htm.
9. *Economist*/Angus Reid Group poll, "NATO and the War in Kosovo/Yugoslavia," Chart 1.
10. Ibid. In Poland, 54 percent approved of NATO's military actions, while 31 percent were opposed. In Hungary, the figures were 48 percent and 41 percent, while the Czechs were the least favorable, with a majority of 57 percent opposed to the intervention, while only 35 percent supported it.
11. See the discussion in Gregory Flynn and Henry Farrell, "Piecing Together the Democratic Peace: The CSCE, Norms and the 'Construction' of Security in Post–Cold War Europe," *International Organization* 53 (summer 1999): pp. 505–35, especially pp. 505 and 520.
12. "In defence of Europe," *Economist,* February 26, 2000, p. 25.
13. "Winning Kosovo's peace," *Economist,* March 18, 2000, p. 20.

Notes on Contributors

The Editors

Pierre Martin is associate professor of political science at the Université de Montréal and a member of the Université de Montréal/McGill University Research Group in International Security (REGIS). At the Université de Montréal, he is also affiliated with the Canadian Center for German and European Studies and the Centre de recherche et développement en économique. In 1999–2000, he was the William Lyon Mackenzie King Visiting Associate Professor of Canadian Studies at Harvard University, as well as a Canada-U.S. Fulbright Scholar. He obtained his Ph.D. from Northwestern University. He has published about 30 articles in books and journals, including the *British Journal of Political Science*, the *Canadian Journal of Political Science*, *Études internationales*, *International Journal*, and *Comparative Politics*.

Mark R. Brawley is professor of political science at McGill University and a member of the Research Group in International Security (REGIS). In 2000–2001, he was visiting professor of government at Harvard University. He obtained his Ph.D. from the University of California, Los Angeles. He is the author of *Liberal Leadership: Great Powers and Their Challengers in Peace and War* (Cornell University Press, 1994), *Turning Points: Decisions Shaping the Evolution of the International Political Economy* (Broadview Press, 1998), and *Afterglow or Adjustment? Domestic Institutions and Responses to Overstretch* (Columbia University Press, 1999). His articles have appeared in several journals, including *International Studies Quarterly*, *Comparative Political Studies*, and the *Canadian Journal of Political Science*.

The Authors

Maurizio Cremasco is scientific adviser in strategic and security studies to the Istituto Affari Internazionali in Rome. He has been a visiting professor at the Johns Hopkins University Bologna Center and visiting Fulbright professor at the University of Nebraska in Lincoln. He teaches in Italy's Interservices War College, has served as a consultant for the Italian Ministries of Defense and Foreign Affairs, and is correspondent for politicomilitary affairs for the daily newspaper *Il Secolo XIX* in Genoa. He has authored six books on security affairs and edited three more, including *La standardizzazione degli armamenti nella NATO*, *Il Fianco Sud della NATO*, and *Lo strumento militare italiano*.

Anne Deighton is a university lecturer in European international politics and a fellow of Wolfson College at Oxford University, where she also holds the Jean Monnet Chair in the History of European Integration. She obtained her Ph.D. from the University of Reading. She has taught at Reading and at the Open University, and also held a position as a senior research fellow at Oxford's Saint Antony's College. She has held visiting professorships at La Sorbonne, Sorbonne-la-Nouvelle, and the Université libre de Bruxelles. Her publications include, notably, *The Impossible Peace: Britain, the Division of Germany and the Origins of the Cold War* (Oxford University Press/Clarendon Press, 1990/1993), and, edited with Alan Milward, *Widening, Deepening and Enlarging: The EEC, 1957–1963* (Nomos Verlag, 1999).

David G. Haglund is director of the Centre for International Relations, Queen's University (Kingston, Ontario), and professor in its Department of Political Studies. He received his Ph.D. from Johns Hopkins University's School of Advanced International Studies. He has held visiting positions at the University of Strasbourg, the University of Bonn, and the Stiftung Wissenschaft und Politik (Ebenhausen). He has written or edited numerous books, including *Alliance Within the Alliance? Franco-German Military Cooperation and the European Pillar of Defense* (1991), *Homeward Bound? Allied Forces in the New Germany* (1992, coedited with Olaf Mager), *From Euphoria to Hysteria: Western European Security After the Cold War* (1993), *Will NATO Go East? The Debate Over Enlarging the Atlantic Alliance* (1996), and *Pondering NATO's Nuclear Options: Gambits for a Post-Westphalian World* (1999). His most recent monograph is entitled *The North Atlantic Triangle Revisited: Canada and the Future of Transatlantic Security* (1999).

Alan K. Henrikson is associate professor of diplomatic history at the Fletcher School of International Law and Diplomacy, Tufts University, where he is director of the Fletcher Roundtable on a New World Order. He earned his Ph.D. in history at Harvard. His research focuses on institutions of regional security in Europe and in the Americas. His recent contributions include *Diplomacy for the 21st Century: "Re-Crafting the Old Guild"* (1998), "Middle Powers as Managers: International Mediation Within, Across, and

Outside Institutions" (in *Niche Diplomacy: Middle Powers After the Cold War*, ed. Andrew F. Cooper, 1997), and "The United Nations and Regional Organizations: 'King Links' of a 'Global Chain.'" He has held visiting appointments in the Foreign Affairs College of the People's Republic of China, the National Institute for Defence Studies in Japan, and the U.S. State Department.

Stanley Hoffmann is the Paul and Catherine Buttenwieser University Professor at Harvard University, where he is a senior faculty associate and the former chairman (1969–95) of the Minda de Gunzburg Center for European Studies. He has published many books and articles, including *Decline or Renewal?* *France since the Thirties* (Viking, 1974), *Primacy or World Order* (McGraw-Hill, 1978), *Duties Beyond Borders* (Syracuse University Press, 1980), *Janus and Minerva* (Westview, 1986), *The European Sisyphus: Essays on Europe 1964–1994* (Westview, 1995), and *World Disorders: Troubled Peace in the Post–Cold War Era* (Rowman & Littlefield, 1998). He is a co-author of *In Search of France* (Harvard, 1963) and of *Living with Nuclear Weapons* (Harvard, 1983), and coeditor of *Rousseau on International Relations* (Oxford, 1991).

Charles A. Kupchan is a senior fellow and director of Europe studies at the Council on Foreign Relations, and an associate professor of international relations at Georgetown University. A graduate of Harvard and Oxford, he held positions at Princeton University and in the U.S. Department of State's Policy Planning Staff before joining the National Security Council as director for European affairs during the first Clinton administration. His publications include *Civic Engagement in the Atlantic Community* (1999), *Atlantic Security: Contending Visions* (1998), *Nationalism and Nationalities in the New Europe* (1995), *The Vulnerability of Empire* (1994), and numerous articles on international affairs. He has been a visiting scholar at Harvard, Columbia, the International Institute for Strategic Studies in London, and the Centre d'Études et de Recherches Internationales in Paris.

S. Neil MacFarlane is the Lester B. Pearson Professor of International Relations at Oxford University, where he is a fellow of St. Anne's College and director of Oxford's Centre for International Studies. He is also a fellow of the Centre for Foreign Policy Studies at Dalhousie University. He received his D.Phil. in international relations from Oxford. Prior to his return to Oxford in 1996, he held positions at the University of Virginia and Queen's University. He has held research posts at the International Institute for Strategic Studies, Harvard, the University of British Columbia, and Berkeley. He has published widely on Soviet and Russian foreign and security policy, and on regional security and international organization. His articles have appeared notably in *World Politics, International Security, International Affairs,* and *Security Studies.*

Alex MacLeod is professor in the Department of Political Science at the Université du Québec à Montréal, where he also is the director of the Centre d'étude des politiques étrangères et de sécurité (CEPES). He has published widely on European security and foreign policy, notably on France, Great Britain, and Japan. His recent publications include *Intérêt national et responsabilités internationales: Six États face au conflit en ex-Yougoslavie (1991–1995)* (co-edited with Stéphane Roussel), as well as recent articles in *International Journal* and *Études internationales* on France's involvement in the Balkan conflict. His current research focuses particularly on the transformations in France's foreign and security policies in the post–Cold War era.

Kim Richard Nossal is a professor in the Department of Political Science at McMaster University (Hamilton, Ontario). He received his Ph.D. from the University of Toronto. From 1992 to 1997 he was editor of *International Journal*. His books and monographs include *The Patterns of World Politics* (1998), *The Politics of Canadian Foreign Policy* (3rd ed. 1997), *Rain Dancing: Sanctions in Canadian and Australian Foreign Policy* (1994), and *The Beijing Massacre: Australian Responses* (1993). He is the coauthor, with Andrew Cooper and Richard Higgott, of *Relocating Middle Powers: Australia and Canada in a Changing World Order* (1993), and, with Carolynn Vivian, of *A Brief Madness: Australia and the Resumption of French Nuclear Testing* (1997).

Louise Richardson is associate professor of government at Harvard University. She is a faculty associate at the Minda de Gunzburg Center for European Studies and the co-chair of the center's British Study Group. She received her B.A. from Trinity College, Dublin, and her Ph.D. from Harvard. She teaches courses on international relations, terrorism, foreign policy, and security issues. Her publications include *When Allies Differ: Anglo-American Relations during the Suez and Falklands Crises* (St. Martin's Press, 1996). She has also written on prospect theory in international relations, on British foreign and defense policy, and on international terrorism. Her current research projects involve a study of terrorist movements and a comparative study of responses to change in the distribution of power in Europe.

Stéphane Roussel is assistant professor of political science at Glendon College, York University, in Toronto. He previously taught at the Université de Montréal, where he obtained his Ph.D. in 1999 and where he remains an associate member of the Research Group in International Security. He has coauthored two monographs and coedited three books, including *Six États face au conflit en ex-Yougoslavie*, *Environnement stratégique et modèles de défense: Une perspective québécoise*, and *Promesses et limites de la coopération régionale en matière de sécurité*. His articles have appeared in *Études internationales*, *International Journal*, the *American Review of Canadian Studies*, and *Canadian Defense Quarterly*. He is preparing a book on the evolution of Canadian-American security relations from 1867 to 1958, based on his recent dissertation.

Peter Rudolf has been a research fellow at the Stiftung Wissenschaft und Politik in Ebenhausen since 1988 and he is now working at its Berlin office. After earning his doctorate from the University of Frankfurt am Main, he has taught at the Universities of Munich and Augsburg and has held research posts at the Frankfurt Peace Research Institute and Harvard's Center for Science and International Affairs. He is the author of *Amerikanische Seemachtpolitik und maritime Rüstungskontrolle unter Carter und Reagan* (Campus, 1990), the coeditor of *Amerikanische Weltpolitik nach dem Ost-West-Konflikt* (Nomos, 1994), and of *Weltmacht ohne Gegner. Amerikanische Außenpolitik zu Beginn des 21. Jahrhunderts* (Nomos, 2000). He has published widely on arms control, U.S. foreign policy, transatlantic relations, and international sanctions.

Milada Anna Vachudová is assistant professor of political science at the University of North Carolina, Chapel Hill. She was previously Jean Monnet Fellow at the European University Institute (Fiesole, Italy) in 2000–2001, and a postdoctoral fellow at the Center for European Studies, Harvard University, and at the EU Center of New York, Columbia University. As a Marshall Scholar, she completed a D.Phil. in international relations at the University of Oxford. Her book titled *Revolution, Democracy and Integration: East Central and South Eastern Europe Since 1989* (Oxford, forthcoming) analyzes the enlargement of the EU and NATO and develops a theory of the influence of international organizations on the domestic politics of democratizing states. She has published on the politics of postcommunist transition, ethnic conflict in democratizing states, and the security and immigration policies of the European Union.

Stephen M. Walt is the Robert and Renee Belfer Professor of International Affairs at the John F. Kennedy School of Government, Harvard University. He was previously professor of political science at the University of Chicago. He received his Ph.D. in political science from the University of California, Berkeley. He has held research and teaching positions at Harvard, Princeton, Brookings, and the Carnegie Endowment for International Peace. He is a member of the board of directors of the *Bulletin of the Atomic Scientists*, on the editorial boards of *Foreign Policy, Security Studies,* and *Journal of Cold War Studies*. He is the author of *The Origins of Alliances* (Cornell, 1987), which received the 1988 Edgar S. Furniss National Security Book Award, *Revolution and War* (Cornell, 1996), and numerous articles on international politics and foreign policy.

Index

Ahtisaari, Martti, 59, 151
Albania, 32–3, 40, 60, 70, 81, 173
Albright, Madeline, 59, 67, 132, 146, 147
alliance persistence, explanations of, x–xii, 1–2, 12–13, 15–19, 91–103
Andreatta, Beniamino, 55, 169
Annan, Kofi, 42–3, 48, 50, 54
Antall, József, 218
Art, Robert, 19
Ashdown, Paddy, 149, 157
Austria, 33, 58, 68, 71
Axworthy, Lloyd, 5, 103, 111, 189, 192–4, 197–9
Azerbaijan, 36
Aznar, José Maria, 106

balance of power theory, 11, 12–13, 79–80
balance of threat theory, 12–13
Basque separatism, 32
Belgium, 70, 106
Berger, Samuel ("Sandy"), 148, 172
Bertinotti, Fausto, 170
Blair, Tony, 4, 63, 78, 83, 106, 122, 145–6, 148–54, 156–61, 163–4, 183, 223, 226
Boniface, Pascal, 94
Boross, Peter, 217
Bosnia, xi, 13, 16, 20, 21–22, 38, 60, 69, 70, 81, 116, 119, 145, 167, 189
Britain, xi, 4, 32, 46, 51, 59, 61, 68, 70, 84, 119–20, 122–3, 125, see Chapter 9 [145–64], 175, 222–3, 230–1
  aid and reconstruction plans, 149
  defense budget, 156
  disagreements over military strategy with U.S., 78–9, 146–8, 150, 153–4
  domestic public opinion, 151, 155–8, 226
  European Security and Defense Identity, 155
Falklands War, 145
Foreign and Commonwealth Office, 112
  military contribution to Operation Allied Force, 151, 153, 163
Persian Gulf War, 153, 157
  "special relationship" with U.S., 152–4
Suez Crisis, 145–6
United Nations, 149
Brown, Harold, 110
Bulgaria, 32, 70, 81, 201–3, 213–16, 219
Bush, George, 145, 161, 181–3

Canada, xi, xii, 4–5, 46, 71, see Chapters 6 and 11 [91–112, 181–99], 225, 230–1
Bosnia, 189–90
  disagreements over military strategy with U.S., 188
  domestic public opinion, 5, 105, 188, 190–1, 226–7
  House of Commons, 183, 188, 190–1, 197–8, 227
  military contribution to Operation Allied Force, 105, 112, 181, 183, 185, 187–8
  military "overstretch," 104–5, 111
  peace-keeping, 103–4
  Persian Gulf War, 181–3, 187–90
  refugees, 34, 193
  "Turbot War," 103
  United Nations, 191
Chernomyrdin, Viktor, 59, 151, 175
Chevènement, Jean-Pierre, 123
Chicago Council on Foreign Relations, 110
China, ix, 3, 19, 23, 41, 46–8, 51, 59, 175
Chirac, Jacques, 49, 63, 84, 119–24, 126–9
Chrétien, Jean, 183–5, 187–8
Christopher, Warren, 132
Churchill, Winston, 152, 154
Ciampi, Carlo Anzeglio, 175

Clark, Joe, 198
Clark, (General) Wesley, 108, 128, 150, 153, 154
Claude, Inis, 44
Clinton, Bill, 75–8, 81–2, 88, 133, 147–50, 174, 181, 185–6
Cohen, William, 49, 147, 150
collective goods theory, 11, 12
Colombo, Emilio, 169
Constrantinescu, Emil, 219
constructivism, 2, 94–9, 184, 192, 195, 222, 225
Contact Group, 47, 59, 61, 117, 126, 132
Cook, Robin, 148, 150, 153, 155, 157–9, 163, 226
Cooper, Robert, 155
Corsica, 32
Cossiga, Francesco, 180
Cossutta, Armando, 170, 173
Cottrell, Robert, 6
Covey, James, 177
Cremasco, Maurizio, 5–6, 224, 228
Croatia, 60, 70, 81, 203
Czech Republic, 6, 32, *see* Chapter 12 [201–20]
  Bosnia, 212
  disagreements over military strategy with U.S., 205, 211–12
  domestic public opinion, 205, 211–13, 216, 218, 223–4, 228, 233
  entry into NATO, 63, 81, 210
  former communists, 206, 210
  military contributions to Operation Allied Force, 205
  Parliament, 212
  split with Slovakia, 33

Daalder, Ivo, 49
D'Alema, Massimo, 61, 169–80, 228
D'Antona, Massimo, 176
Dayton Accords, 59, 70, 93, 117
Defence Capabilities Initiative, 64, 71, 72
Deighton, Anne, 3, 216, 233
Delian League, 91–2, 97, 107, 232
democratic peace theory, 17–18, 24, 97
Denmark, 70–1, 226
Deutsch, Karl, x, 18
Dini, Lamberto, 173, 175, 178
Dregger, Alfred, 142
Dyer, Gwynne, 190

Eden, Anthony, 159
Eggleton, Art, 186, 188, 196, 199, 227, 233
Estonia, 32
Euro–Atlantic Partnership Council, 53
European Bank for Reconstruction and Development, 71
European Defence Community, 68, 71
European Investment Bank, 71
European Monetary Union, 63, 68, 80
European Union, xi, 3, 20, 28–31, 39, 47, 53, *see* Chapter 4 [57–72], 80, 83, 86, 117, 121–2, 125–6, 140, 168–9
  aid and reconstruction plans, 59, 60–1, 78
  Amsterdam Treaty, 58, 63, 64, 71, 117
  Bosnia, 63, 69, 84, 119, 167
  Commission, 58, 60
  Common Foreign and Security Policy, 63–4, 83–4, 94, 132, 140
  Council, 64, 120, 138
  enlargement possibilities, 60, 83, 203–4
  European Security and Defense Identity, 3, 38, 93–4, 108, 113, 117, 119–20, 125, 155
  Maastricht Treaty, 63, 69
  Schengen agreement, 33–4

Finland, 58–9, 68–9, 71
Fischer, Joschka, 59, 61–2, 71, 133–5, 137–8, 143
France, xi, 5, 22, 32, 46, 49, 51, 59–61, 68, 70, 84, *see* Chapter 7 [113–30], 148, 150, 173–4, 222–3
  Bosnia, 116
  concern with international standing, 113–16
  disagreements over military strategy with U.S., 78, 113, 118–19, 122, 129
  domestic public opinion, 123–5, 129–30, 228
  Eurocorps, 72
  military contribution to Operation Allied Force, 127
  Persian Gulf War, 116, 123
  Socialists' allies in government, 123
  Suez Crisis, 114
  United Nations, 115–19, 122, 127

G7/G8, 47, 57, 60, 61, 117, 126, 175
Galbraith, John Kenneth, 67
de Gaulle, Charles, 22, 114

Gee, Marcus, 186
Geneva Conventions, 48
Georgia, 36, 40
Germany, 5, 19, 27–8, 32, 48, 50–1, 58–9, 61, 68, 70, 84–5, 100, 121–2, *see* Chapter 8 [131–43], 148, 150, 173–4, 222–3, 225
    Bosnia, 139
    Bundestag, 134, 148
    Constitutional limits, 134–5
    defense budget, 94
    disagreements over military strategy with U.S., 138–9
    domestic public opinion, 96, 135–7, 140, 227
    Eurocorps, 72
    Fischer Plan, 139, 143
    governing coalition, 131–3, 135–40
    integration into Europe, 82–3
    military contribution to Operation Allied Force, 138
    refugees, 33–4, 132
    Russia, 138–9
    United Nations, 132–3, 135, 137–40
Greece, ix, xi, 57, 70, 148, 172, 205, 228
Guichard, Catherine, 50

Habermas, Jürgen, 142
Haglund, David, 5, 71, 196, 222, 227, 232
Haiti, 78
Havel, Vaclav, 211–13, 228
Helsinki Final Act, 49
Henrikson, Alan, 2–3
Holbrooke, Richard, 51, 133–4, 141, 147
Holbrooke-Milosevic agreement, 51
Hombach, Bodo, 177
human security agenda, 5, 103–4, 192–4
humanitarian interventions, ix–x, 42–3, 52, 117–18, 184, 192, 232
Hungary, 6, 32, 70, *see* Chapter 12 [201–20]
    Bosnia, 208, 217
    domestic public opinion, 204, 207, 209, 216–17, 223–4, 233
    entry into NATO, 63, 81
    former communists, 205–6
    Hungarian minorities abroad, 207–9, 219
    military contributions to Operation Allied Force, 202, 204–5, 208–9
    NATO bases in, 208, 217
Huntington, Samuel, 19

Iceland, 71, 95
Iliescu, Ion, 203, 214, 219
institutionalism, 2, 12, 15–17, 21, 23
International Criminal Tribunal for the Former Yugoslavia, 54
International Monetary Fund, 71
Iran, xi
Iraq, ix, xi, 35, 78
Ireland, 58, 68, 71
irrendta, 32
Islamic world, xi, 19
Israel, xi
Italy, ix, 5–6, 50, 57, 61, 70, 122, 148, 150, *see* Chapter 10 [165–80], 224
    Bosnia, 167–8, 171
    Chamber of Deputies, 177, 179
    coalition governments, 165–7, 169–70, 173, 175
    disagreements over military strategy with U.S., 174–5, 179
    domestic public opinion, 165, 170, 172, 179–80, 228
    NATO bases in, 168, 170–1, 174
    Persian Gulf War, 167, 171
    Red Brigades, 176
    refugees, 33
    Somalia, 167
    United Nations, 168–71, 173, 177
Ivanov, Igor, 48

Jackson, (General Sir) Michael, 108, 153
Japan, 19, 51, 60, 71, 83, 102
Joffe, Joseph, 82
Jospin, Lionel, 119, 122, 127–8
Jovanovic, Zivadin, 112
Juppé, Alain, 126
just war theory, x

Kasza, Jozsef, 209
Katzenstein, Peter, 195
Kavan, Jan, 212
Kennan, George, 72
Kinkel, Klaus, 48, 132–3, 135
Kissinger, Henry, 77
Klaus, Vaclav, 206, 210, 212, 218
Kohl, Helmut, 84, 133
Kosovo Liberation Army, 51, 77, 175, 196
Kouchner, Bernard, 120, 122, 177
Kupchan, Charles, 4
Kuwait, ix

Laden, Osama bin, 34
Lafontaine, Oskar, 137
Lansky, Egon, 212
Latvia, 32
Laurier, Wilfrid, 187, 197
Layne, Christopher, 13, 15
liberal theory, 12
Libya, 224
Lithuania, 32
Lott, Trent, 174
Luttwak, Edward, 102
Luxembourg, 70, 95

Macedonia, 31–2, 60, 70, 77, 81, 148, 173, 185, 219
MacFarlane, Neil, 2, 224
Macleod, Alexander, 5, 162
Major, John, 159
Martin, Keith, 198
Martonyi, Janos, 209, 217
Mastanduno, Michael, 102
McKay, John, 187
Mearsheimer, John, 13, 15
Meciar, Vladimir, 203, 214, 218
Meyer, Paul, 187
migration of refugees, 33–4, 40, 156, 190–1, 217
Milosevic, Slobodan, x, 31, 50–2, 59, 60, 66, 70, 77, 91, 97, 134–5, 146–7, 172–5, 189
Montenegro, 31, 60, 77, 120, 122, 173, 185
Mulroney, Brian, 183–5
Mussi, Fabio, 171
Mutates, Abel, 112

Netherlands, 70
North American Aerospace Defense Command (NORAD), 225
North Atlantic Cooperation Council, 63
North Atlantic Treaty Organization (NATO)
 bases in Italy, 168, 170–1, 174
 future enlargement, 37, 81, 201–3, 213–15
 interoperability, 31, 38, 64, 204
 non-Article 5 operations, 6, 64, 230–1, *also see* Petersberg Tasks
 North Atlantic Council, 53, 70
 Persian Gulf War, 35–6
 Strategic Concepts, 16, 22, 25, 27–40, 63–4, 100, 110

Northern Ireland, 32
Norway, 226
Nossal, Kim, 4

O'Hanlon, Michael, 49
oil reserves, 35–6, 40
Orban, Viktor, 208, 210
O'Reilly, John, 198
Organization for Economic Cooperation and Development (OECD), 71
Organization of Petroleum Exporting Countries (OPEC), 35
Organization for Security and Cooperation in Europe (OSCE), 28, 30–1, 33, 39, 49, 53, 58, 61, 70, 120–1, 126

Partnership for Peace, 36, 63
Pearson, Lester B., 192, 198
Pelley, Robert, 198
Petersberg Tasks, 62, 64–5, 67, 71
Pinochet, (General) Augusto, 70
Poland, 6, 32, *see* Chapter 12 [201–20]
 domestic public opinion, 205–6, 216, 223–4, 227–8, 233
 entry into NATO, 63, 81
 former communists, 205–6
 military contribution to Operation Allied Force, 204
Portugal, 51, 70, 106
Price, David, 191, 196, 198
Prodi, Romano, 68, 178

Qin Huasun, 51
"Quint" group, 61

Racak massacre, 51, 59, 135
Rambouillet negotiations, 51–2, 59, 70, 117, 135, 146–7, 162, 182, 198
realism, 2, 11–12, 13–15, 20, 21, 101, 108, 184, 192, 222, 225
refugees, *see* migration of
Revolution in Military Affairs, 63, 104
Richard, Alain, 122
Richardson, Louise, 4, 226
Risse-Kappen, Thomas, 97–8
Robertson, George, 64, 71, 148, 150, 157, 162
Romania, 31–2, 70, 81, 201–3, 207–8, 213–15, 216, 219
Rose, Gideon, 108

Rothstein, Robert, 7
Roussel, Stéphane, 4
Rudolf, Peter, 5, 227
Ruehe, Volker, 133, 136
Ruggie, John G., 115
Rugova, Ibrahim, 174–5
Russia, ix, x–xi, 3, 5, 17, 23, 28, 30, 32, 36–7, 41, 46–8, 51, 59–61, 70, 85, 117, 119, 126, 133, 173, 175, 203, 214–15, 224
 information leaks to Serbs, 150–1
 Partnership for Peace, 36
 public opinion, 36
 Stability Pact, 71
 troops in Pristina, 108
Rwanda, x, 42, 114, 194

Saint-Malo Declaration, 63, 64, 66–7, 71, 120–1, 155
Santer, Jacques, 58
Scalfaro, Oscar Luigi, 170, 178
Scharping, Rudolf, 133, 135–6, 142–3
Schäuble, Wolfgang, 136, 142
Schroeder, Gerhard, 19, 48, 133–4, 136–7, 143, 148–9, 175
Scowcroft, Brent, 147
security (definitions of), 28–9, 39
security communities, x, 11, 18, 23–4
Serbia, x, 5, 31–2, 47, 50–2, 55, 59, 95, 120, 146–7, 168, 178, 182, 185, 192–4, 202–3
Serbian Unity Congress, 112
Shea, Jamie, 153, 226
Short, Clare, 146
Single European Act, 62
Slovakia, 31–3, 201, 203, 207–8, 213–19
Slovenia, 70, 81
Solana, Javier, 50, 64–5, 83, 149
Soviet threat, x, 2, 11, 16, 20, 27, 29–30, 81, 99, 102
Spain, 5, 32, 70, 95, 105–7, 225
 military contribution to Operation Allied Force, 105–6
 public opinion, 5, 105, 228
 "Turbot War," 103
Srebrenica, 135, 193
Stability Pact, 60, 65, 70–1, 121, 177, 210
Stalin, Joseph, 20
Stoiber, Edmund, 136
Sweden, 51, 58, 68, 71
Switzerland, 33

terrorism, xi, 31, 34–5, 156
Thatcher, Margaret, 145, 159, 161
Todd, Emmanuel, 91, 93
Tudjman, Franjo, 203
Turkey, xi, 29, 70–1
Turp, Daniel, 191, 194

Ukraine, 32
unipolarity, 14, 21
United Nations, 2–3, 30, 38, *see* Chapter 3 [41–55], 117, 119, 168, 177
 Charter, 41–4, 52, 118
 Declaration of Human Rights, 48
 General Assembly, 45–6
 High Commissioner for Refugees, 34, 71
 Korean War, 41
 Persian Gulf War, 41, 44–5
 Security Council, ix-x, 41–2, 44–7, 51–2, 61, 117–19, 122, 126, 168–9, 172–3
 Suez Crisis, 43
United Nations Interim Mission in Kosovo (UNMIK), 61, 65
United States, *see* Chapter 5 [75–89]
 Bosnia, 21–2, 65, 132, 145
 Caspian region, 40
 casualties (fear of), 76–7, 79, 81–2, 226
 domestic public opinion, 14–15, 21–2, 67, 80, 110, 148
 economy, 22, 81
 generational change in, 82
 isolationist tendencies, 92–3, 107–8
 House of Representatives, 77, 81–2
 Lewinsky Affair, 161
 military forces compared with Europe, 64, 71, 79, 85, 91–3
 military overstretch and retrenchment, 72, 79–82
 National Missile Defense, 110, 225
 NATO enlargement, 75
 Persian Gulf War, 22, 116, 145, 153
 Senate, 76, 78, 81–2, 88
 "special relationship" with Britain, 152–4
 Suez Crisis, 43, 145–6
 and U.N., 46–7, 49, 51, 66

Vachudová, Milada, 6, 224
Védrine, Hubert, 91, 114–15, 120–2, 125–30, 132
Voigt, Karsten, 95–6, 143

Wagnière, Frederic, 186
Walt, Stephen, 2, 101, 222
Waltz, Kenneth, 13, 15, 20, 101
Weapons of Mass Destruction (WMD), 30, 35
Wendt, Alexander, 96–7
West European Union, 28, 39, 62–4, 69, 71, 117, 125, 168–9

Wohlforth, William, 14–15, 21
Wolfers, Arnold, 43
World Bank, 71

Yeltsin, Boris, 48

Zeman, Milos, 212

Rothstein, Robert, 7
Roussel, Stéphane, 4
Rudolf, Peter, 5, 227
Ruehe, Volker, 133, 136
Ruggie, John G., 115
Rugova, Ibrahim, 174–5
Russia, ix, x–xi, 3, 5, 17, 23, 28, 30, 32, 36–7, 41, 46–8, 51, 59–61, 70, 85, 117, 119, 126, 133, 173, 175, 203, 214–15, 224
  information leaks to Serbs, 150–1
  Partnership for Peace, 36
  public opinion, 36
  Stability Pact, 71
  troops in Pristina, 108
Rwanda, x, 42, 114, 194

Saint-Malo Declaration, 63, 64, 66–7, 71, 120–1, 155
Santer, Jacques, 58
Scalfaro, Oscar Luigi, 170, 178
Scharping, Rudolf, 133, 135–6, 142–3
Schäuble, Wolfgang, 136, 142
Schroeder, Gerhard, 19, 48, 133–4, 136–7, 143, 148–9, 175
Scowcroft, Brent, 147
security (definitions of), 28–9, 39
security communities, x, 11, 18, 23–4
Serbia, x, 5, 31–2, 47, 50–2, 55, 59, 95, 120, 146–7, 168, 178, 182, 185, 192–4, 202–3
Serbian Unity Congress, 112
Shea, Jamie, 153, 226
Short, Clare, 146
Single European Act, 62
Slovakia, 31–3, 201, 203, 207–8, 213–19
Slovenia, 70, 81
Solana, Javier, 50, 64–5, 83, 149
Soviet threat, x, 2, 11, 16, 20, 27, 29–30, 81, 99, 102
Spain, 5, 32, 70, 95, 105–7, 225
  military contribution to Operation Allied Force, 105–6
  public opinion, 5, 105, 228
  "Turbot War," 103
Srebrenica, 135, 193
Stability Pact, 60, 65, 70–1, 121, 177, 210
Stalin, Joseph, 20
Stoiber, Edmund, 136
Sweden, 51, 58, 68, 71
Switzerland, 33

terrorism, xi, 31, 34–5, 156
Thatcher, Margaret, 145, 159, 161
Todd, Emmanuel, 91, 93
Tudjman, Franjo, 203
Turkey, xi, 29, 70–1
Turp, Daniel, 191, 194

Ukraine, 32
unipolarity, 14, 21
United Nations, 2–3, 30, 38, *see* Chapter 3 [41–55], 117, 119, 168, 177
  Charter, 41–4, 52, 118
  Declaration of Human Rights, 48
  General Assembly, 45–6
  High Commissioner for Refugees, 34, 71
  Korean War, 41
  Persian Gulf War, 41, 44–5
  Security Council, ix-x, 41–2, 44–7, 51–2, 61, 117–19, 122, 126, 168–9, 172–3
  Suez Crisis, 43
United Nations Interim Mission in Kosovo (UNMIK), 61, 65
United States, *see* Chapter 5 [75–89]
  Bosnia, 21–2, 65, 132, 145
  Caspian region, 40
  casualties (fear of), 76–7, 79, 81–2, 226
  domestic public opinion, 14–15, 21–2, 67, 80, 110, 148
  economy, 22, 81
  generational change in, 82
  isolationist tendencies, 92–3, 107–8
  House of Representatives, 77, 81–2
  Lewinsky Affair, 161
  military forces compared with Europe, 64, 71, 79, 85, 91–3
  military overstretch and retrenchment, 72, 79–82
  National Missile Defense, 110, 225
  NATO enlargement, 75
  Persian Gulf War, 22, 116, 145, 153
  Senate, 76, 78, 81–2, 88
  "special relationship" with Britain, 152–4
  Suez Crisis, 43, 145–6
  and U.N., 46–7, 49, 51, 66

Vachudová, Milada, 6, 224
Védrine, Hubert, 91, 114–15, 120–2, 125–30, 132
Voigt, Karsten, 95–6, 143

Wagnière, Frederic, 186
Walt, Stephen, 2, 101, 222
Waltz, Kenneth, 13, 15, 20, 101
Weapons of Mass Destruction (WMD), 30, 35
Wendt, Alexander, 96–7
West European Union, 28, 39, 62–4, 69, 71, 117, 125, 168–9

Wohlforth, William, 14–15, 21
Wolfers, Arnold, 43
World Bank, 71

Yeltsin, Boris, 48

Zeman, Milos, 212